ADOBE® PREMIERE® ELE

CLASSROOM IN A BOOK®

The official training workbook from Adobe Systems

Adobe

Writer: Jan Ozer
Editor: Connie Jeung-Mills
Development Editor: Stephen Nathans-Kelly
Production Editor: Tracey Croom
Copyeditor: Anne Marie Walker
Keystroker: Bob Lindstrom
Compositor: Kim Scott, Bumpy Design
Indexer: Rebecca Plunkett
Cover design: Eddie Yuen
Interior design: Mimi Heft

Printed and bound in the United States of America

ISBN-13:   978-0-321-68638-1
ISBN-10:   0-321-68638-1

9 8 7 6 5 4 3 2 1

WHAT'S ON THE DISC

Here is an overview of the contents of the Classroom in a Book disc

Lesson files … and so much more

The *Adobe Premiere Elements 8 Classroom in a Book* disc includes the lesson files that you'll need to complete the exercises in this book, as well as other content to help you learn more about Adobe Premiere Elements 8 and use it with greater efficiency and ease. The diagram below represents the contents of the disc, which should help you locate the files you need.

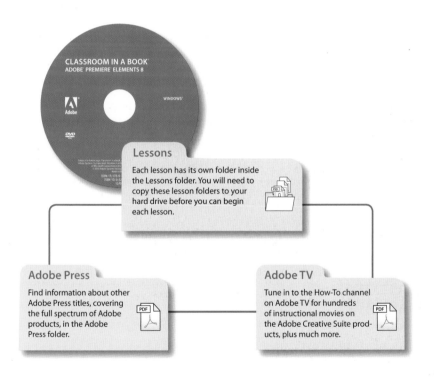

Lessons

Each lesson has its own folder inside the Lessons folder. You will need to copy these lesson folders to your hard drive before you can begin each lesson.

Adobe Press

Find information about other Adobe Press titles, covering the full spectrum of Adobe products, in the Adobe Press folder.

Adobe TV

Tune in to the How-To channel on Adobe TV for hundreds of instructional movies on the Adobe Creative Suite products, plus much more.

CONTENTS

GETTING STARTED

Adobe Premiere Elements 8 delivers video editing tools that balance power and versatility with ease of use. Adobe Premiere Elements 8 is ideal for home users, hobbyists, business users, and professional videographers—anyone who wants to produce high-quality movies and DVDs.

If you've used earlier versions of Adobe Premiere Elements, you'll find that this Classroom in a Book covers the many new advanced skills and innovative features that Adobe Systems introduces in this version. If you're new to Adobe Premiere Elements, you'll learn the fundamental concepts and techniques that help you master this application.

About Classroom in a Book

Adobe Premiere Elements 8 Classroom in a Book is part of the official training series for Adobe graphics and publishing software developed by Adobe product experts. Most lessons in this book include self-paced projects that give you hands-on experience using Adobe Premiere Elements 8.

The *Adobe Premiere Elements 8 Classroom in a Book* includes a DVD attached to the inside back cover. On the DVD, you'll find all the files used for the lessons in this book. As an overview, in the first two lessons, you'll learn your way around Adobe Premiere Elements' interface, how to set up a project, and how to customize critical preferences.

In Lesson 3, you'll learn how to capture and otherwise import video into Adobe Premiere Elements. Starting with Lesson 4 and continuing through Lesson 13, you'll open projects on the DVD and learn how to convert your raw, captured clips into a polished movie.

Prerequisites

Before you begin working on the lessons in this book, make sure that you and your computer are ready.

Requirements for Your Computer

You'll need about 4.3 gigabytes (GB) of free space on your hard disk for the lesson files and the work files you'll create. For some lessons, you will need to have 2 GB RAM installed on your computer. Note that the lessons assume that you installed all templates and associated content available with the DVD version of Adobe Premiere Elements 8. If you see a template that's not installed on your computer, you should be able to simply choose another template and continue with the lesson.

Required Skills

The lessons in this *Adobe Premiere Elements 8 Classroom in a Book* assume that you have a working knowledge of your computer and its operating system. This book does not teach the most basic and generic computer skills. If you can answer *yes* to the following questions, you're probably well qualified to start working on the projects in these lessons. You will almost certainly get the most benefit from working on the lessons in the order in which they occur in the book.

- Do you know how to use the Microsoft Windows Start button and the Windows task bar? Can you open menus and submenus, and choose items from those menus?

- Do you know how to use My Computer, Windows Explorer, or Internet Explorer to find items stored in folders on your computer, or to browse the Internet?

- Are you comfortable using the mouse to move the pointer, select items, drag, and deselect? Have you used context menus, which open when you right-click items?

- When you have two or more open applications, do you know how to switch from one to another? Do you know how to switch to the Windows desktop?

- Do you know how to open, close, and minimize individual windows? Can you move them to different locations on your screen? Can you resize a window by dragging?

- Can you scroll (vertically and horizontally) within a window to see contents that may not be visible in the displayed area?

- Are you familiar with the menus across the top of an application and how to use those menus?

- Have you used dialogs (special windows in the interface that display information), such as the Print dialog? Do you know how to click arrow icons to open a menu within a dialog?

- Can you open, save, and close a file? Are you familiar with word processing tasks, such as typing, selecting words, backspacing, deleting, copying, pasting, and changing text?

- Do you know how to open and find information in Microsoft Windows Help?

If there are gaps in your mastery of these skills, see the Microsoft documentation for your version of Windows. Or, ask a computer-savvy friend or instructor for help.

Installing Adobe Premiere Elements 8

Adobe Premiere Elements 8 software (sold separately) is intended for installation on a computer running Windows Vista or Windows XP. For system requirements and complete instructions on installing the software, see the Adobe Premiere Elements 8 application CD and documentation. To get the most from the projects in this book, you should install all the templates included with the software. Otherwise, you may notice missing-file error messages.

● **Note:** The videos on the DVD are practice files provided for your personal use in these lessons. You are not authorized to use these videos commercially or to publish or distribute them in any form without written permission from Adobe Systems, Inc., or other copyright holders.

Copying the Classroom in a Book Files

The DVD attached to the inside back cover of this book includes a Lessons folder containing all the electronic files for the lessons in this book. Follow the instructions to copy the files from the DVD, and then keep all the lesson files on your computer until after you have finished all the lessons.

Copying the Lessons Files from the DVD

1 Insert the *Adobe Premiere Elements 8 Classroom in a Book* DVD into your DVD-ROM drive. If a message appears asking what you want Windows to do, select Open folder to view files using Windows Explorer, and click OK.

   If no message appears, open My Computer and double-click the DVD icon to open it.

2 Locate the Lessons folder inside the Adobe Premiere Elements 8 folder on the DVD and copy it to any convenient folder on your computer. Just remember where you copied it, because you'll be opening the lesson files frequently throughout the book. Inside the Lessons folder you will find individual folders containing project files needed for the completion of each lesson.

3 When your computer finishes copying the Lessons folder (which could take several minutes), remove the DVD from your DVD-ROM drive, and store it in a safe place for future use.

Additional Resources

Adobe Premiere Elements 8 Classroom in a Book is not meant to replace documentation that comes with the program, nor is it designed to be a comprehensive reference for every feature in Adobe Premiere Elements 8. For additional information about program features, refer to any of these resources:

- Premiere Elements Help, which is built into the Adobe Premiere Elements 8 application. You can view it by choosing Help > Premiere Elements Help.

- The Premiere Elements 8 Quick Reference Card, which is included either in the box with your copy of Adobe Premiere Elements 8 or in PDF format on the installation DVD for the application software. If you don't already have Adobe Reader (or if you don't have the latest version of Adobe Reader, formerly called Acrobat Reader) installed on your computer, you can download a free copy from the Adobe Web site (www.adobe.com).

- Visit Adobe Premiere Elements Help and Support Web page (www.adobe.com/designcenter/premiereelements), which you can view by choosing Help > Adobe Premiere Elements Help. You can also choose Help > Online Support for access to the Premiere Elements Support Center on the Adobe Web site. Both of these options require that you have Internet access.

- The Adobe Premiere Elements 8 User Guide, which is included either in the box with your copy of Adobe Premiere Elements 8 or in PDF format on the installation DVD for the application software (E:\English\User Documentation |Adobe Premiere Elements Help.pdf). If you don't already have Adobe or Acrobat Reader installed on your computer, you can download a free copy from the Adobe Web site (www.adobe.com).

Photoshop.com

Various chapters in this book will refer to features of and services provided by Photoshop.com. Please note that currently, Photoshop.com services are available only for Adobe Premiere Elements and Adobe Photoshop Elements users in the United States.

Adobe Certification

The Adobe Training and Certification Programs are designed to help Adobe customers improve and promote their product-proficiency skills. The Adobe Certified Expert (ACE) program is designed to recognize the high-level skills of expert users. Adobe Certified Training Providers (ACTP) use only Adobe Certified Experts to teach Adobe software classes. Available in either ACTP classrooms or on-site, the ACE program is the best way to master Adobe products. For Adobe Certified Training Programs information, visit the Partnering with Adobe Web site at http://partners.adobe.com.

1 THE WORLD OF DIGITAL VIDEO

This lesson describes how you'll use Adobe Premiere Elements 8 to produce movies and introduces you to the key panels, workspaces, and views within the application. You'll also learn the benefits of subscribing to Adobe Photoshop.com.

This lesson will introduce the following concepts:

- Navigating the Adobe Premiere Elements workspaces
- Importing and tagging media
- Uploading and sharing content with Photoshop.com

 This lesson will take approximately 45 minutes.

The Adobe Premiere Elements workspace.

How Adobe Premiere Elements Fits into Video Production

All video producers are different, and each will use Adobe Premiere Elements differently. At a high level, however, all producers will use Adobe Premiere Elements to import and organize footage (video, stills, and audio)—whether from a camcorder, digital camera, or other source—and then edit the clips into a cohesive movie. If you have both Adobe Premiere Elements and Adobe Photoshop Elements, you have an extraordinarily flexible and well-featured platform for projects combining still images and video.

From a video perspective, such editing will include trimming away unwanted sections of your source clips, correcting exposure and adjusting color as needed, and then applying transitions and special effects and adding titles. On the audio front, perhaps you'll add narration to your productions or a background music track. Once your movie is complete, you may create menus for recording to DVD and/or Blu-ray discs, and then output the movie for sharing with others via disc (such as DVD or Blu-ray) and/or file-based output.

Adobe Premiere Elements facilitates this workflow using a simple three-panel interface with custom workspaces for each of the four production steps: clip acquisition and organization, editing, disc menu creation, and sharing. This chapter will introduce you to the Adobe Premiere Elements interface and these four workspaces.

You undoubtedly purchased Adobe Premiere Elements to start producing movies as soon as possible. Taking a few moments now to read through this overview will not only get you up and running in Adobe Premiere Elements more quickly, but it will also help you understand how this book is organized and where to find the content that details the operations you'll be performing in future projects.

The Adobe Premiere Elements Workspace

When you launch Adobe Premiere Elements, a Welcome screen appears. From here, you can open the Organizer, start a new project, or open a project. On the bottom, the Welcome screen displays the status of your Photoshop.com Membership and provides access to your Account Details, your Shared Gallery, and Adobe Premiere Elements Tutorials. The large center screen will also contain information about tutorials available to Plus members on Photoshop.com.

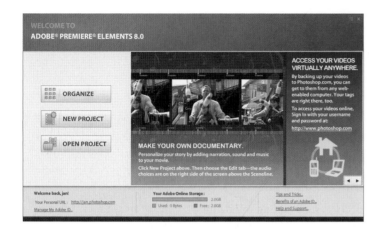

One of the most significant enhancements to this version of Adobe Premiere Elements is that Adobe now includes a complete version of the Elements Organizer. In contrast, previous versions of Adobe Premiere Elements contained only a limited-function version. The Organizer is a great place to start many projects. It offers excellent tagging and search tools, the ability to view all your media in one place irrespective of its actual location on your hard drive, and the ability to easily share and archive your collections of video and still images. If you also own Photoshop Elements, you'll share the same Organizer, so you can access all your content from either Adobe Premiere Elements or Adobe Photoshop Elements, and you can launch a range of activities and workflows from either application from within one common content database.

Let's load some video files to see how starting projects in the Organizer works. Specifically, let's load only the video files from the Lesson 04 and 05 subfolder that you copied to your hard disk from the DVD.

1   Start Adobe Premiere Elements and click the Organize button in the Welcome screen. The Organizer opens. If this is the first time you've worked with the Organizer, it will be empty, and may ask you to identify folders where your media is located. If you've worked with it previously, it will contain other content that you've used before.

2   In the Organizer, choose File > Get Photos and Videos > From Files and Folders. The Get Photos and Videos from Files and Folders dialog opens.

3   Navigate to your Lesson04 and 05 folder.

4   Click the View menu, and choose Details.

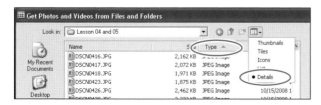

5 On the top of the file list window, click Type to sort the files by file type.

6 All video files should now be listed consecutively, although you may have to use the scroll bar on the right to view them. Find the video files, click to select the top file with an .AVI extension, press and hold the Shift key on your keyboard, and then click to select the last video file with an .AVI extension. All video files with an .AVI extension should be highlighted.

● **Note:** The Organizer can input video footage directly from all camcorders except for tape-based camcorders, like DV and HDV, and analog camcorders. Footage from these devices must be captured before importing the video into the Organizer. For this reason, if your project involves video from DV, HDV, or analog camcorders that you previously haven't captured to hard disk, you should start your projects by clicking New Projects in the Welcome screen, as shown in "Setting Up a New Project" in Chapter 2. Otherwise, if you're working with footage from any camcorder or digital camera that stores video onto a hard disk, DVD, SD media, or similar nontape-based storage, you can input that footage directly from the Organizer.

7 On the bottom right of the Get Photos and Videos from Files and Folders dialog, click Get Media. The Organizer loads the video into the Browser pane. If this is the first time you've used the Organizer, you may get a status message stating, "The only items in the main window are those you just imported. To see the rest of the Catalog, click Show All." Click OK to close the message; do not click Show All.

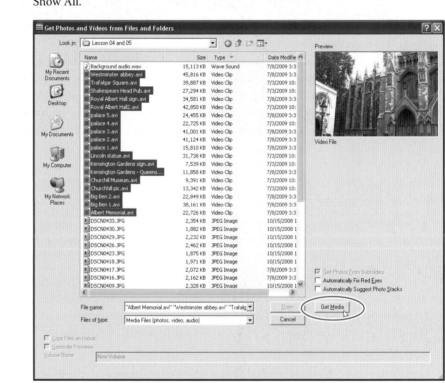

Working in the Organizer

In the Organizer workspace, the main work area is the Browser pane where you can find, sort, and organize your video, audio, photos, and other media files. On the right is the Task pane, which includes four tabs that open the Organize, Fix, Create, and Share panels. You'll learn the operation of all four panels in Chapter 4; for now, here are a couple of highlights.

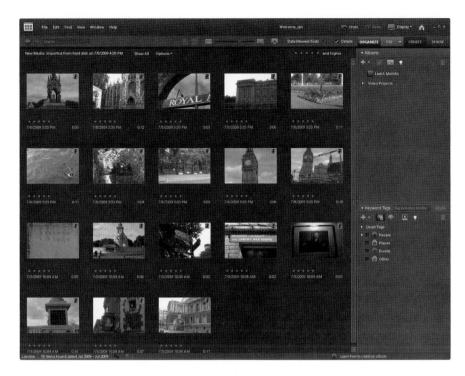

In the Organize panel, shown on the right, you can apply tags to your videos to help organize them, or run the Auto Analyzer, which applies Smart Tags to the clips. Smart Tags assist in multiple activities, including creating InstantMovies (Chapter 4) and directing Smart Trimming (Chapter 5) and SmartFix (Chapter 6). To run the Auto Analyzer function, select a clip or clips, right-click, and choose Run Auto Analyzer.

In addition, in the Create panel, you can start a number of projects, including InstantMovies and DVDs with menus, as well as a host of photo-related projects. In the Share panel, you can launch Adobe Premiere Elements to upload video to YouTube or to a mobile phone. And in the Fix panel, you can send all selected videos to Adobe Premiere Elements for editing. Let's do that and start our tour of the Adobe Premiere Elements workspace.

1   In the Organizer, click the Fix tab to open the Fix panel.

2   Press Ctrl-A to select all videos currently in the Organizer (only those videos that you just imported should be displayed).

3 In the Fix panel, click the down triangle on the top right of the Fix tab, and choose Edit Videos.

4 If this is the first time you've used this function, you'll see the status message in the next figure. Click OK to close the message.

5 Adobe Premiere Elements opens the New Project panel. Type *Lesson01* in the Name field (Adobe Premiere Elements will add the necessary extension), and click the Browse button to change the location of the project, if desired.

6 Check the Project Settings in the lower-left corner of the New Project panel. If the Project Settings field shows NTSC-DV-Standard 48kHz, proceed to step 9. If not, click the Change Settings button to open the Setup screen.

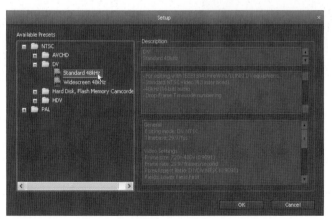

Premiere
ialog asks

king
lowing

B

C

A. Monitor panel. **B.** Tasks panel (Organize workspace selected. Note that your Organize workspace may contain different items). **C.** My Project panel (Sceneline selected).

The Adobe Premiere Elements workspace is arranged in three main panels: the Monitor panel, the Tasks panel, and the My Project panel. The following sections give you an overview of these panels and the role they play when you are working on a movie project.

Monitor Panel

The Monitor panel serves multiple purposes. It enables you to edit as well as to view your movie in one convenient place. You can navigate to any position in the movie and preview a section or the entire movie. In this role, the Monitor panel previews the movie that you are building in the My Project panel, using the VCR-like controls beneath the playback window. Other chapters will detail the Monitor panel's controls and operation; here you can experiment with the playback controls to get a feel for how to use them.

In other roles, the Monitor panel also offers tools to trim unwanted footage and split clips. You can drag one scene onto another to create picture-in-picture effects, and add titles and other text directly in the Monitor panel. The Monitor panel adjusts its appearance for some editing tasks. When creating menus, the Monitor panel switches to become the Disk Layout panel; in title-editing mode, the Monitor panel displays additional tools to create and edit text.

My Project Panel

The My Project panel lets you assemble your media into the desired order and edit clips. This panel has two different views:

- **Sceneline:** In the Sceneline of the My Project panel, the initial frame represents each clip. This display makes it easy to arrange clips into a coherent series without regard to clip length. This technique is referred to as *storyboard-style editing.* The Sceneline is useful when you first start editing a movie because it allows you to quickly arrange your media into the desired order, to trim unwanted frames from the beginning and ends of each clip, and to add titles, transitions, and effects.

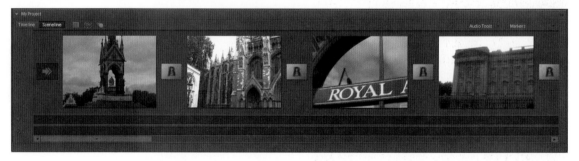

- **Timeline:** The Timeline of the My Project panel presents all movie components in separate horizontal tracks beneath a timescale. Clips earlier in time appear to the left, and clips later in time appear to the right, with clip length on the Timeline representing a clip's duration. The Timeline is useful later in the project and for more advanced editing, because it lets you better visualize content on different tracks, such as picture-in-picture effects and titles, or narration and background music.

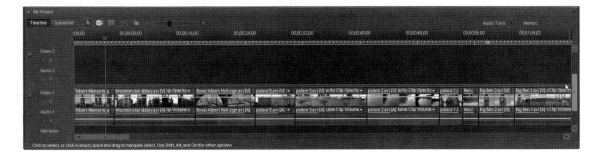

Tasks Panel

The Tasks panel is the central location for adding and organizing media; finding, applying, and adjusting effects and transitions; creating DVD and Blu-ray disc menus; and sharing your finished projects. It's organized into four main task workspaces: Organize, Edit, Disc Menus, and Share. Within each workspace are all the tools you need to accomplish your tasks.

Organize workspace

The Organize workspace is divided into four views to input media, create an InstantMovie, tag your media, and view the content included in your project. There's also an icon that opens the stand-alone Organizer. If you don't start your projects in the Organizer, you'll typically start by clicking Get Media in the Organize workspace.

The Organize workspace (Get Media view selected).

- **Get Media:** This view shows buttons to access all the different methods for acquiring media for your movie: DV Camcorder, HDV Camcorder, DVD (Camcorder or PC DVD Drive), AVCHD or other hard disk/memory camcorder, Digital Still Camera, Mobile Phone and Players, Webcam or WDM Device, and PC Files and Folders, which you'll use to retrieve files already existing on your hard disk.

- **Organizer:** Clicking this icon opens the Organizer, where you can create and apply keyword tags and albums to manage and organize your media (videos, still images, and audio files). Tags, Smart Tags, Albums, Smart Albums, and any combination of these let you limit what appears in the Organizer so that you can easily and quickly find the files you want. You can add keywords for anything, such as people's names, places, or events.

- **InstantMovie:** This view automatically and quickly steps you through the selection and editing portion of movie creation, adding theme-based effects, title, transitions, and audio.

- **Media:** This icon displays the current contents of the Organizer with simple tools for filtering and searching.

- **Project:** In this view you can view, sort, and select media you have captured or imported into your project. Media can be presented in List view or Icon view, selected by buttons at the lower-left corner of Project view. Note that in Adobe Premiere Elements 7, the Project view was presented in the Edit workspace, not the Organizer.

Edit workspace

If you were working on a real project, after importing and tagging your media, you'd be ready to edit. Click Edit to enter the Edit workspace, which is divided into five views to access effects and transitions, create movie titles from templates, select and apply movie themes, and choose from available clip art libraries.

- **Effects:** This view shows video and audio effects and presets you can use in your movie. You can search for effects by typing all or part of the name into the search box, browse through all available effects, or filter the view by type and category. The menu in the upper-right corner of the panel lets you choose between List view and Thumbnail view. You can apply video effects to adjust exposure or color problems, apply perspective or pixelate, or add other special effects. Audio effects help you improve the sound quality, add special effects like delay and reverb, and alter volume or balance.

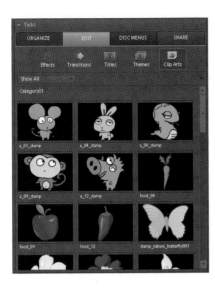

The Edit workspace
(Clip Art view selected).

- **Transitions:** This view shows video and audio transitions you can use in your movie. You can search for transitions by typing all or part of the name into the search box, browse through all available transitions, or filter the view by type and category. The menu in the upper-right corner of the panel lets you choose between List view and Thumbnail view. Transitions between clips can be as subtle as a cross-dissolve, or quite emphatic, such as a page turn or spinning pinwheel.

- **Titles:** This view shows groups of preformatted title templates you can use in your movie. You can browse all available templates or filter the view by categories such as Entertainment, Travel, and Wedding. Title templates include graphic images and placeholder text that you can modify freely, delete from, or add to, without affecting the actual templates.

- **Themes:** This view displays movie themes that you can use to instantly and dramatically enhance your movies. Using Themes enables you to create professional-looking movies quickly and easily. Themes come preconfigured with effects, transitions, overlays, title and closing credit sequences, intros, sound effects, and more. You can choose to simply apply all the available options in a theme or select just the options you want.

- **Clip Art:** This view displays clip art libraries that you can drag and drop into your projects. Clip art libraries include items like those shown in the screenshot, as well as thought bubbles and similar text-oriented clip art.

Disc Menus workspace

Use the Disc Menus workspace to add menus to your movies before burning them onto DVDs or Blu-ray discs. The Disc Menus workspace lets you preview and choose preformatted menu templates you can use for your movie. You can browse the available templates by categories such as Entertainment, Happy Birthday, Kid's Corner, and New Baby.

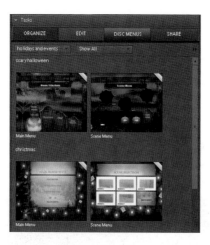

These are templates in the holidays and events category. Note that the templates you see on your computer may be different.

Share workspace

After you've finished editing your movie, and you're ready to burn a disc or save your movie for viewing online or on a mobile phone, PC, videotape, or other device, click Share. The Share workspace shows buttons for accessing all the different methods for exporting and sharing your movie: Disc, Online, Personal Computer, Mobile Phones and Players, and Tape. Quick Share lets you create and reuse sharing options.

Properties View

Often during editing or when producing disc menus, you'll need to customize effect parameters or menu components after applying or selecting them. Properties view (Window > Properties) lets you view and adjust parameters of items—such as video or audio clips, transitions, effects, or menus—when selected in the Monitor or My Project panel.

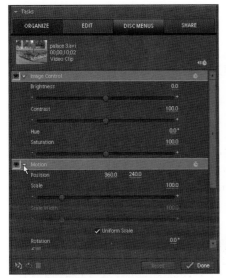 

Info and History Panels

The Info panel displays information about a selected clip in the My Project panel. Among other things, the Info panel can be helpful in identifying the duration of a clip.

● **Note:** The Info panel is dynamic, and the fields can vary slightly depending on what is selected. For clips selected in the Timeline, the Info panel lists a start and end point; for clips selected in Project view, it lists In and Out points.

1 To open the Info panel, choose Window > Info. Once it's opened, you can drag the Info panel by its title bar to reposition it on the screen, if necessary.

2 Click to select a clip in Project view or the My Project panel. The Info panel displays the clip's name, type, start and end points, duration, video and audio attributes, and location in the Timeline/Sceneline, and the position of the Cursor.

The History panel (Window > History) keeps a running list of every step you take during a project and adds each action to the bottom of its list. To undo an editing step, click it in the History panel. To undo multiple steps, click the earliest step that you'd like to undo, and Adobe Premiere Elements will also undo all editing steps after that point.

These are the most prominent panels and workspaces within Adobe Premiere Elements. Now let's take a brief look at Photoshop.com, which is where you'll back up and share your photos and movies.

▶ **Tip:** In addition to the History panel, Adobe Premiere Elements supports multiple undos by choosing Edit > Undo or by pressing Ctrl+Z. Each time you press Ctrl+Z, you are undoing another step and working back through your edits in order, starting with the most recent. You can also redo a step by choosing Edit > Redo or pressing Ctrl+Shift+Z.

Working with Photoshop.com

Photoshop.com is an online photo and video hosting, editing, and sharing site. If you're using Adobe Premiere Elements in the United States, you can register for a free Basic Membership or opt for the Plus Membership (check www.photoshop.com for pricing). All members can back up images and movies on the site. Basic members are allocated 2 gigabytes (GB) of storage space, and Plus members have access to 20 GB of storage, or about four hours of DVD-quality video, with the option to purchase more online storage.

If you're already a member of Photoshop.com, you can log in from Adobe Premiere Elements by clicking Sign In on the upper-right toolbar. If not, you can click Create New Adobe ID to register for the service.

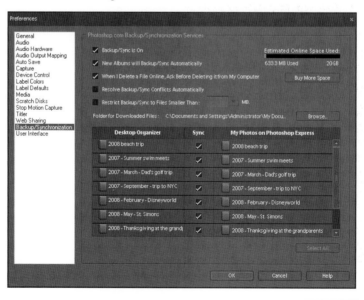

All members control the content that is uploaded to their Photoshop.com accounts with this Preferences panel, which you access in the Elements Organizer by choosing Edit > Preferences > Backup/Synchronization.

Photoshop.com Plus members also receive free access to online moviemaking ideas and tutorials. If you have a Plus Membership, Adobe Premiere Elements will display these tutorials in the Welcome screen that opens when you first run the program and, from time to time, on the lower right of the My Project panel.

Click the tutorial title to display a short description of the tutorial, and then click See how to view the tutorial in the Adobe Photoshop.com Inspiration Browser.

Plus members all receive free content from Photoshop.com, such as the titles shown above. Note that Adobe Premiere Elements will download these files automatically once they're available and will display them in the Photoshop.com folder. The titles shown here are from the two themes added during Fall 2008, Scary Halloween and Autumn Leaves.

Review Questions

1 What are the three main panels in Adobe Premiere Elements, and what function does each serve?

2 What types of projects should you consider starting from the Organizer, and why?

3 What are the two views of the My Project panel, and what are their respective strengths?

4 What are the three major benefits of the Plus Membership of Photoshop.com?

Review Answers

1 The three main panels are the Monitor, Tasks, and My Project panels. You build your movies by adding clips to the My Project panel. The Monitor panel serves multiple roles, allowing you to preview your movies and create titles and other effects. The Tasks panel has four workspaces that allow you to organize your clips, create InstantMovies, and render your movies for sharing with others. It also contains content like effects, transitions, themes, titles, and disc menus.

2 Any project that doesn't involve capture from tape should start from the Organizer. Starting work in the Organizer provides faster access to tagging and sort tools, and direct access to production activities like creating an InstantMovie or uploading a video to Photoshop.com.

3 Adobe Premiere Elements offers two views in the My Project panel: Sceneline and Timeline. The Sceneline shows only the first frame of the clip and is ideal for quickly arranging the order of your clips and performing basic edits. The Timeline displays clips on separate tracks and is superior for advanced edits like picture-in-picture and other overlay effects, and for adding background music or narration to your productions.

4 Plus members receive up to 20 GB of storage space (compared to 2 GB for the Basic Membership), access to tutorials, ideas, and additional content when released by Adobe.

2 GETTING READY TO EDIT

Now that you're familiar with the Adobe Premiere Elements interface, you'll learn how to create a project, set relevant user preferences, and configure the interface to your liking. For those tempted to skip this chapter, understand that while Adobe Premiere Elements is a wonderfully flexible and customizable program, once you choose a project setting and start editing, you can't change the setting.

While you can often work around this issue, in some instances you may have to abandon the initial project and start again using a different setting to achieve the desired results. Invest a little time here to understand how Adobe Premiere Elements works with project settings so you can get your project done right the first time.

In this lesson, you'll learn to do the following:

- Create a new project
- Choose the optimal setting for your project
- Set preferences for Auto Save, Scratch Disks, and the user interface
- Customize window sizes and locations in the workspace
- Restore the workspace to its default configuration

 This lesson will take approximately one hour.

Collecting assets for your movie.

Setting Up a New Project

Adobe Premiere Elements can work with video from any source, from DV camcorders shooting 4:3 or 16:9 (widescreen) standard-definition (SD) video to the latest AVCHD and HDV high-definition (HD) camcorders. For the best results, you should choose a project setting that matches your source footage, following the procedure described here.

After you choose a setting, Adobe Premiere Elements will automatically use the same setting for all future projects, which should work well if you use the same source video format for all subsequent projects. Should you change the format, however—for example, from DV to HDV—remember to change your project setting as well.

1 Launch Adobe Premiere Elements and click the New Project button in the Welcome screen. If Adobe Premiere Elements is already open, choose File > New > Project.

● **Note:** For more information on a Preset, click the setting, and Adobe Premiere Elements will display technical details in the Description field.

2 Check the Project Settings in the lower-left corner of the New Project screen. If the Project Settings match your source footage, proceed to step 4. If not, click the Change Settings button to open the Setup screen.

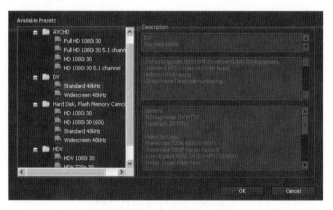

3 Click the Preset that matches your source footage.

4 After choosing a Preset, click OK to close the Setup screen.

5 In the New Project panel, choose a name and storage location for the new project. Then click OK to save the new project file.

Diagnosing Settings-related Issues

If you've chosen the wrong project setting, the most common problem you'll encounter concerns differences in the aspect ratio of your video. This is evidenced by black bars across the sides or top and bottom of the video in the Monitor panel, which is a display technique called letterboxing. Adobe Premiere Elements will letterbox a 4:3 video displayed in a 16:9 window, producing the black bars on the sides of the video in the Monitor panel below.

1   To view the current project setting, choose Edit > Project Settings > General. In this project with the letterboxing issue, as you can see in the Project Settings screen, the Editing Mode is DV NTSC, but the Pixel Aspect Ratio is D1/DV NTSC Widescreen (1.2), which is 16:9 video. Your project Pixel Aspect Ratio should be D1/DV NTSC (0.9091), and you shouldn't see letterboxing. Both fields are grayed out and inactive, indicating that you can't change their values. Click OK to close the Project Settings screen.

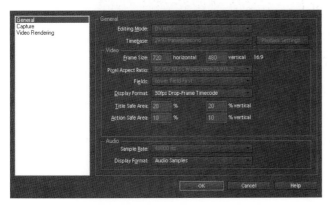

2 To view aspect ratio-related information about clips in the My Project panel, choose Window > Info. If you don't have any clips in the My Project panel, drag one down from the Media view into the Sceneline or Timeline in the My Projects panel.

3 Click any clip in the Timeline or Sceneline. In the Video description line in the Info panel, you can see that the video has a frame rate of 29.97 frames per second (fps) and a resolution of 720x480, but the aspect ratio is .9091, which designates 4:3 video.

To display the 4:3 video in a 16:9 project, Adobe Premiere Elements inserts letter-boxes on the sides of the 4:3 video. You can eliminate the letterboxes using the controls discussed in "Reframing a Clip with Motion Controls" in Lesson 6, which is a good solution when including one 4:3 clip in a 16:9 movie. If all your clips are 4:3, however, you should restart the project using a 4:3 setting.

Choosing the Correct Setting

There are many different video formats, several with multiple flavors, which can make it challenging to choose the correct setting. This sidebar will identify and detail the most frequently used settings in Adobe Premiere Elements to simplify your selection. Note that you may have to consult the documentation that came with your camcorder for details on the video format captured by the camcorder.

Before beginning, understand that there are two aspect ratios that relate to cam-corder video. The *display aspect ratio* is either 4:3 (standard) or 16:9, which is also called widescreen or sometimes anamorphic. These are the aspect ratios that you're most familiar with, because they're identical to the two common aspect ratios of TV sets.

The other aspect ratio is the *pixel aspect ratio*, which describes how the pixels that comprise the video must be adjusted during display. For example, all AVCHD video displays at 1920x1080. However, "HD" AVCHD video is stored by the camcorder at a resolution of 1440x1080, and each horizontal pixel must be stretched by a factor of 1.33 during display to achieve full resolution. For this reason, AVCHD video stored at a resolution of 1440x1080 has a pixel aspect ratio of 1.33.

In contrast, "Full HD" AVCHD video is captured at 1920x1080 resolution, so no stretching is required to produce the full1920x1080 display. Full HD video has a pixel aspect ratio of 1.0.

Adobe Premiere Elements can work with virtually any source of video, and once you choose the proper setting, you'll never have to worry about these aspect ratios again. However, to identify the setting that matches your source video, you may have to learn these highly technical details, especially if you're working with AVCHD:

- **AVCHD:** There are four AVCHD presets, differentiated by the resolution of video stored by the camcorder and audio channels. The two "Full HD" presets are for AVCHD video stored by the camcorder at 1920x1080 resolution (pixel aspect ratio of 1.0), whereas the "HD"  presets are for AVCHD video captured and stored at 1440x1080 resolution (pixel aspect ratio of 1.33). Both formats have a display aspect ratio (as opposed to pixel aspect ratio) of 16:9, as do all HD formats. The two 5.1 channel presets are for video recorded with 5.1-surround sound, and the other two presets are for video recorded with stereo audio.

- **DV:** There are two types of DV footage. Standard DV has a display aspect ratio of 4:3 and a pixel aspect ratio of .9, whereas widescreen DV has a display aspect ratio of 16:9 and a pixel aspect ratio of 1.2.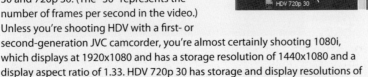

- **HDV:** There are two varieties of HDV, 1080i 30 and 720p 30. (The "30" represents the number of frames per second in the video.) Unless you're shooting HDV with a first- or second-generation JVC camcorder, you're almost certainly shooting 1080i, which displays at 1920x1080 and has a storage resolution of 1440x1080 and a display aspect ratio of 1.33. HDV 720p 30 has storage and display resolutions of 1280x720, and a display aspect ratio of 1.0.

- **Hard disk and Flash memory camcorders:** Adobe Premiere Elements has four presets for hard disk and Flash Memory camcorders. Use HD 1080i 30 for HD camcorders that shoot in that mode, and use HD 1080i (60) for  camcorders that shoot in that mode. Otherwise, use Standard 48kHz (kilohertz) for standard-definition (720x480 resolution) video with a display aspect ratio of 4:3, irrespective of pixel aspect ratio. Use Widescreen 48kHz for SD (720x480 resolution) video with a display aspect ratio of 16:9, irrespective of pixel aspect ratio.

Working with Project Preferences

For the most part, once you have the right project setting selected, you can jump in and begin editing with Adobe Premiere Elements. However, at some point you may want to adjust several program preferences that impact your editing experience. Here are the preferences that will prove relevant to most video editors.

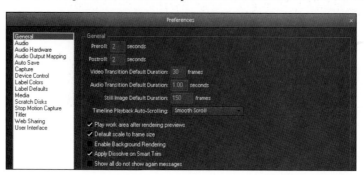

● Note: Adjusting these default durations will impact only edits made after the adjustment. For example, if you change the Still Image Default Duration to 120 frames, Adobe Premiere Elements will assign this duration to all still images added to the project thereafter, but won't change the duration of still images already inserted into the project.

1 To open the General Preferences panel, choose Edit > Preferences > General. Multiple preferences are in this panel; most important are the Video and Audio Transition Default Durations and the Still Image Default Duration, the latter of which controls the duration of all still images added to your project.

Better Saved than Sorry

With Auto Save enabled, Adobe Premiere Elements automatically saves a copy of your project at the specified duration, which you can customize. You can also change the number of separate projects that Adobe Premiere Elements saves.

Adobe Premiere Elements saves all Auto Save files in a separate subfolder titled Adobe Premiere Elements Auto-Save, which is located in the folder containing your current project file.

It's good practice to manually save your project periodically during editing to preserve your work in the event of a power outage or other random crash. Should a crash occur, you may be able to recover some of the editing that you've done subsequent to your last manual save by loading the most recent project automatically saved by Adobe Premiere Elements.

You load these just like any other project: click File > Open Project, navigate to the Adobe Premiere Elements Auto-Save folder, and choose the newest project file.

2 Click Auto Save to view Auto Save preferences.

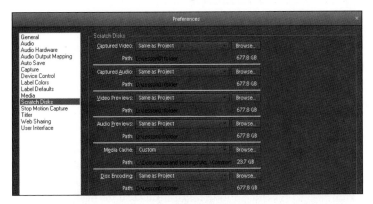

3 Click Scratch Disks to view the Scratch Disk preferences. This preference identifies the folders used to store audio and video clips that Adobe Premiere Elements creates while producing your project. This includes clips captured from your camcorder, video and audio previews, and media encoded for recording onto DVD or Blu-ray disc. By default, Adobe Premiere Elements stores this content in the same folder as the project file. If you run short of disk space, you can change the location of the scratch disk by clicking the Browse button next to each category of content and choosing a different location on a separate disk.

4 Click User Interface. Drag the User Interface Brightness slider to the right to make the interface brighter and to the left to make it darker. These adjustments can be useful when editing under varying lighting conditions, like in a dark or extremely bright room.

5 If desired, select the Use Windows Background Color check box to substitute the Windows default background color for Adobe Premiere Elements' background colors, and click OK to close the Preferences panel.

These are the most critical preferences to consider before starting your first project. With these configured, let's explore other options for customizing your workspace.

Customizing the Workspace

Adobe Premiere Elements uses a docking system to fit all the panels into the available space of the application window. However, panels can be moved and resized so that you can create a workspace that best fits your needs.

With Adobe Premiere Elements open, notice that the Monitor panel, the Tasks panel, and the My Project panel are separated by solid vertical and horizontal dividing lines. These dividers can be quickly repositioned to give you more space to work in one of the panels when you need it.

1   To increase the height of the My Project panel, hover your pointer over the dividing line between the My Project and Monitor panels until it converts to a two-headed cursor, and then drag it up toward the Monitor panel.

You can use a similar technique to expand the size of the Monitor panel by dragging it to the right, or expand the Tasks panel by dragging it to the left.

2   To reset the panels to their default layout, choose Window > Restore Workspace. Notice how everything snaps back to its original position. Consider restoring your workspace if you find your screen becomes cluttered.

To save some space on your screen, the docking headers of the panels, which contain title and sometimes panel menu and Close buttons, are hidden by default in Adobe Premiere Elements.

3 To show the docking headers, choose Window > Show Docking Headers. To hide them again, choose Window > Hide Docking Headers.

While the default workspace layout has every panel docked into a specific position, you may find it helpful from time to time to have a more flexible environment. To do this, you can undock, or float, your panels.

4 If the docking headers are not currently visible, choose Window > Show Docking Headers. Then click the docking header of the My Project panel and drag it a short distance in any direction. As you drag the header, the panel becomes translucent. When you release the pointer, the My Project panel becomes a floating window, allowing the Monitor panel and the Tasks panel to expand toward the bottom of the main window.

● **Note:** The Tasks panel is the only panel that cannot be undocked.

▶ **Tip:** When you work with multiple monitors, you can choose to display the application window on the main monitor and place floating windows on the second monitor.

5 Close the My Project panel by clicking its Close button (✖) in the upper-right corner.

6 Reopen the panel by choosing Window > My Project. Notice that the panel opens where you have previously placed it. This is because Adobe Premiere Elements remembers the locations of the panels and retains them as part of the customized workspace.

7 Choose Window > Restore Workspace to return to the default workspace layout.

● **Note:** The Tasks panel is the only panel that cannot be closed.

● **Note:** To learn more about customizing your workspace, choose Help > Adobe Premiere Elements Help, and then search for "Customizing the workspace" in the Adobe Help Center window.

Review Questions

1 What's the most important factor to consider when choosing a project setting?

2 Why is it so important to choose the right setting at the start of the project?

3 What is letterboxing, and what's a common cause for having letterboxes appear in your project?

4 What is Auto Save, and where do you adjust the Auto Save defaults in Adobe Premiere Elements?

5 What command do you use for restoring your workspace to the default panel configuration?

Review Answers

1 Choose a setting that matches the primary video that you will use in the project. For example, if you're shooting in widescreen DV, you should use a Widescreen DV project setting.

2 It's critical to choose the right setting when starting a project because unlike most Adobe Premiere Elements configuration items, you can't change the Project Setting after you create the project. In some instances, you may have to start the project over using the correct setting to produce optimal results.

3 Letterboxing is a display technique characterized by black bars on the sides or on the top and bottom of video in the Monitor panel. One of the most common causes of letterboxing is a discrepancy between the display aspect ratio of the project setting and the display aspect ratio of a video file imported into the project. For example, if you import 4:3 video into a 16:9 project, Adobe Premiere Elements will display letterboxes on both sides of the video in the Monitor panel.

4 Adobe Premiere Elements' Auto Save function automatically saves a copy of the project file at specified intervals, guarding against loss of work due to power outages or other random crashes. You can adjust the Auto Save defaults in the Preferences panel accessed by choosing Edit > Preferences.

5 Choose Window > Restore Workspace.

3 VIDEO CAPTURE AND IMPORT

This lesson describes how to capture and import video from your camcorder and other devices for editing in Adobe Premiere Elements, and introduces the following key concepts:

- Connecting a camcorder to your PC

- Capturing video from a camcorder

- Using the Media Downloader to import video from an AVCHD camcorder, digital still camera, DVD, or DVD-based camcorder or other similar devices

- Importing audio, video, or still images already on your hard drive into an Adobe Premiere Elements project

 This lesson will take approximately 1.5 hours.

Capturing video from your DV camera.

Capturing Video with Adobe Premiere Elements

When videographers and video enthusiasts started editing video on computers, the typical source was an analog camcorder. Today, while some Adobe Premiere Elements users still shoot analog video, most will start with DV or HDV source footage, AVCHD, video shot with a digital still camera, or even video imported from a previously created DVD.

Whatever the source, Adobe Premiere Elements includes all the tools necessary to capture or import your footage so you can begin producing movies. Though the specific technique will vary depending on the source, Adobe Premiere Elements guides your efforts with device-specific interfaces. All you have to do is connect the device to your computer as described in this lesson, and choose the appropriate icon from Get Media view in the Organize workspace.

Adobe Premiere Elements has two basic interfaces for capturing or importing video. After a quick overview of these interfaces, this lesson will detail how to capture video from a tape-based camcorder and then explain how to import content from an AVCHD camcorder or any other device that stores video on a hard disk, CompactFlash media (such as an SD card), or optical media. All the concepts in this section and the specific Adobe Premiere Elements features that support them are described in more detail in the Adobe Premiere Elements User Guide.

● **Note:** Adobe Premiere Elements lets you add video, audio, graphics, and still images to your project from numerous sources. In addition to capturing footage, you can import image, video, and audio files stored on your computer's hard disk, card readers, mobile phones, DVDs, Blu-ray discs, CDs, digital cameras, other devices, or the Internet.

Capture Interfaces

When you shoot video, it's stored locally on your camcorder, whether on tape, SD media, a hard drive, or even an optical disc like a DVD. Before you can edit your movie in Adobe Premiere Elements, you must transfer these clips to a local hard disk. In addition to capturing or importing video from a device, you may have existing content on your hard disk to import into the project.

Tape and Live Capture vs. Clip-based Import

Adobe Premiere Elements provides three interfaces for accomplishing captures and imports. If you're capturing video footage from a tape-based camcorder, such as a DV or HDV model, or live from a webcam or WDM (Windows Device Model) device, you'll use the Capture panel.

If you're importing video clips from a hard disk, flash media, or optical media, you use the Media Downloader. Again, to open the appropriate interface, just connect your device and click the correct icon in Get Media view in the Organize workspace; Adobe Premiere Elements will do the rest.

(See illustration on next page.)

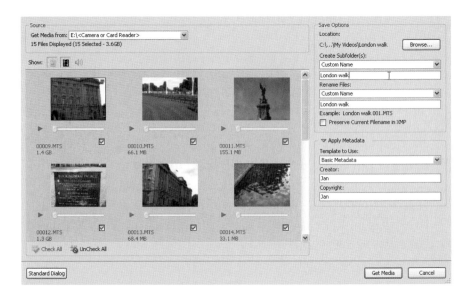

If the audio, video, or still image files are already on your computer's hard drive, click the PC Files and Folders icon in Get Media view in the Organize workspace, navigate to the files, and select them as you normally would. This lesson details this procedure at the end of the chapter.

Capturing Tape-based or Live Video

If you're capturing from a DV or HDV camcorder, or a webcam, you'll use the Capture panel. This lesson will discuss some preliminary concepts relating to these devices and then detail the procedure.

Connecting Your Device

The simplest way to capture DV or HDV video is to connect the camcorder to a computer with an IEEE 1394 port. Adobe Premiere Elements supports a wide range of DV devices and capture cards, making it easy to capture DV source files.

Some DV and HDV camcorders also have USB 2.0 ports. USB 2.0 is a high-speed transfer protocol similar to IEEE 1394. When present on a DV/HDV camcorder, the USB 2.0 connector is typically used only for transferring digital still images rather than tape-based video shot by the camcorder to the computer. When both connectors are present, use the IEEE 1394 connector for video capture.

● **Note:** Though it's extremely rare, sometimes when connecting your computer to your camcorder via an IEEE 1394 connector, an electrical charge from the computer can damage the camcorder. To minimize this risk, always turn off both devices before capture, connect the IEEE 1394 cable, turn on your computer, and then turn on the camcorder.

System Setup

Before you attempt video capture, make sure your system is set up appropriately for working with digital video. The following are some general guidelines for ensuring that you have a DV-capable system:

- **IEEE 1394 port:** Make sure your computer has an IEEE 1394 port. This port may either be built into your computer or available on a PCI or PC card (often referred to as capture cards) that you install yourself. Many computers manufactured now include onboard IEEE 1394 cards.

- **High data transfer rate:** Make sure your hard disk is fast enough to capture and play back digital video. The speed at which digital video files transfer information—the *data transfer rate* (often shortened to *data rate*)—is 3.6 megabytes per second (MB/sec). The sustained (not peak) data transfer rate of your hard disk should meet or exceed this rate. To confirm the data transfer rate of your hard disk, see your computer or hard disk documentation.

- **Extra storage:** Consider using a secondary hard disk for extra capacity during capture and production and to enhance capture performance. In general, most internal hard disks should be sufficiently fast for capture and editing. However, external drives that connect via USB 2.0 and IEEE 1394, though excellent for data backup chores, may be too slow for video capture. If you're looking for an external drive for video production, a newer technology called eSATA offers the best mix of performance and affordability, but you may have to purchase an internal eSATA adapter for your computer or notebook.

- **Sufficient hard disk space:** Make sure you have sufficient disk space for the captured footage. Five minutes of digital video occupies about 1 gigabyte (GB) of hard disk space. The Capture panel in Adobe Premiere Elements indicates the duration of footage that you can capture based on the remaining space on your hard disk. Be certain beforehand that you will have sufficient space for the intended length of video capture. Also, some capture cards have size limits on digital video files ranging from 2 GB and up. See your capture card documentation for information on file size limitations.

- **Defragment:** Make sure you periodically defragment your hard disk. Writing to a fragmented disk can cause disruptions in your hard disk's transfer speed, causing you to lose or drop frames as you capture. You can use the defragmentation utility included with Windows or purchase a third-party utility.

- **Updates:** The state of high-end video hardware changes rapidly; consult the manufacturer of your video capture card for suggestions about appropriate video storage hardware.

Capture Video

How to connect your DV camcorder to your computer

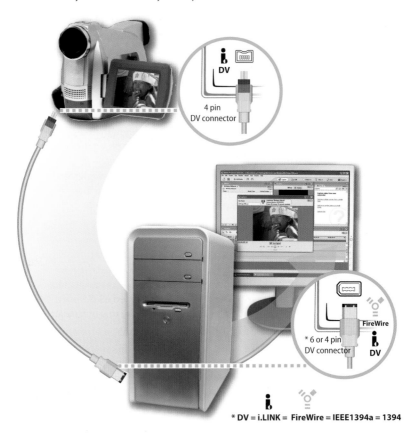

Most DV/HDV camcorders have a four-pin IEEE 1394 connector, whereas most computers have a larger, six-pin connector. Note, however, that some computers—particularly notebooks—may also have a four-pin IEEE 1394 connector. When purchasing an IEEE 1394 cable, make sure that it has the appropriate connectors.

If you're capturing from a webcam or WDM device, Adobe Premiere Elements will capture the video from the USB 2.0 connector used to connect the device with your computer.

Capture Options

The Capture settings dialog

When you capture video from a tape or live source, you have multiple capture options, including whether to capture audio and video, capture to the Timeline, split scenes, and apply Smart Tagging. Let's briefly discuss each option before working through the capture process.

About Timecode

When capturing video, it's important to understand the basics about timecode. Timecode numbers represent the location of a frame in a video clip. Many camcorders record timecode as part of the video signal. The timecode format is based on the number of frames per second (fps) that the camcorder records and the number of frames per second that the video displays upon playback. Video has a standard frame rate that is either 29.97 fps for NTSC video (the North American and Japanese TV standard) or 25 fps for PAL video (the European TV standard). Timecode describes a frame's location in the format of hours:minutes:seconds:frames. For example, 01;20;15;10 specifies that the displayed frame is located 1 hour, 20 minutes, 15 seconds, and 10 frames into the scene.

—From Adobe Premiere Elements Help

Capturing video or audio only

By default, Adobe Premiere Elements captures both audio and video when capturing a clip. You can change this default in the Capture Settings dialog that appears in the Capture panel, which opens after you select your video source. In the top line of the dialog, both Video and Audio are selected by default. To capture only audio, deselect the Video check box. To capture only video, deselect the Audio check box.

Note that you can easily remove either the audio or video portion of the captured clip during editing. Unless you're absolutely certain that you won't use either the audio or the video, capture both and remove the undesired media during editing.

Capture to Timeline

The Capture to Timeline option automatically inserts all captured clips into the My Project panel. By default, this option is selected. If you'd prefer to manually drag all clips to the My Project panel, deselect this option.

Capturing video clips with Scene Detect

During capture, Adobe Premiere Elements can split the captured video into scenes, which makes it much easier to find and edit the desired content. Adobe Premiere Elements can use one of two scene-detection techniques to detect scenes: Timecode-based and Content-based.

Timecode-based scene detection is available only when capturing DV source video. As the name suggests, this technique uses timecodes in the video to break the capture clips into scenes. Specifically, when you record DV, your camcorder automatically records a time/date stamp when you press Stop or Record. During capture, Adobe Premiere Elements creates a new scene each time it detects a new time/date stamp and creates a separate video file on your hard drive for each scene.

Content-based scene detection, which is your only option for HDV or webcam videos, analyzes the content after capture to identify scene changes. For example, if you shot one scene indoors and the next outdoors, Adobe Premiere Elements would analyze the video frames and detect the new scene.

When detecting scenes using Content-based scene detection, Adobe Premiere Elements stores only one video file on your hard drive and designates the scenes in the Organize and Edit workspaces. After capture, while scanning the captured video for scene changes, Adobe Premiere Elements displays a status panel describing the operation and apprising you of its progress.

During capture, Adobe Premiere Elements will default to Timecode-based scene detection for DV source video and default to Content-based scene detection for HDV and webcam-based videos. I suggest leaving Scene Detect enabled during video capture and using these defaults. To change these defaults in the Capture panel (which you'll learn how to open shortly), do the following:

1   To disable Scene Detect entirely, deselect the Split Scenes check box in the Capture settings on the right of the Capture panel.

2   If you're capturing DV, you can opt for either the Timecode-based or Content-based scene detection. In most instances, the former will be faster and more accurate. To change from Timecode-based to Content-based scene detection, select the Split Scenes check box, twirl the By: triangle if necessary to view both options, and click the Content radio button.

Capturing video clips with the Auto Analyzer

The Auto Analyzer feature analyzes captured video clips and adds quality tags, such as shaky or bright; or interest tags, such as faces or motion. You can use these tags to quickly find your highest-quality video. In addition, features such as InstantMovie and Automatic Quality Enhancement use Smart Tags when performing their respective functions.

The roles that Smart Tags play in video production are detailed in the section titled "Running the Auto Analyzer" in Lesson 4. In general, the Auto Analyzer takes relatively little time and produces a wealth of useful information about your clips. We suggest leaving the Auto Analyzer enabled during capture with all tags enabled, because this is the default setting.

To completely disable the Auto Analyzer, deselect the Auto Analyzer check box in the Capture settings on the right of the Capture panel. To change the Smart Tags that the Auto Analyzer searches for, twirl the Analyze: triangle to view all Smart Tags, and select all desired Smart Tags.

With Smart Tagging enabled, Adobe Premiere Elements will scan the video after capture and display a status window describing the operation and apprising you of its progress.

With these options covered, let's discuss one more capture-related feature and then capture video.

Capturing clips with device control

When capturing clips, device control refers to the ability to control the operation of a connected video deck or camcorder using controls within the Adobe Premiere Elements interface rather than using the controls on the connected device. This mode of operation is more convenient because Adobe Premiere Elements offers controls like Next Scene or Shuttle that may not be available on your camcorder's controls.

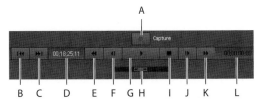

Capture panel controls: **A.** Capture. **B.** Previous Scene. **C.** Next Scene. **D.** Current Position – Timecode Display. **E.** Rewind. **F.** Step Back (Left). **G.** Play/Pause. **H.** Shuttle. **I.** Step Forward (Right). **J.** Fast-Forward. **K.** Stop. **L.** Capture Duration (active only during capture)

You probably know most of these controls because they're similar to your camcorder or VCR. You may not be familiar with the Shuttle control, which you can drag with your pointer to the left or right to rewind or fast-forward the video. This control is position-sensitive; the farther you drag the shuttle widget from the center, the faster the tape fast-forwards or rewinds. The Previous Scene and Next Scene controls use Timecode-based scene detection to advance backwards or forwards to the previous or next scenes.

Adobe Premiere Elements should be able to establish device control with all DV and HDV camcorders, but it's not available when capturing from webcams, WDM devices, or analog camcorders. You can still capture video from these sources without device control, but the capture procedure is slightly different. Procedures for capturing both with and without device control are detailed in the following section.

Debugging Device Control Issues

As mentioned, Adobe Premiere Elements should be able to establish device control with all DV and HDV camcorders. If you see the error message "No DV camera detected" or "No HDV camera detected," Adobe Premiere Elements can't detect your camcorder. In this case, you won't be able to establish device control and may not be able to capture video. Here are some steps you can take to attempt to remedy this situation.

1 Exit Adobe Premiere Elements and make sure your camcorder is turned on and running (and hasn't timed out due to inactivity) in VCR, Play, or other similar mode. Also check to see that your IEEE 1394 cable is firmly connected to both the camcorder's and computer's IEEE 1394 ports. Then run Adobe Premiere Elements again and see if the program detects the camcorder.

2 If not, check your Project Settings and make sure they match your camcorder (DV project if DV camcorder; HDV project if HDV camcorder).

3 If Adobe Premiere Elements still doesn't detect your camcorder, determine if Windows detects your camcorder, which is necessary for Adobe Premiere Elements to detect the device. When you turn your camcorder on and off, Windows should respond, usually with an audible alert, and often by opening a Digital Video Device dialog.

In addition, check to see if your camcorder is identified in Windows Explorer. If Windows doesn't respond when you turn your camcorder on and off, if your camcorder isn't identified in Windows Explorer, or both, it's likely that there's a hardware issue, like a defective cable or faulty IEEE 1394 port on your camcorder or computer. Try substituting new devices (cable, camcorder, computer) until you identify the faulty component.

4 If Windows does recognize your camcorder, you may have a configuration problem within Adobe Premiere Elements. In the Capture panel, choose Capture Settings, which opens the Project Settings dialog to the Capture Format.

5   In this dialog, choose the correct capture device, either DV or HDV. Close and reopen the Capture panel. If Adobe Premiere Elements still doesn't detect your camcorder, try step 6.

6   In the Capture panel menu, choose Device Control, which opens the Preferences dialog with the Device Control view visible.

7   In this dialog, choose the format that matches your connection, DV/HDV for IEEE 1394 or USB Video Class 1.0 for USB. Close and reopen the Capture panel. If Adobe Premiere Elements still doesn't detect your camcorder, try step 8.

8   Most HDV camcorders can also record and play DV video. However, if you're capturing DV video and your camcorder is set to record HDV, Adobe Premiere Elements may detect an HDV camcorder rather than DV (or vice versa). For example, if you shot HDV in your last shoot but were capturing DV video from a previous shoot, Adobe Premiere Elements may detect an HDV camcorder rather than a DV camcorder. In this situation, set the camcorder to record DV video, and once you return to VCR or Play mode, play a few seconds of DV video, which may enable Adobe Premiere Elements to detect the DV camcorder.

Capturing with the Capture Panel

With the preceding information in this lesson as a prologue, let's look at the process for capturing video via Adobe Premiere Elements' Capture panel.

1   Connect the DV camcorder to your computer via an IEEE 1394 cable.

2   Turn on the camera and set it to the playback mode, which may be labeled VTR, VCR, or Play.

3   Launch Adobe Premiere Elements. Click New Project in the Welcome screen, and choose a project name and the appropriate preset.

4   In the Organize workspace, click Get Media.

● **Note:** This exercise assumes that a DV camera has been successfully connected to your computer and that you have footage available to capture. If this is not the case, you can still open the Capture panel to review the interface; however, you will not be able to access all the controls.

Note: If your DV camera is connected but not turned on, your Capture panel will display Capture Device Offline in the status area. Although it is preferable to turn on your camera before launching Adobe Premiere Elements, in most cases turning on your camera at any point will bring it online.

Note: When capturing DV and webcam footage, you will see video in the Preview area of the Capture panel. When capturing HDV, you won't see any video in the Preview area and will have to watch the LCD screen on your camcorder to determine when to stop capture.

5 In Get Media view, select DV Camcorder ( ) to follow along with this procedure. Selecting HDV Camcorder ( ) or Webcam or WDM Device ( ) will also open the Capture panel, though some settings will be different from this example.

The Capture panel appears. Note that if you're capturing from videotape, your preview screen will be black until you actually start to play the video.

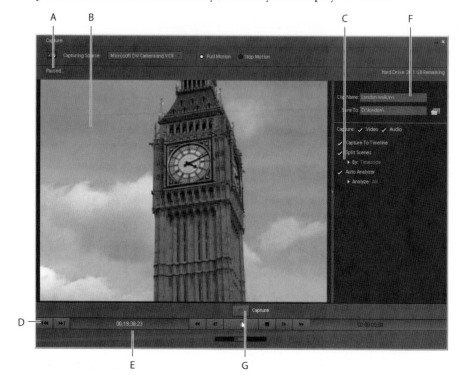

A. Status area—Displays status information about your camera. **B.** Preview area—Displays your current video as played through your camera. **C.** Capture settings—Enables you to change the capture settings. **D.** Device controls—Contains buttons used to directly control your camera. **E.** Current position—Timecode display. Shows you the current frame of your video, measured in the format of hours;minutes;seconds;frames. **F.** Clip name—By default, Adobe Premiere Elements uses the project name to name the AVI movie clips. **G.** Capture/Pause button

6 On the upper-right area of the Capture panel, type the desired Clip Name and Save To location for the captured files. Note that Adobe Premiere Elements defaults to the project name for Clip Name and uses the folder where you stored your project file for the default Save To location. If desired, change any of the default Capture settings.

7 At the bottom of the Capture panel, use the navigation controls to navigate to the first scene you'd like to capture.

Tip: See "Capture stop-motion and time-lapse video" in Adobe Premiere Elements Help for more information.

Capturing Stop-motion and Time-lapse Video

Using stop-motion and time-lapse video, you can make inanimate objects appear to move, or show a flower grow and bloom in seconds. In this mode, you capture single video frames at widely spaced time intervals for later playback at normal frame rates.

You create stop-motion animations or time-lapse videos by using the Stop Motion button in the Capture panel. You can capture frames either from pre-recorded tape or from a live camera feed. Stop-motion capture lets you manually select the frames you want to capture; Time Lapse capture automatically captures frames at set intervals. Using Time Lapse mode you can reduce a lengthy event, such as a sunset or a flower blooming, to a very short span.

Note: You cannot capture stop-motion video from an HDV source.

—*From Adobe Premiere Elements Help*

To capture stop-motion from a tape-based device, do the following:

1   Connect your tape device to your computer and turn it on. Then do one of the following:

   • If capturing live from a camcorder, place the camcorder in Camera mode.

   • If capturing from videotape, place the device in Play, VTR, or VCR mode.

2   In the Capture panel, click the Stop Motion button.

3   Click the Create New Stop Motion button in the middle of the Capture panel preview pane.

4   If capturing from videotape, use the camcorder's controls to move to the desired frame. If capturing live, adjust your scene as desired. Click Grab Frame whenever the Capture panel displays a frame that you want to save to the hard disk. Each frame you grab will appear as a .bmp file in Project view with a sequential number in its filename.

5   Close the Capture panel and in the dialog that appears, save the still images as a movie file.

8   Click the Capture button ( ), and Adobe Premiere Elements automatically starts playing video on the DV camcorder, captures each scene as an individual movie clip, and adds it to your project.

9 After clicking the Capture button, it converts into the Pause button (). To stop capturing video, either click the Pause button or press the Esc key on your keyboard. If enabled, the Auto Analyze window will appear as Adobe Premiere Elements analyzes the clip and then close. Any clips you have already captured will remain in your project.

● **Note:** When capturing without device control, use the camcorder's playback controls to navigate to a position about 20 seconds before the first scene you want to capture. Then click Play, and about 10 seconds before the actual scene appears, click the Capture button ( ). Adobe Premiere Elements will start capturing the video. Capture the desired scenes, and about 10 seconds after the last target frame, click the Stop button ( ) to stop capture.

● **Note:** If you receive the error message "Recorder Error - frames are dropped during capture," or if you're having problems with the device control, it's likely that your hard disk is not keeping up with the transfer of video. Make sure you're capturing your video to the fastest hard disk available; for example, an external IEEE 1394 drive rather than a hard disk inside a laptop computer.

10 After you've completed capturing your video, close the Capture panel by clicking the Close button ( ) in the upper-right corner. Your captured clips appear in the Organize workspace in both the Media and Project views. If you enabled Capture to Timeline, Adobe Premiere Elements will also place each clip into your Sceneline in sequential order.

Converting Analog Video to Digital Video

Before DV camcorders were widely manufactured, most people used camcorders that recorded analog video onto VHS, 8mm, or other analog tape formats. To use video from analog sources in your Adobe Premiere Elements project, you must first convert (digitize) the footage to digital data, because Adobe Premiere Elements accepts only direct input from digital sources. To digitize your footage, you can use either your digital camcorder or a stand-alone device that performs analog-to-digital (AV DV) conversion.

You can perform a successful conversion using the following methods:

- **Output a digital signal.** Use your digital camcorder to output a digital signal from an analog input. Connect the analog source to input jacks on your digital camcorder and connect the digital camcorder to the computer. Not all digital camcorders support this method. See your camcorder documentation for more information.

- **Record analog footage.** Use your digital camcorder to record footage from your analog source. Connect your analog source's output to the analog inputs on your digital camcorder. Then record your analog footage to digital tape. When you are finished recording, Adobe Premiere Elements can then capture the footage from the digital camcorder. This is a very common procedure. See your camcorder documentation for more details on recording from analog sources.

- **Capture sound.** Use your computer's sound card, if it has a microphone (mic) input, to capture sound from a microphone.

- **Bridge the connection.** Use an AV DV converter to bridge the connection between your analog source and the computer. Connect the analog source to the converter and connect the converter to your computer. Adobe Premiere Elements then captures the digitized footage. AV DV converters are available in many large consumer electronics stores.

Note: If you capture using an AV DV converter, you might need to capture without using device control.

—From Adobe Premiere Elements Help

Using the Media Downloader

As mentioned at the start of this lesson, you will use Adobe Premiere Elements' Media Downloader to import clips from DVDs, DVD-based camcorders, AVCHD camcorders, digital still cameras, and mobile phones and players. In essence, if the video is stored on a hard drive, SD card, optical disc, or other storage media other than tape, you'll import it with the Media Downloader.

● **Note:** This connection procedure will vary by device: Some AVCHD camcorders require that you set the camcorder to PC Mode before connecting the USB 2.0 cable, others the reverse. Please check the documentation that came with your camcorder for additional details.

In this exercise you'll use the Media Downloader to import video from an AVCHD camcorder. If you don't have an AVCHD camcorder, you can follow along using video captured on a digital still camera, DVD camcorder, or mobile phone, or even a nonencrypted DVD, such as one that you've previously produced with Adobe Premiere Elements. Note that Adobe Premiere Elements will not import video from DVDs that are encrypted, such as most Hollywood DVD titles.

1 Connect your AVCHD camcorder to your computer via the USB 2.0 port.

2 Turn on the camcorder and set it to PC mode, or whichever mode is used to transfer video from camcorder to computer.

3 Launch Adobe Premiere Elements. Click New Project in the Welcome screen, and choose a project name and the appropriate preset.

4 In the Organize workspace, click Get Media.

5 In Get Media view, select AVCHD Camcorder ( ) to follow along with this procedure. Selecting DVD Camcorder or PC DVD Drive ( ), or Digital Still Camera ( ), or Mobile Phones and Players ( ) will also open Media Downloader, though some settings will be different from this example.

The Media Downloader opens using the Advanced dialog. (If the Advanced dialog doesn't appear, click Advanced Dialog in the lower left of the Adobe Premiere Elements - Media Downloader window.)

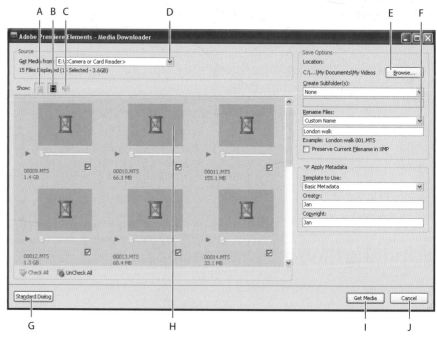

Adobe Premiere Elements Media Downloader (Advanced dialog): **A.** Show/hide image files. **B.** Show/hide video files. **C.** Show/hide audio files. **D.** Available drives and devices. **E.** Location for saved files. **F.** Naming convention. **G.** Standard Dialog button. **H.** Importable files. **I.** Get Media button. **J.** Cancel button.

6 Under Source, choose the drive or device from the Get Media view menu.

Once you choose the drive or device, Adobe Premiere Elements will populate the Media Downloader. When importing video from most devices, including DVDs and most digital still cameras, thumbnails of all available video and still image files will appear in the dialog. When importing video from an AVCHD camcorder, Adobe Premiere Elements will not show video thumbnails, although the Media Downloader will display thumbnails of digital still images captured by the AVCHD camcorder.

7 To show or hide specific file types, click the Show/Hide Images button (🖼), the Show/Hide Video button (🎞), or the Show/Hide Audio button (🔊) located above the thumbnail area.

8 To preview a video file, click the black triangle in the lower-left corner of the video thumbnail image.

9 To specify a location for the saved files, do one of the following:

- To save files to the default location—which is the location where you previously stored files captured by the Media Downloader—leave the location unchanged.

- To specify a new location for saving the files, click Browse and choose a folder, or click Make New Folder to create a new folder.

- Optionally, Adobe Premiere Elements saves imported files to one or more subfolders with multiple naming options.

- To create a single folder with a name of your choice, select Custom Name from the Create Subfolder(s) menu and enter the name of the folder in the text box that appears.

10 To rename the files using a consistent name within the folder, select an option other than Do Not Rename Files from the Rename Files menu. When the files are added to the folder and to the Media panel, the file numbers are incremented by 001. For example, if you enter *London walk* as Custom Name under Rename Files, Adobe Premiere Elements will change the filenames to London walk 001.MTS, London walk 002.MTS, and so on.

11 In the thumbnail area, select individual files to add to the Media panel. A check mark below a file's thumbnail indicates that the file is selected. By default, all files are selected. Only selected files are imported. Click a check box to deselect it, thus excluding the related file from being imported.

● **Note:** When you import a DVD using the Media Downloader, files for menus are distinguished from video files by the word Menu, as in Menu_Epgc_Esf_938876809.psd.

● **Note:** You cannot preview AVCHD video in the current version of Adobe Premiere Elements.

12 Click Get Media. This transfers the
media to the destination location,
which is typically your hard disk. You
can click Stop in the Copying dialog at
any time to stop the process.

Files that you import using the Media
Downloader appear in the Organize workspace, as well as Project view in the Edit
workspace.

Importing Content from Your Hard Disk

Follow this procedure to import audio, video, or still-image content that's already
on your hard disk.

1 In the Organize workspace, click Get Media.

2 Click PC Files and Folders ( ).

Adobe Premiere Elements opens the Add Media panel.

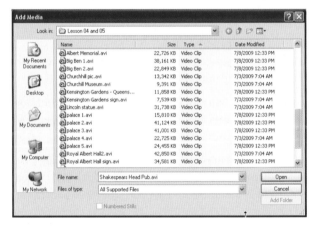

3 To change to a new disk or folder, click the Look In list box and navigate to a
new location.

4 To display only certain files types in the dialog, click the Supported Files of type
list box, and choose the desired file type. The dialog displays only files of the
selected type.

5 To change the file view in the dialog, click the View menu.

6 To import files, choose them in the dialog as you normally would, and click
Open.

Files that you import using the Add Media dialog appear in the Organize workspace, as well as in Project view in the Edit workspace.

Review Questions

1   How do you access the Capture panel in Adobe Premiere Elements?

2   Why is having a separate hard disk dedicated to video a good idea?

3   What is Scene Detect, and how would you turn it on or off if you wanted to?

4   What is the Media Downloader, and when would you use it?

5   What is device control?

Review Answers

1   Click Get Media from the Organize Workspace, and then click the appropriate capture icon.

2   Video files take up large amounts of space compared to standard office and image files. A hard disk stores the video clips you capture and must be fast enough to store your video frames. Although office-type files tend to be fairly small, they can clutter a hard disk when scattered throughout the available space; the more free, defragmented space you have on a hard disk, the better the performance of real-time video capture will be.

3   Scene Detect is Adobe Premiere Elements' ability to detect scene changes in your video (based on timecode or by content) during video capture and save each scene as an individual clip in your project. You can select or deselect Scene Detect by Timecode and Scene Detect by Content in the Capture panel menu.

4   The Media Downloader is a feature of Adobe Premiere Elements that enables you to import media from AVCHD camcorders, digital still cameras, mobile phones and players, and DVDs, whether from a camcorder or PC DVD driver.

5   Device control is the ability of Adobe Premiere Elements to control the basic functions of your digital video camera (such as play, stop, and rewind) through the interface in the Capture panel. It's available on most DV and HDV camcorders.

4 ORGANIZING YOUR CONTENT

After you've captured or imported your content, you can drag it to the My Project panel from either the Media view or Project view in the Edit workspace. Why two locations? As you'll read in this chapter, each has its own unique strengths.

For example, Media view and its big brother the Organizer are ideal for tagging your clips for easy search and retrieval, for creating InstantMovies, and for creating albums to back up to Photoshop.com. Project view works well when you'd like to sort and trim your clips before adding them to the Sceneline or Timeline.

Fast and efficient movie production is all about organization. In this lesson, you'll learn how to do the following:

- Manually tag your clips in the Organizer

- Apply Smart Tagging in the Organizer

- Create an Album for backing up your projects to Photoshop.com

- Create an InstantMovie using manual and Smart Tagging

- Create a "rough cut" of your movie in Project view

- Trim clips using the Preview window in Project view

- Drag clips to the My Project panel from either Media view or Project view

 This lesson will take approximately two hours.

Tagging content in the Organizer.

Getting Started

Before you start working with the footage, let's review a final version of the movie you'll be creating.

1   To begin, make sure that you have correctly copied the Lesson04 and 05 folder from the DVD in the back of this book onto your computer's hard disk. For more information, see "Copying the Classroom in a Book files" in the "Getting Started" section at the beginning of this book.

2   Launch Adobe Premiere Elements.

3   In the Welcome screen, click the Open Project button. If necessary, click Open in the pop-up menu. The Open Project dialog opens.

4   In the Open Project dialog, navigate to the Lesson04 and 05 folder you copied to your hard disk. Within that folder, select the file Lesson04_Start.prel, and then click Open. Make sure that you don't select the Lesson05_Start.prel file, which is in the same folder. If a dialog appears asking for the location of rendered files, click the Skip Previews button.

Your project file opens with the Monitor, Tasks, and My Project panels open.

5   Choose Window > Restore Workspace to ensure that you start the lesson with the default window layout.

Viewing the Completed Movie Before You Start

To see what you'll be creating in this lesson, you can take a look at the completed movie.

1   In the Organize workspace of the Tasks panel, click the Project button. In Project view, locate the file Lesson04_Movie.wmv (which should be the only file), and then double-click it to open the video into the Preview window.

2   In the Preview window, click the Play button ( ) to watch the video about the sites in London, which you'll be building in this lesson.

3   When finished, close the Preview window by clicking the Close button (☒) in
    the upper-right corner of the window.

Working in the Organize Workspace

When you first open Adobe Premiere Elements, you'll find yourself in the Organize
workspace. I described the separate views and functions within this workspace back
in Chapter 1, but since you're here now, let's review.

As you saw in the previous chapter, if you click Get Media (![icon]), you'll enter the Get Media view, where you'll capture or import video into your project.

The Media view (![icon]) should be open when you first run Adobe Premiere Elements. This is a customized view of the Organizer, which you can open by clicking the Organizer icon (![icon]).

The InstantMovie icon (![icon]) starts a wizard that automatically and quickly steps you through the selection and editing portion of movie creation, allowing you to add theme-based effects, title, transitions, and audio. You'll produce an InstantMovie of the London tour later in this chapter.

In the Project view (![icon]) you can view, sort, and select media you have captured or imported into your current project. Note that in Adobe Premiere Elements 7, the Project view was presented in the Edit workspace, not the Organize workspace.

There's some overlap between the Media and Project views and the Organizer program, so let's cover that. The Organizer is a separate application that contains all audio, video, and still image content that you've input into either Adobe Photoshop Elements or Adobe Premiere Elements since you first installed the programs. It's a great place to start many projects and provides access to a wide range of organization and collection functions.

The Media view works neatly within Adobe Premiere Elements' Organize workspace. It doesn't offer the breadth of capabilities enabled by the full Organizer, but it's convenient and provides a customized subset of functions that let you efficiently find and deploy media within your movie projects.

As mentioned, the Media view is the default view in the Tasks panel and should be open when you run Adobe Premiere Elements for the first time. If it's not showing now, click Media in the Organize workspace, or choose Window > Organizer.

When you first run Adobe Premiere Elements, either loading an existing project or starting with a new project, the Media view will display all files currently contained in the Organizer, so you can easily reuse this content if desired. As you import content into the project, Media view will show only the newly imported content.

In contrast, Project view displays all content that you've imported into the project. Clips appearing in the Media view and Organizer when you first run Adobe Premiere Elements won't appear in the Project view until you either import them or drag them to the My Project panel. Let's load some files from the lesson folder to reinforce this point.

Follow this procedure to import audio and video clips from the Lesson04 and 05 folder.

1 In the Organizer, click the Get Media button (![icon]).

2 Click PC Files and Folders (![icon]).

    Adobe Premiere Elements opens the Add Media panel.

3 Navigate to the Lesson04 and 05 folder. In the "Files of type" pop-up menu on the bottom of the Add Media window, choose AVI Movie (*.avi) and select all the visible files. Click Open to import the clips.

After importing the clips, Media view should display only the clips you just imported. Project view, which previously contained only the one WMV file, should contain all the new files that you just imported plus Lesson04_Movie.wmv.

 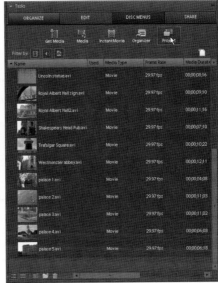

If you compare the two panels, you will see the same files in both. However, if you closed the project file and later reopened it, the Organizer and Media view will again contain *all* files previously imported into *all* previous Adobe Premiere Elements projects, whereas Project view will contain only those files imported into *that specific* Adobe Premiere Elements project.

With this background information, let's take a deeper look into both workspaces, starting with the Media view.

Finding Clips in Media View

The role of the Media view is to help you find files using different search methods. Some basic search methods are available without any action on your part, and advanced methods are available after you've rated the clips or have applied keyword or Smart Tags to your clips; all of which are discussed later in this lesson. In this short section, you'll learn how to use the basic tools in Media view to find the desired file.

1 To find files in Media view, *do any or all of the following*:

- Browse through the entire catalog by using the scroll bar at the right side of Media view.

- Select either Newest First or Oldest First from the Media Arrangement According to Date menu located in the upper-right corner of Media view to sort the files in chronological or reverse-chronological order.

- Select which media type to show—or not to show—using the icons just below the Ratings field.

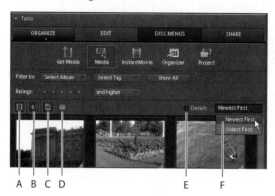

A. Show/Hide Video. **B.** Show/Hide Audio. **C.** Show/Hide Still Image.
D. Set Date Range. **E.** Details check box. **F.** Media Arrangement According to Date.

- Restrict your search to files created within a period of time by choosing Set Date Range and then entering a start and end date in the Set Date Range dialog.

- Select the Details check box to show star ratings, filename, and other details in Media view.

- Use the Media Arrangement According to Date list box to display the newest clips first or the oldest clips first.

- Click the Filter By: list box and choose either an Album () or Project (▣). Media view will display content from that Album or Project.

- To show all content in the Media view, click the Show All button.

2   To add a still image, video, or audio file from Media view to your project, drag the file from Media view into the Timeline or Sceneline of the My Project panel. This will also automatically add the file to Project view.

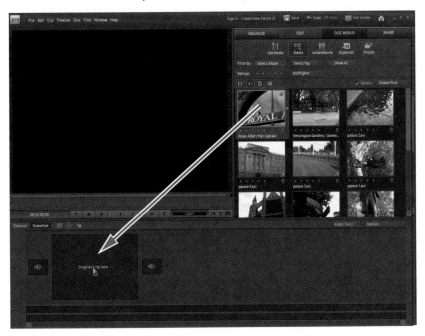

Tagging in the Organizer

Media view is great for quickly finding clips, but the Organizer is Adobe Premiere Elements' best tool for serious organization and search and retrieval work. You can open the Organizer by clicking the Organizer icon ( ) in the Organize workspace. This exercise will detail how to perform manual and Smart Tagging in the Organizer, and then how to search for clips using those tags in the Organizer.

Let's start with a brief description of tagging, which you perform in one or more of three ways, via star ratings (1–5), applying keyword tags, and using Smart Tags. At a high level, all tags allow you to more easily find the clips to include in a particular movie. For example, if you review and rate all your clips on a scale of 1–5, you can later search for only clips that you rated 4 or above—an easy way to find high-quality clips and eliminate poor-quality clips.

Keyword tags allow you to tag a clip by person, location, event, or other tag, with customizable categories. For example, in this exercise, you'll apply several keyword tags to the clips from this project, and then search for clips containing these keyword tags.

When you run the Auto Analyzer on a clip, Adobe Premiere Elements analyzes the video to detect scenes based on content; hunt for scenes with faces; and identify scenes that are out of focus, shaky, underexposed, or overexposed. Using this qualitative data, Adobe Premiere Elements then categorizes all clips as high-, medium-, or low-quality. This serves a valuable triage function that you can later use to search for the best clips for your movie. This analysis is also used for features like Smart Trimming, which you'll learn in Chapter 5, and Automatic Quality Enhancement, as discussed in Chapter 6.

For example, if you shot an hour of video on your last vacation, Smart Tagging allows you to identify medium-quality and higher clips containing faces (presumably family members), and produce a movie containing only these clips. What would literally take you hours to accomplish manually, Smart Tagging can produce in a few moments.

Using all these tags in any combination, you can hunt for clips to manually produce into a movie, or create an InstantMovie, which is a professional-looking edited movie, complete with titles, soundtrack, effects, and transitions that you'll produce using a fast and simple step-by-step process.

Tagging Clips in the Organizer

Let's open and explore operations in the Organizer. To open the Organizer, click the Organizer icon ( ) in the Organize workspace. To make your Organizer look like the one in the figure, click the View menu and make sure that Details,

Show File Names, Show Grid Lines, and Show Borders around Thumbnails are
all enabled.

1   Double-click the video Albert Memorial.avi to open the file in the Organizer's
    Preview view.

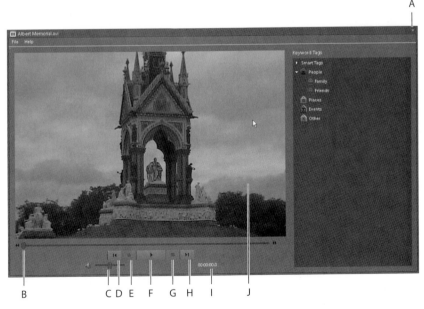

A. Close Player (and return to Organizer). **B.** Current-time Indicator. **C.** Volume Adjustment.
D. Beginning. **E.** Record. **F.** Play (spacebar). **G.** Stop. **H.** End. **I.** Timecode. **J.** Preview window.

2   Click Play to play the video file, and use the playback controls to fast-forward, rewind, and otherwise experiment with these controls.

3   In the upper right of the Preview view, click the Close icon (■) to return to the Organizer.

● **Note:** You can position the Organizer anywhere onscreen by grabbing the docking header and moving the panel to the new location. You can also resize the panel by grabbing and dragging any edge to the desired size.

Working with Star Ratings

Follow these procedures to apply and delete star ratings, and to search for clips based on the star ratings. Ratings range from 1 (on the extreme left) to 5 (on the extreme right).

1   In the upper-right corner of the Organizer (or Media view), select the Details check box.

2   Hover your pointer over the star ratings beneath any clip, and click the star that corresponds with the desired rating for that clip. Go ahead and rate a few clips so you can sort by rating in step 5.

3   To change a rating, use the same procedure and choose a different rating.

4   To delete the star rating, click and drag the pointer from right to left, starting at the rating and extending to the left of the first star.

5 To find clips based on their assigned ratings in the Organizer (or in Media view), click the number of target stars and adjust the list box as desired. Adobe Premiere Elements displays only those files that meet the selected criteria.

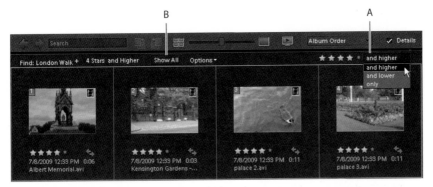

A. Target Stars list box. **B.** Show All button.

6 Click the Show All button to view all clips in the Organizer (or the Media view).

Working with Keyword Tags

Adobe Premiere Elements includes general categories of keyword tags that you can apply as is or customize with your own categories or subcategories. In this lesson, you'll create and apply two custom categories in the Organizer, and then search for clips based on those keywords in Media view.

1 Under Keyword Tags in the Organizer, click and select Places.

2 Under Keyword Tags, click the Create New button () and choose New Sub-Category.

3   In the Create Sub-Category panel, type *London Trip – June 2009* in the Sub-Category Name field. Then click OK.

Adobe Premiere Elements creates the new subcategory.

4   Repeat steps 2–3 to create two subcategories beneath *London Trip – June 2009*, *Buckingham Palace* and *Downtown*.

5   In the Browser panel, click the clip Palace 1.avi to select it. Then press and hold the Ctrl key, and click Palace 2.avi through Palace 5.avi.

6   Drag the Buckingham Palace keyword tag to any of the selected clips. When you release the pointer, Adobe Premiere Elements applies the keyword tag to all selected clips.

7   Use the same procedure to apply the Downtown tag to all other clips in the Organizer.

8 In Media view (shown below on the left) and Organizer (on the right), or both, select the box next to the keyword tags to show only those files tagged with the selected keyword tags. In both panels, Adobe Premiere Elements will show only the Palace clips.

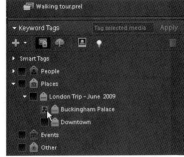

Running the Auto Analyzer

When you run the Auto Analyzer on a clip or clips, Adobe Premiere Elements analyzes the clip to detect scenes based on content, hunt for certain content types like faces, and rank the quality of your clips. Then you can use this information just like keyword tags to include or exclude clips from the Organizer or Media view. Adobe Premiere Elements also uses this information to apply features like Smart Trimming, which you'll learn in Chapter 5, and Automatic Quality Enhancement, as discussed in Chapter 6.

Follow these steps to apply Smart Tags to the project clips.

1 If necessary, click the Organizer icon (![icon]) in the Organize workspace to open the Organizer.

2 Click to select all clips and then right-click and choose Run Auto Analyzer. This can take awhile, so you might want to try one or two clips first.

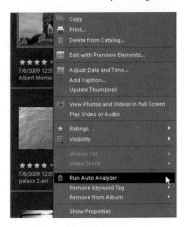

3 Adobe Premiere Elements starts analyzing the clips and reports its progress in the Elements Organizer. The duration of the process will vary by clip length, clip format, and the speed of your computer. After completion, Adobe Premiere Elements will open the Auto Analyzer window to let you know the process has completed; click OK to close that window.

▶ **Tip:** As with keyword tagging, you can use the tags created via Smart Tagging in either the Organizer or Media view. You can use these tags by themselves or in conjunction with keyword tags or even star ratings. For example, in the Organizer, click Four Stars and Higher in the top toolbar, click the Buckingham Palace tag in the Keyword tags, and click Medium Quality in Smart Tags. Adobe Premiere Elements will display only those clips that meet these criteria.

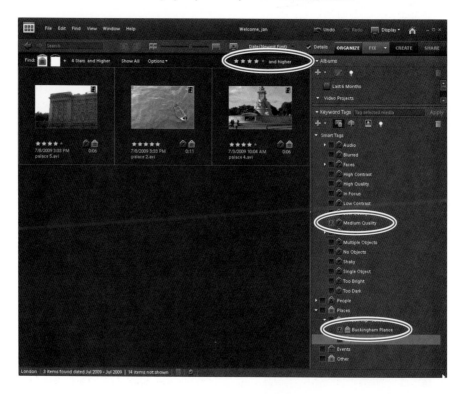

● **Note:** When you close the Organizer, the search criteria from that panel are applied to Media view, so that only the clips appearing in the Organizer before you closed it will appear in Media view.

4 Make sure the Details check box on the upper right of the Organizer (and Media view) is selected. In both panels, a purple tag (🏷) beneath the clip's thumbnail indicates that Smart Tagging has been applied. Tags of different colors (🏷) indicate that keyword tags have been applied. To view which tags have been applied, double-click the clip in either the Organizer or Media view. Tagging details will appear beneath the Preview window.

5 To remove a tag, right-click the tag in the Organizer and delete the tag, or right-click the thumbnail in Media view, and choose the tag to remove.

● Note: When you close the Organizer, the search criteria from that panel are applied to the Organizer, so that only the clips appearing in the Organizer before you closed it will appear in the Organizer.

6 Close the Organizer by clicking the Close button (⊠) in the upper-right corner of the panel.

Working with Clips After Smart Tagging

Let's take a moment to understand what happens to clips after Smart Tagging. To review, during Smart Tagging, Adobe Premiere Elements breaks the clip into different scenes based on content changes (as opposed to timecode, like DV files); finds different types of content like faces; and rates the quality of each clip based on factors like exposure, focus, and stability.

In the Organizer, you'll know that the clip has been split into multiple scenes if there is a Step Forward icon (▮▶) on the right of the clip. Click that icon, and Adobe Premiere Elements displays all scenes separately in the Organizer, surrounded by a border that's a lighter gray than the rest of the Organizer. This lets you know that all the scenes are part of a single clip.

In this view, you can treat each scene as a separate clip, for example, dragging it to the My Project panel to include it in a project or double-clicking it to play it in the Preview window. You can consolidate all scenes back into a single frame by clicking the Step Backward icon to the right of the final scene (◀▮). Note that Adobe Premiere Elements will show these detected scenes separately in Project view.

Creating an InstantMovie

In this exercise, you'll create an InstantMovie from the clips that you tagged for the London walk in a previous exercise. Again, an InstantMovie is a professional-looking edited movie, complete with titles, soundtrack, effects, and transitions that you'll create by following a simple wizard.

1 In Media view, click the Show All button (if showing) to display all clips available in the Organizer. If the button is not visible, all available content is already displayed.

2 Click the second Filter By: list box, click the twirl-triangle next to Places, and then select the check box next to London Trip – June 2009. The Organizer will display only those clips previously tagged with the London Trip – June 2009 tag or clips tagged with a subcategory of the London Trip – June 2009 tag.

3 Click to select all clips in the Organizer, and then click the InstantMovie (![InstantMovie]) button. Adobe Premiere Elements opens the InstantMovie Wizard. You can preview any Style by clicking it, and stop the preview by clicking it again.

4 Choose Road Trip and click Next. If this theme is not available, choose another.

5 Customize the Theme as desired. Accept the options as is, *or do any or all of the following*:

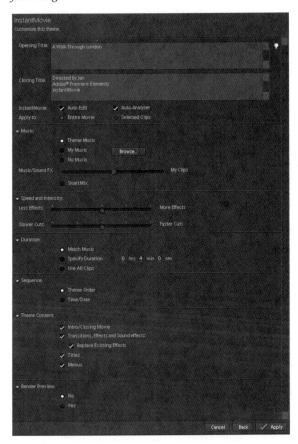

● **Note:** The Apply to: radio buttons become active only when you apply a Theme to clips already inserted into the My Project panel, not when you create an InstantMovie from the Organizer.

- Customize the Opening and Closing Titles.

- Select the Auto Edit check box to have Adobe Premiere Elements analyze your clips and edit them to fit the selected theme, which is recommended. If you don't select Auto Edit, Adobe Premiere Elements uses the clips as is and doesn't edit them. Also choose whether to Apply the Auto Analyzer or not to clips that you haven't previously analyzed.

- In the Music box, choose the Theme Music radio button to use the background music from the selected Theme, or choose the No Music radio button. To use your own background music, click the My Music radio button, and then click the Browse button to choose the target song. Then drag the Music/Sound FX slider to the desired setting, dragging to the right to prioritize audio captured with the video clips and to the left to prioritize the selected background music. If you have dialogue in your project (which this clip doesn't), select the SmartMix check box and Adobe Premiere Elements will reduce the volume of the music track when it detects dialogue.

- In the Speed and Intensity dialog, adjust the Effects and Cuts sliders as desired.

- In the Duration box, choose the desired option. Match Music produces a movie that matches the duration of the selected music and is recommended. Or, you can specify a duration or choose Use All Clips, which uses all clips at their original duration with no background music.

- In the Sequence box, choose Theme Order (recommended), which allows Adobe Premiere Elements to use clips as they best match the theme, or choose Time/Date, which uses the clips in the order that they were shot.

- In the Theme Content box, choose the content to incorporate into the InstantMovie and whether to replace any existing content with theme-based content.

- In the Render Preview box, choose Yes to render a preview of the InstantMovie after completion or No to preview in real time from the My Project panel (recommended).

6 After selecting your options, click Apply to create the InstantMovie. Click No when the InstantMovie dialog opens and asks if you want to select more clips. Adobe Premiere Elements creates the InstantMovie and inserts it into the My Project panel.

7 Use the playback controls in the Monitor panel to preview the InstantMovie.

A. Docking Header.
B. Preview area.
C. Panel menu. **D.** Current Time. **E.** Clip Representation in Mini-Timeline. **F.** Go to Previous Edit Point.
G. Rewind. **H.** Step Back (left). **I.** Play/Pause (spacebar). **J.** Step Forward (right). **K.** Fast-Forward. **L.** Go to Next Edit Point. **M.** Shuttle.
N. Split Clip (Ctrl-K).
O. Add Default Text.
P. Freeze Frame.

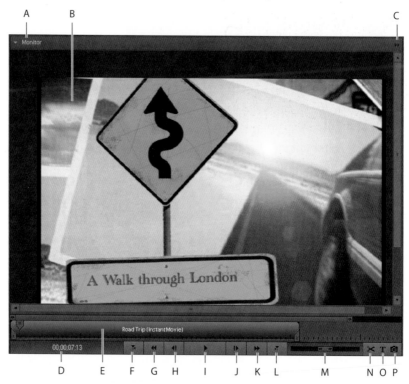

8 Adobe Premiere Elements adds the InstantMovie to the My Project panel (either Timeline or Sceneline, whichever was selected) in consolidated form. To separate the InstantMovie into its components to edit them, click to select the new InstantMovie, right-click, and choose Breakapart InstantMovie.

Uploading Files to Photoshop.com

Depending on your membership level in Photoshop.com, you can back up at least 2 gigabytes (GB) of video, audio, and still image files to the site. To upload files, you must first create an Album, and then add the video file to that Album.

Follow this procedure to back up video files to Photoshop.com.

1 If necessary, click the Organizer icon ( ) in the Organize workspace to open the Organizer.

2 Under Albums in the Organizer, click the Create New Album or Album Group button ( ) and choose New Album. Adobe Premiere Elements opens the Create Album panel.

● **Note:** Photoshop.com services are currently available only for Adobe Premiere Elements users in the United States.

3 In the Album Name field, type *London Trip – June 2009*, and make sure that the Backup/Synchronize check box is selected. Then click Done to close the panel.

4 Since you also named a subcategory in Places London Trip – June 2009, Adobe Premiere Elements will open a dialog asking if you want to create an album of that name as well. Click OK to close that dialog. If you're not signed in, you will see a dialog to enter your account info or to register.

5 In the Keyword tags box, select the check box next to the London Trip – June 2009 tag. The Organizer will display only those clips previously tagged with the London Trip – June 2009 tag or a tag from either of the two subcategories.

6 Select all clips (Ctrl-A).

7 Drag the London Trip - June 2009 album tag to any of the selected clips. When you release the pointer, the album tag is applied to all selected clips.

Note: Once you create the Album, you may be prompted to log into www. Photoshop.com. If you haven't created an account, you can do so by clicking Join Now on the www.Photoshop. com homepage. If you don't have an account or aren't currently logged in, you'll get an error message in your Preferences panel.

8 In the Organizer menu, choose Edit > Preferences > Backup/Synchronization. In this panel, if not already selected, *do the following:*

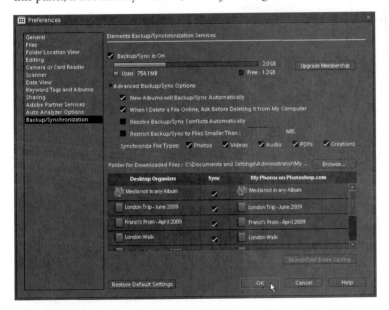

- Select the Backup/Sync is On check box.

- Twirl the Advanced Backup/Sync Options to reveal the advanced options. Here's where you can set options like which file types to archive and how to resolve conflicts between your online and desktop albums. Adjust these options as desired.

- Select the Sync check box for London Trip - June 2009.

9 Click OK to close the Preferences window.

Note: You must be logged into Photoshop.com to view this screen.

10 Unless you have a burning desire to store random videos of another family on your Photoshop.com site, under Album in the Organizer, click the London Trip - June 2009 album, and then click

the Delete Album button (🗑). Adobe Premiere Elements will delete the Album and remove any files from that Album previously uploaded to Photoshop.com.

Working with Smart Albums

You know the drill. It's holiday time or perhaps birthday time, and you're thinking, man, I've gotta create a year-in-review video or perhaps a new photo collection. If you've been applying tags to your video all year long, you should be able to quickly search for what you want via some combination of tags, Smart Tags, star ratings, and date selection.

Alternatively, using a Smart Album, you can see all the relevant content with the click of a button. Simply stated, a Smart Album contains information based on search criteria that you insert when you create the Smart Album.

To create a Smart Album, click the Create New Album or Album Group button (⊞) and choose New Smart Album. Adobe Premiere Elements opens the New Smart Album panel.

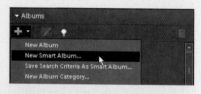

In the New Smart Album panel, you can add any number of search criteria, including keyword tags, date tags, and Smart Tags. The New Smart Album will identify all content tagged for either of my two daughters (Eleanor Rose and Whatley) that was shot during 2009 and is judged either Medium or High Quality by Adobe Premiere Elements. When I'm ready to produce that year-end video, all I have to do is click the Kids – 2009 Album, and the content will be there waiting for me.

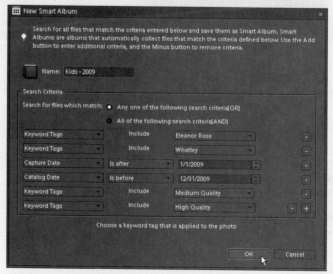

Working with Project View

As discussed previously, Project view is where Photoshop Elements stores all clips captured or imported into a project. The filenames in Project view identify the files imported into the project.

It's important to note that files listed in Project view are simply references to the clips you import, not the actual clips. The original clips you import are on your hard disk and are untouched by Adobe Premiere Elements. Cutting or editing a clip in Adobe Premiere Elements does not affect the original file. Adobe Premiere Elements records your modifications along with the reference to the original file in Project view. This means that a 20 MB clip takes up 20 MB of space on your hard disk whether you use only a portion of the clip—by trimming away unwanted sections—or whether you use this clip in its full length (or even two or more times) in a project.

Note: By clicking the column headers, you can choose to sort by other attributes or toggle between ascending and descending order. You can customize which columns you want shown in Project view by choosing Edit Columns from the panel menu in the docking header of the Tasks panel.

1 In Adobe Premiere Elements, to show Project view, select the Organize tab and then click Project. Or, choose Window > Available Media. Project view lists all the source clips imported to your Adobe Premiere Elements project. When you capture video or import files, the individual clips are automatically placed in Project view in alphabetical order, as shown here.

2   If necessary, use the scroll bar on the right side of Project view to scroll down toward the bottom of the list.

3   If the docking headers are not currently visible, choose Window > Show Docking Headers. Then choose View > Icon from the panel menu (▶▶) located at the right end of the Tasks panel docking header, or click the Icon View button (■) in the lower-left corner of Project view. This will change your view from the default List view to Icon view, which offers a larger thumbnail preview and an ability to sort files in Project view that you'll explore in a future lesson.

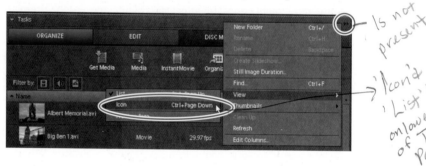

is not present

'Icon' 'List' buttons on lower of Task Panel

4   Return to List view by choosing View > List from the panel menu or by clicking the List View button (■) in the lower-left corner of Project view.

Trimming a Clip in the Preview Window

● **Note:** Trimming a clip in the Preview window does not change the In and Out points of instances of that clip already included in the My Project panel. It only sets the In and Out points for all subsequent instances of that clip placed in the My Project panel.

One of the most important editing tasks is removing unwanted footage from the beginning and end of your clips. Adobe Premiere Elements has multiple ways of accomplishing this task, but you can access one of the simplest techniques in Project view.

1   Locate the Palace 4.avi clip in Project view. Double-click the clip to open it in the Preview window. Note that the name of the clip is displayed in the title bar of the Preview window.

A. Docking Header. B. Preview area. C. Close window. D. In Point Handle. E. Current Time in Movie. F. Set In Point. G. Rewind. H. Step Back (left). I. Play/Pause (spacebar). J. Step Forward (right). K. Set Out Point L. Clip Representation in Mini-Timeline. M. Fast-Forward. N. Clip Duration. O. Current-time Indicator. P. Out Point Handle.

2   Click the Play button ( ) and play this clip from beginning to end. You'll notice a car passing that marred the beginning of the video, and a few moments of shakiness at the end of the clip. You'll trim that out below.

The timecode in the lower-left corner of the Preview window displays the timecode of that clip on the original DV tape, whereas the timecode in the lower-right corner shows clip duration. You can navigate through this clip by clicking the timecode in the lower-left corner of the Preview window and then dragging left or right.

3 Place your pointer over the current-time indicator ( ) in the lower-left corner of the Preview window and drag it to the right until the current time in movie timecode beneath the window reads 00;01;17;23. Note that you can also use the left and right arrow keys on your keyboard for precise positioning.

4 To set a new In point, click the Set In Point button ( ). You'll see the In Point handle ( ) jump to the selected frame. Note that you could have also set the In point simply by clicking and dragging the In point handle to the desired location.

5 Next, trim out the shaky frames at the end of the clip. To set a new Out point, click and drag the Out point handle ( ) to the desired location on the mini-timeline in the Preview window (about 00;01;21;25 as shown in the lower-left corner). Or, position the current-time indicator ( ) at the desired position (00;01;21;25), and then click the Set Out Point button ( ).

6 Click the Close button ( ) to close the Preview window. Note: When you set In and Out points in the Preview window, they're automatically applied–prospectively–to all clips that you drag into the My Project panel, but these In and Out points aren't retroactively applied to clips already in the My Project panel. You'll learn how to trim clips in the My Project panel in the next chapter.

Creating a Rough Cut in Project View

After trimming your clips, it's often convenient to arrange them in the desired order, which is called a *rough cut* of your movie, before dragging them to the My Project panel. This is very easy to accomplish in Project view using Icon view as discussed earlier. In this exercise you will create a rough cut and then drag it to the My Project panel.

1 If you still have the InstantMovie in your My Project panel, delete it by right-clicking the movie, and *doing one of the following:*

• If you're working in the Sceneline, choose Delete Scene and its objects.

• If you're working in the Timeline, choose Clear.

2 In the lower-left corner of Project view, click the Icon View button ( ).

3 Drag the clips into the order shown in the preceding figure, leaving out
Lesson04_Movie.wmv and any content relating to the InstantMovie that you
created, which will be named after the selected template.

▶ **Tip:** To increase the
workspace, you can
drag the horizontal
dividing line between
the Tasks panel and the
Monitor panel to the
left. To snap all clips
back into view and to
close any gaps between
the clips, choose Clean
Up from the panel
menu. Or choose
Window > Restore
Workspace to restore
your workspace to its
default layout.

4 Click to select all clips and then drag them to the first clip target in the Sceneline in the My Project panel. When you release the pointer, Adobe Premiere Elements will open the SmartFix dialog and ask if you want to fix the quality problems in the clips. Click No (we'll examine these in the next chapter) and Adobe Premiere Elements will insert the clips into the Sceneline.

5 Click Play to watch the rough cut that you just created.

Review Questions

1 What's the difference between Media view and Project view?

2 What's the difference between the Organizer that ships with Adobe Premiere Elements and the Organizer that ships with Adobe Photoshop Elements?

3 What is Smart Tagging? Are there any situations in which you wouldn't want to apply Smart Tagging?

4 After creating an InstantMovie, how do you break up the movie to edit it further?

5 What is a rough cut, and where would you create one?

6 How do you upload your clips to Photoshop.com?

Review Answers

1 Media view contains clips that you've imported into all projects and has multiple tools to help you find your clips. Project view contains only those clips that you've imported into the project.

2 This is a trick question—there is no difference. If you have Adobe Premiere Elements and Adobe Photoshop Elements installed, both programs can insert content into the same shared database and sort through and retrieve data from that database.

3 When you apply Smart Tagging to a clip, Adobe Premiere Elements analyzes the clip to detect scenes based on content, hunt for certain content types like faces, and rank the quality of your clips. Other than processing time, there's very little downside to applying Smart Tagging. Your video clips will be divided into useful scenes, and you can find high-quality clips much faster than you could manually.

4 Click the clip with your pointer to select it, and then right-click and choose Breakapart InstantMovie.

5 A rough cut is a collection of clips in the desired order. You can create a rough cut using the Icon view in Project view.

6 To upload clips to Photoshop.com, create an Album in the Organizer and drag the new Album tag onto the target clips. Then enter the Organizer Preferences panel and make sure that that Album is synched with Photoshop.com.

5 EDITING VIDEO

In the previous lesson, you learned to organize your video in the Organizer and Project views. In this lesson, you'll learn how to take that footage and shape it into a refined final version. You'll apply these basic editing techniques:

- Insert, delete, and rearrange clips in the Sceneline and Timeline

- Trim and split clips

- Use Smart Trim mode to quickly remove lower-quality segments from your videos

Over the course of this lesson, you'll work on a short travel movie. You'll be working with video and audio clips provided on the DVD included with this *Adobe Premiere Elements 8 Classroom in a Book*. If you were producing an actual project of your own, you would be working with your own source videos.

 This lesson will take approximately two hours.

Working in the Sceneline.

Getting Started

To begin, launch Adobe Premiere Elements, open the Lesson05 project, and review a final version of the movie you'll be creating.

1 Before you begin, make sure that you have correctly copied the Lesson04 and 05 folder from the DVD in the back of this book onto your computer's hard disk. For more information, see "Copying the Classroom in a Book Files" in the Getting Started section at the start of this book.

2 Launch Adobe Premiere Elements.

3 In the Welcome screen, click the Open Project button, and then click the Open Project folder.

4 In the Open Project dialog, navigate to the Lesson04 and 05 folder you copied to your hard disk.

5 Within that folder, select the file Lesson05_Start.prel, and then click Open. Be sure not to select Lesson04_Start.prel. If a dialog appears asking for the location of rendered files, click the Skip Previews button.

Your project file opens with the Monitor, Tasks, and My Project panels open.

6 Choose Window > Restore Workspace to ensure that you start the lesson with the default panel layout.

Viewing the Completed Movie Before You Start

To see what you'll be creating in this lesson, you can take a look at the completed movie.

1 In the Organize tab of the Tasks panel, click Project ( ). In Project view, locate the file Lesson05_Movie.wmv, and then double-click it to open the video in the Preview window.

2 In the Preview window, click the Play button ( ) to watch the video about sites in London, which you will build in this lesson.

3 When done, close the Preview window by clicking the Close button ( ) in the upper-right corner of the window.

Setting Up Your DV Hardware

If you're working with a DV camcorder, you can preview your work on an external monitor. Note that this procedure is optional; it's not required to complete any of the lessons in this Classroom in a Book.

Sending video/audio output from Adobe Premiere Elements to an external monitor takes a bit of setup but is often worthwhile. Computer monitors and TV monitors use two different methods for displaying video; therefore, the color and brightness levels you see on your computer monitor often do not match those on a standard TV set. Previewing your video on a TV will allow you to spot early in a project potential issues such as the length of shots, transitions, titles, and so on.

To connect your computer to your VCR and TV, do the following:

1   Connect your DV camcorder to the IEEE 1394 port or a USB (Universal Serial Bus) port on your PC.

2   Using an AV connector (which should have come with your DV camcorder), connect your camcorder to your TV set.

3   Turn on your camcorder and set it to the VCR setting.

4   Depending on your TV, you will most likely have to change the Video input to "Video 1" or "Line 1."

5   Preview a project in Adobe Premiere Elements to make sure you are viewing the output on your TV set or video monitor.

Working with the Monitor Panel

When you open the project for this lesson, you'll see multiple clips in the My Project panel, in either Storyboard or Sceneline view. Regardless of which view you choose, you'll preview your work in the Monitor panel. The Timeline and Sceneline are different panels for arranging clips and applying effects, and can show different views of the project.

In contrast, the Monitor panel shows one frame of the project, and one frame only. The displayed frame is at the location of the current-time indicator ( ). In the Sceneline, the current-time indicator is in the mini-timeline just below the preview area. In the Timeline, the current-time indicator is positioned directly on the Timeline.

Now let's explore the functions of the Monitor panel, particularly the multiple ways that you can move around the content presented in the My Project panel.

1 Select the first clip in the Sceneline, and then click the Play button (▶)
   in the Monitor panel to begin playback. As the movie is playing, notice that
   the timecode in the lower-left corner of the Monitor panel is advancing. To
   pause playback, press the spacebar, or once again click the Play button, which
   becomes the Pause button (▮▮) during playback.

2 You can locate a specific frame in your movie by changing your position in time.
   Place your pointer over the timecode in the lower-left corner of the Monitor
   panel, and your Selection tool (⬉) will change to a hand with two arrows (✥).

3 Drag the hand with two arrows icon to the right, advancing your video. The
   pointer will disappear while you are dragging and reappear when you stop. As
   long as you keep holding down the mouse button you can move backward and
   forward through the video. This is known as *scrubbing* through your video.

Previewing in Adobe Premiere Elements

Adobe Premiere Elements attempts to preview all movies at full frame rate.
Typically, the effects that you apply to your clips in the My Project panel are what
slow down preview, as I'll discuss in Lesson 6. To help ensure real-time preview irrespective of the effects applied, Adobe Premiere Elements 8 can render these effects
in the background if you select that option in the Preferences panel. To enable the
Preference, choose Edit > Preferences > General, and click the Enable Background
Rendering check box.

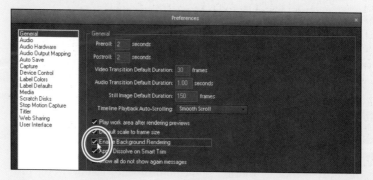

Once background rendering is enabled, Adobe Premiere Elements will start rendering all effects applied to your clips. On a very fast computer, you probably won't
notice any difference, except that every time you preview, you'll see the video play
at full frame rate. On slower computers, you may notice some lack of responsiveness
during editing, because rendering in the background consumes CPU cycles normally allocated for dragging videos around, adjusting controls, or performing other

typical editing tasks. If you find these delays irritating, you can disable background rendering by deselecting the Enable Background Rendering check box.

As with all background processes, on older computers or computers with less than 1 GB of RAM, there's a small chance that background rendering could make your computer a little less stable. Keep this in mind if you enable background rendering; save your projects more frequently, and if Adobe Premiere Elements starts to crash, background rendering might be the culprit. Disable the feature, and see if the crashes stop.

With background rendering disabled, while working with the sample DV clips provided in these lessons, you should be able to preview at full frame rate with any computer that meets the system requirements as specified on the retail box, Adobe Web site, and elsewhere. However, with high-definition formats such as AVCHD and HDV and more advanced effects, preview may slow down considerably, especially on older computers. If this occurs, check the Adobe Premiere Elements Help file, in particular the section titled "Render an area for preview."

A. Docking Header **B.** Preview area **C.** Panel menu **D.** Current-time Indicator **E.** Current Time **F.** Clip Representation in Mini-Timeline **G.** Playback controls.

About Timecode

Timecode represents the location of the frames in a video. Cameras record time-code onto the video. The timecode is based on the number of frames per second (fps) that the camera records and the number of frames per second that the video displays upon playback. Digital video has a standard frame rate that is either 29.97 fps for NTSC video (the North American broadcast video standard) or 25 fps for PAL (the European broadcast video standard). Timecode describes location in the format of hours;minutes;seconds;frames. For example, 01;20;15;10 specifies that the displayed frame is located 1 hour, 20 minutes, 15 seconds, and 10 frames into the scene.

—From Adobe Premiere Elements Help

4 The Shuttle control located in the lower-right corner of the Monitor panel lets you navigate through the movie in a similar fashion. To move forward through your video, drag the Shuttle control to the right. The farther to the right you move the Shuttle control, the faster you move through the video. This method is useful for quickly scanning a project for edit points.

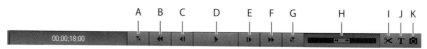

A. Go to Previous Edit Point. **B.** Rewind. **C.** Step Back. **D.** Play/Pause. **E.** Step Forward.
F. Fast-Forward. **G.** Go to Next Edit Point. **H.** Shuttle. **I.** Split Clip (Ctrl-K). **J.** Add Default Text.
K. Freeze Frame.

● **Note:** To move to a specific frame in the movie—say, 9 seconds, 15 frames in—type the number 915. This tells Adobe Premiere Elements to move to the ninth second and fifteenth frame of the movie.

5 You can move to a specific point in your movie by entering the time in the Timecode control. Click the timecode in the lower-left corner of the Monitor panel, and it will change to an editable text field. Type the number *900* and then press Enter to move to the nine-second point of your project.

6 Click the Step Forward button ( ) repeatedly to advance your video one frame at a time. Video is simply a series of frames shown at a rate of approximately 30 frames per second. Using the Step Forward ( ) or Step Back ( ) button enables you to locate moments in time very precisely. You also can use the right and left arrow keys on the keyboard to accomplish the same functions.

7 Click the Go to Next Edit Point button ( ) to jump to the first frame of the next clip. Notice in the mini-timeline that the current-time indicator ( ) jumps to the beginning of the next clip representation. Click the Go to Previous Edit Point ( ) to jump to the previous edit. Or, you can use the Page Up and Page Down keys on your keyboard to accomplish the same functions.

8 Reposition the current-time indicator in the mini-timeline by clicking and dragging it to the left or to the right.

9 The Zoom control, located just above the mini-timeline in the Monitor panel, enables you to zoom in to get a more detailed view of the clips, zoom out to see more of the entire movie in the mini-timeline, or scroll through the mini-timeline to find a clip. To work with the Zoom control, *do any of the following:*

- To zoom in, drag the left Zoom Claw (⊛) to the right, or drag the right Zoom Claw to the left.

- To zoom out, drag the left Zoom Claw to the left, or drag the right Zoom Claw to the right.

- Scroll through the mini-timeline by clicking and dragging the gray center bar of the Zoom control.

10 Press the Home key on your keyboard to position the current-time indicator at the beginning of the movie. Press the End key on your keyboard to position the current-time indicator at the end of the movie. This is useful when you want to add content to the existing sections of your movie.

[handwritten margin note: Does not work on Sceneline but works on timeline]

Working with the My Project Panel in the Sceneline

As mentioned, the My Project panel has two views: a Sceneline for basic movie editing and a Timeline for more advanced techniques. You can switch between the two views by clicking either the Sceneline or the Timeline button in the upper-left corner of the My Project panel.

Adding Clips in the Sceneline

In the Sceneline, each clip is represented by its first frame. This display makes it easy to arrange clips into coherent sequences without regard for clip length. This technique is referred to as *storyboard-style* editing.

1 If the My Project panel is not already in the Sceneline, click the Sceneline button.

The Sceneline: **A.** Switch to Timeline. **B.** Sceneline (selected). **C.** Properties. **D.** Smart Trim mode. **E.** Motion Tracking mode. **F.** Audio tools. **G.** Markers. **H.** Change Track Volume (Scenes). **I.** Change Track Volume (Narration). **J.** Change Track Volume (Soundtrack).

2 To add clips in the Sceneline, do *any of the following*:

- **To add a clip at the end of the movie:** Use the scroll bar at the bottom of the My Project panel to scroll to the end of the movie. In Media view, click any clip, and then drag it onto the empty clip target at the end of the movie. If the SmartFix dialog opens and asks if you want to fix quality problems in the clip, answer No.

- **To add a clip before another:** In Project view, click a clip, and then drag it onto an existing clip in the Sceneline. If the SmartFix window opens and asks if you want to fix quality problems in the clip, answer No. Adobe Premiere Elements will insert the new clip before the clip it was dropped onto and will push the clip it was dragged onto and all subsequent clips to the right.

- **To add a clip after another in the Sceneline:** Select the clip after which you want to add the new clip. To do so in Media view, click the clip you want, and then drag it onto the Monitor panel. If the SmartFix window opens and asks if you want to fix quality problems in the clip, answer No. Adobe Premiere Elements will insert the new clip after the clip currently selected in the Sceneline and will push all subsequent clips to the right.

3   Choose Edit > Undo three times to remove the clips that you added to the project during this exercise.

Moving Clips in the Sceneline

Working in the Sceneline makes it easy to move clips in your movie. Here's how it works.

1   To move a clip to a new position in the movie, click the clip in the Sceneline, and then drag it to a position before or after another clip. Release the pointer when a vertical blue line appears at the desired position.

2 To move several adjacent clips to a new position in the movie, Ctrl-click to select multiple clips in the Sceneline, and then drag them before or after another clip. Release the pointer when a vertical blue line appears at the desired position.

● **Note:** Though not shown in this exercise, a transition following a scene moves with the scene.

3 Choose Edit > Undo twice to undo the changes you made in this exercise.

Deleting Clips in the Sceneline

You may find, as your project develops, that you want to remove scenes you've imported into the Sceneline.

1 To delete a scene, right-click it in the Sceneline, and then choose one of the following from the context menu:

- **Delete Scene and its objects:** This option deletes the scene and any overlays it might have. Overlays are any item included above the scene, like a title, graphic, or a picture-in-picture video. Note that the sample project that you're working with doesn't have any scenes with objects, so choose the next option, Delete just Scene.

- **Delete just Scene:** This option deletes the clip but leaves the overlays in place.

  The clips following the deleted clip move to the left to close the gap. This is the default behavior when deleting clips in Adobe Premiere Elements and is called a *ripple deletion*.

● **Note:** When a clip is deleted from the Sceneline, the transition following the clip is also deleted; when a clip is deleted from the Timeline, the preceding and following transitions are deleted.

2 Choose Edit > Undo to restore the Scene that you just deleted.

Trimming Clips in the Sceneline

Although deleting unnecessary clips and thoughtfully rearranging the order of clips will make a better video, you will inevitably want to shorten the length of some clips to create a more compelling movie. Here's how you'll accomplish this task.

Every clip has a beginning and an end. In editing terminology these are referred to as the *In points* and *Out points*. Setting In and Out points does not actually delete frames from the hard drive but instead isolates a portion of the clip for use in your movie. When you trim a clip in Adobe Premiere Elements, you are simply changing the In and Out points.

1 Click Royal Albert Hall sign.avi, the eleventh clip in the Sceneline, and then press the spacebar to play the clip. As you'll see, the clip contains two left-to-right passes along the title, and we need only one in the movie. So we'll trim frames from the start and end of the clip to isolate the best pass through the sign.

2 Watching the timecode in the bottom left of the Monitor panel, drag the In point handle ( ) to the right until you see the 00;00;04;14 mark, which means that you're trimming 4 seconds and 14 frames from the start of the clip. Notice that your Monitor panel has changed to a split screen: On the left, the Monitor displays the final frame of the scene *before* the one that you're trimming, and on the right, the first frame of the scene that you're trimming. This gives you an ideal view of the transition from the first scene to the second.

3   Watching the timecode in the bottom left of the Monitor panel, click the Out
    point handle ( ), located on the right side of the current clip representation in
    the mini-timeline, and then drag it to the left until you see the 00;00;01;28 mark,
    which means that you're trimming 1 second and 28 frames from the end of the
    clip. The Monitor panel stays in split-screen view: On the left it displays the final
    frame of the clip you're trimming, and on the right it displays the initial frame of
    the *next* clip on the Sceneline.(while you are keeping mouse button pressed)

4   Click the Royal Albert Hall sign.avi clip again in the Sceneline. If necessary, click
    the Go To Previous Edit Point ( ) button in the playback controls (or press
    the Page Up key on your keyboard) to move the current-time indicator to the
    start of the clip, and then press the spacebar to play the clip. Notice that you've
    trimmed away frames from the start and end of the clip, and have isolated the
    most usable segment.

Using the Split Clip Tool in the Sceneline

The Split Clip tool allows you to cut single clips into multiple clips. You can use
this tool to split a clip into sections so you can delete one of them, an alternative
to trimming that you'll perform in this exercise. You can also use it to split a long
clip into separate clips to edit them individually, although if you elected to Auto
Analyze your clips, Adobe Premiere Elements would split most longer clips into
separate scenes for you.

1 Click Palace 2.avi, which is the fourteenth clip in the Sceneline, and then press the spacebar to play the clip. This was meant to be an artsy transition to Buckingham Palace, but it spends too much time on the ducks up front.

2 Position the current-time indicator at the 00;01;30;01 mark, which marks the beginning of the section that we want to use after splitting.

3 To split the clip at the position of the current-time indicator, click the Split Clip button (✂), located near the right end of the Monitor panel just below the mini-timeline. You might have to resize the Monitor panel to its full width to see this icon. Or, choose Timeline > Split Clip. Adobe Premiere Elements will split the clip into two segments, both named Palace 2.avi.

4 Delete the first clip. Click the Palace 2.avi clip, right-click the clip representation, and choose Delete Just Scene.

● **Note:** After you split a clip, Adobe Premiere Elements treats each subclip as a completely separate clip, which you can trim or reorder—just as with any other clip.

5 When you're finished reviewing the movie, choose File > Save As.

6 In the Save Project dialog, name the file *Lesson05_Work* and save it in your Lesson04 and 05 folder.

Working with the My Project Panel in the Timeline

While most basic editing tasks can be performed in the Sceneline together with the Monitor panel, you'll use the Timeline for many advanced editing tasks, especially those that involve *layering*, which means having multiple clips in the project at the same location.

The Timeline graphically represents your movie as video and audio clips arranged in vertically stacked tracks. Before beginning to work with the Timeline, follow the instructions at the start of this lesson to load Lesson05_Start.prel.

1   In the My Project panel, click the Timeline button to switch to the Timeline. Depending on your monitor size, you might want to increase the height of the My Project panel to have more space to display additional video and audio tracks.

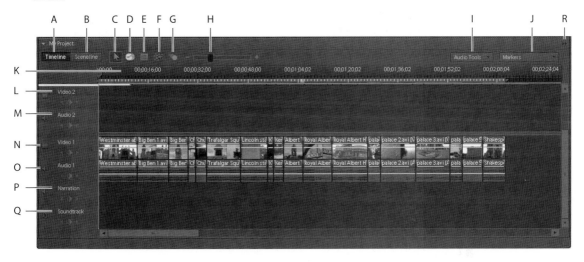

The Timeline: **A.** Timeline (selected). **B.** Switch to Sceneline. **C.** Selection tool. **D.** Time Stretch tool. **E.** Properties. **F.** Smart Trim mode. **G.** Motion Tracking mode. **H.** Zoom slider. **I.** Audio Tools. **J.** Markers. **K.** Time ruler. **L.** Video track. **M.** Audio track. **N.** Set Video Track Display Style. **O.** Set Audio Track Display Style. **P.** Narration track. **Q.** Soundtrack. **R.** Panel Menu.

The Timeline displays time horizontally. Clips that fall earlier in time appear to the left, and clips that come later in time appear to the right. Time is indicated by the time ruler near the top of the Timeline.

The Zoom controls in the Timeline let you change the timescale, allowing you to zoom out to see your entire video or zoom in to see time in more detail.

2   Click the Zoom In button () once to zoom into the Timeline. Drag the Zoom slider to the right to zoom in farther.

Zooming in enables you to make precise edits in the Timeline. In doing so, however, you cannot see the entire Timeline at once.

3   To see other parts of your project, drag the scroll bar at the bottom of the Timeline to scroll through the Timeline.

4   Adobe Premiere Elements has keyboard shortcuts that enable you to quickly zoom in and out. Press the equals sign (=) to zoom in one step per keystroke; press the minus sign (-) to zoom out one step per keystroke. Press the backslash (\) key to fit the entire video into the Timeline.

These shortcuts Do work!!

Adding and Deleting Tracks

The Timeline consists of vertically stacked tracks where you arrange media clips. Tracks let you layer video or audio and add compositing effects, picture-in-picture effects, overlay titles, soundtracks, and more.

You'll perform most of your editing in the Video 1 and the Audio 1 tracks. Directly above these are the Video 2 and Audio 2 tracks. Note that the stacking order of video tracks is important. The Monitor panel displays (and Adobe Premiere Elements produces) the tracks from the top down. Accordingly, any opaque areas of the clip in the Video 2 track will cover the view on the clip in the Video 1 track.

Conversely, the clip in the Video 1 track will show through any transparent areas of the clip in the Video 2 track. Below the Video 1 and Audio 1 tracks are two more audio tracks, Narration and Soundtrack. Audio tracks are combined in playback, and their stacking order is not relevant.

Adobe Premiere Elements starts with three open video tracks (Video 1, 2, and 3) and five open audio tracks (Soundtrack; Narration; and Audio 1, 2, and 3), which should be sufficient for most projects. Should you need additional video or audio tracks, you can add them by choosing Timeline > Add Tracks. You can delete any empty tracks by choosing Timeline > Delete Empty Tracks.

Changing the Height of Tracks

You can change the height of each track in the Timeline for better viewing and easier editing of your projects. As a track enlarges, it displays more information. Let's adjust the height of the Video 1 track.

1   If necessary, scroll down in the Timeline to see the Video 1 track.

2 At the left side of the Timeline, place
   your pointer between the Audio 2 and
   the Video 1 tracks. Your pointer should
   change to two parallel lines with two
   arrows (). Drag up to expand the
   height of this track.

3 Choose Window > Show Docking Headers if the docking headers are not
   currently visible. From the My Project panel menu (the double arrow icon on
   the extreme right hand side of the My Project panel docking header, choose
   Track Size > Small, Track Size > Medium, or Track Size > Large to change the
   track size for all tracks in the Timeline at the same time.

Customizing Track Views

You can display clips in the Timeline in different ways, depending on your preference or the task at hand. You can choose to display a thumbnail image at just the
beginning of the clip; at the head and tail of the clip; or along the entire duration
of the clip, as shown in the previous figure. For an audio track, you can choose to
display or hide the audio waveform of the audio contents. Toggle through the various views of the video and audio tracks until you find the one that best suits your
eye and working style.

1 By default, Adobe Premiere Elements
   displays all the frames in a video clip.
   However, at times you may find you
   would like to work with fewer visual
   distractions in your clip. Click the Set
   Display Style button () to the left of
   the Video 1 track to set the display style to Show Head and Tail. This will show
   you the first frame and last frame of all the clips in Video 1.

2 Click the Set Display Style button again to view only the head of the clip.

3 Click the Set Display Style button again to view the clip by its name only. No
   thumbnails will be displayed on the clip.

4 Click the Set Display Style button one more time to view the default style of all
   the frames.

Editing in the Timeline

Editing in the Timeline is very similar to editing in the Sceneline, although several
controls are in different places. Most notably, when you switch to Timeline view,
the mini-timeline beneath the Monitor panel moves to the Timeline, as does the
current-time indicator. Other than that, all playback controls are identical.

(See illustration on next page.)

A. Docking Header.
B. Preview area.
C. Playback controls.
D. Panel menu.
E. Current Time.
F. Time ruler.
G. Current-time Indicator.

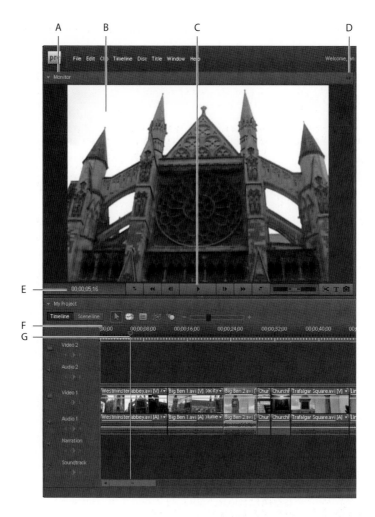

Beyond the interface issues, most of the basic clip-related operations are also identical. For example, you add clips to the Timeline the same way you add them to the Sceneline. You move clips around the same way, and you delete clips the same way. If you repeat the exercises you've already completed in this chapter using the Timeline rather than Sceneline, you'll quickly become adept at all of these operations.

Trimming and splitting clips is also very similar, but because these operations are so critical to everyday editing, let's run through them again in the Timeline.

Trimming Clips in the Timeline

Every clip has a beginning and an end. In editing terminology these are referred to as the *In points* and the *Out points*, as described earlier in this lesson. Setting In and Out points does not actually delete frames from the hard drive but instead isolates a portion of the clip for use in your movie. When you trim a clip in Adobe Premiere Elements, you are simply changing the In and Out points.

1 Press the Home key to move the current-time indicator to the first frame of the project.

2 Press the Page Down key 10 times to move to the start of Royal Albert Hall sign. avi, the eleventh clip in the Timeline, and then press the spacebar to play the clip. As you can see, I shot the sign twice to make sure I got a good take; Let's remove the first pass.

3 Click the Zoom In button (![+]) at the top of the Timeline to magnify your view, and if necessary, drag the scroll bar on the bottom of the Timeline to center the Palace 2.avi clip in the Timeline. Trimming in the Timeline is easier when you're zoomed into the clip. Zooming in and out to make these adjustments will feel awkward at first but will quickly become second nature.

4 Let's trim away unnecessary frames from the start of the clip. Hover the pointer over the left edge of Royal Albert Hall sign.avi in the Timeline. The pointer changes to a two-headed drag pointer (![drag]), with the direction depending upon the direction of your trim. Watching the current timecode in the bottom left of the Monitor panel, or in the text box that appears beneath the drag pointer, drag the edge of the clip to the right until you see the 00;00;04;14 mark, which means that you're trimming 4 seconds and 14 frames from the start of the clip. Notice that your Monitor panel has changed to a split screen: On the left, the Monitor displays the final frame of the scene *before* the one that you're trimming, and on the right, the first frame of the scene that you're trimming. This gives you an ideal view of the transition from the first scene to the second.

5   Now let's trim the unnecessary frames from the end of the clip. Hover the pointer over the right edge of Royal Albert Hall sign.avi in the Timeline. The pointer changes to a two-headed drag pointer ( ). Watching the current timecode in the bottom left of the Monitor panel, or the text box that appears beneath the drag pointer, drag the edge of the clip to the right until you see the 00;00;01;28 mark, which means that you're trimming 1 second and 28 frames from the end of the clip. The Monitor panel stays in split-screen view: On the left it displays the final frame of the clip you're trimming, and on the right it displays the initial frame of the *next* clip on the Timeline.

6   Click the Royal Albert Hall sign.avi clip again in the Timeline. If necessary, click the Go To Previous Edit Point ( ) button in the playback controls (or press the Page Up key on your keyboard) to move the current-time indicator to the start of the clip, and then press the spacebar to play the clip. Notice that you've trimmed away frames from the start and end of the clip, and have isolated the most usable segment.

Using the Split Clip Tool in the Timeline

The Split Clip tool allows you to cut single clips into multiple clips. You can use this tool to split a clip into sections so you can delete one of them, an alternative to trimming that you'll perform in this exercise. You can also use it to split a long clip into separate clips to edit them individually, though if you elect to Auto Analyze your clips, Adobe Premiere Elements will split most longer clips into separate scenes for you.

1 Press the Home key, and then press the Page Down key 13 times, which should take you to the start of Palace 2.avi. Then press the spacebar to play the clip. This was meant to be an artsy transition to Buckingham Palace, but it spends too much time on the ducks up front. We'll correct it again using the Split Clip tool.

2 Click the Zoom In button ( ) at the top of the Timeline to magnify your view, and (if necessary) drag the scroll bar on the bottom of the Timeline to center the Palace 2.avi clip in the Timeline.

3 Position the current-time indicator at the 00;01;30;01 mark, which marks the beginning of the section that we want to use after splitting.

4 To split the clip at the position of the current-time indicator, click the Split Clip button ( ), located near the right end of the Monitor panel just below the mini-timeline. You might have to resize the Monitor panel to its full width to see this icon. Or, choose Timeline > Split Clip. Adobe Premiere Elements will split the clip into two segments, both named Palace 2.avi.

5   Delete the first clip. Click the Palace
    2.avi clip, right-click the clip, and
    choose Delete and Close Gap.

6   When you're finished reviewing the
    movie, choose File > Save As.

7   In the Save Project dialog, name the
    file *Lesson05_Work* and save it in your Lesson04 and 05 folder.

Working in Smart Trim Mode

Smart Trim is an editing mode that can help you identify suboptimal regions within
your videos so that you can either fix or delete them. Smart Trim relies on infor-
mation gathered while Adobe Premiere Elements analyzes your clips, so you must
Auto-Analyze your clips before entering Smart Trim mode. You can operate Smart
Trim either automatically or manually, although I recommend that you use Smart
Trim manually until you understand how it works.

You can work with Smart Trim in either the Timeline or Sceneline; this exercise
will demonstrate how it works in Timeline view. If necessary, to make your screen
look like the figures in this exercise, click the Timeline button (Timeline) on the top
left of the My Project panel to view the Timeline. Then adjust the size and positioning as necessary to place the Trafalgar Square clip in the Video 1 track below the
Monitor, as shown in the following figure. Once the clip is positioned, click the
Smart Trim icon ( ) atop the My Project panel to enter Smart Trim mode. If
you haven't run the Auto-Analyzer, Adobe Premiere Elements will run it now.

As you can see in the preceding figure, Smart Trim identifies problem areas via a zebra pattern. If you hover your mouse over the zebra pattern, a tool tip will detail the problems with the clip. You have multiple options regarding any clip, or portion of a clip, that Adobe Premiere Elements flags as a problem area.

You can right-click the clip, and choose Trim, Keep, or Select All. Trim will delete the selected portion; Keep will retain it and turn off the zebra striping; and Select All will select multiple suboptimal regions within the same clip so you can trim or keep them all. In addition to these options, you can trim away any or all of the suboptimal portions of your clip by clicking and dragging an edge to the desired new starting point, just as you would trim any other clip in the Timeline.

How Smart Trim Works

Another approach is to choose Smart Trim Options and adjust these options. Let's view the choices available by right-clicking the Big Ben 2.avi clip (or another clip identified as having problems), and choosing Smart Trim Options.

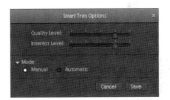

As you can see, atop the Smart Trim Options window Adobe Premiere Elements uses two variables to identify suboptimal clips: Quality Level and Interest Level. Quality is simple to understand: If a clip is shaky, blurry, has poor contrast or lighting, or has other deficits that mar quality, Adobe Premiere Elements identifies the clip in Smart Trim mode as being below the Quality Level threshold, depending on how flawed the clip is and where you positioned the Quality Level slider.

By contrast, Interest Level analyzes qualities such as the amount of motion in a clip, the presence or absence of dialogue, and other criteria that tend to identify clips that are interesting to watch. If you shot a picture of a blank wall that was sharp, well lit, and completely stable, the Quality Level would be perfect, but Adobe Premiere Elements would flag it as lacking in the Interest Level department. That doesn't do much for those boring conversations with Uncle Harold, so you'll still have to delete those manually.

You can adjust the sliders to set the tolerance levels for either criteria: Moving the slider to the left will increase the threshold for suboptimal clips, so that fewer and fewer clips will be flagged. Moving it to the right reduces the threshold so that more clips will be flagged.

For example, if you examine the clips in your project and find that most clips flagged by Adobe Premiere Elements look good to you, move the slider to the left and Adobe Premiere Elements will set the threshold higher and flag fewer clips. If clips left unflagged in Smart Trim mode look suboptimal to you for either Quality Level or Interest Level reasons, move the slider to the right.

Operating Modes

Note that there are two operating modes in the Smart Trim Options window: Manual and Automatic. In Manual mode, which is the default, Adobe Premiere Elements will display all subop-timal regions via the zebra stripes shown and dis-cussed previously. If you opt for Automatic mode, Adobe Premiere Elements will immediately delete all suboptimal regions present on the Timeline. Thereafter, when you drag clips with suboptimal regions to the My Project window, Adobe Premiere Elements will present a dialog asking if it's OK to remove Smart Trim sections.

Perspective

There's an awful lot of bad video out there, and Smart Trim mode presents a very efficient way to identify it. Unfortunately (or perhaps fortunately, depending on your point of view), given the fixed capacity of the DVD accompanying this book, I was unable to pack a lot of boring and/or problem-filled video on the DVD for Smart Trim mode to identify.

In a real project, however, when you've shot 30–60 minutes of footage and want to quickly isolate the best 3–5 minutes to include in your movie, Smart Trim mode can be a godsend. So check it out on your own projects and see how it works for you.

Two final points: First, when Smart Trim flags quality-related problems, you can either delete the offending sections or try to fix them, which we'll attempt to do in

Lesson 6. So even if you decide to leave suboptimal clips in the project, Smart Trim helps by identifying sequences you can improve with corrective effects.

Second, to reiterate a comment I made earlier, I recommend that you *not* use Smart Trim in Automatic mode. Lots of "must have" sequences in your movies—such as your son blowing out the candles on his birthday cake or your daughter accepting her diploma—may not meet Adobe Premiere Elements' quality thresholds, but you still don't want to delete them. In Automatic mode, you don't get that choice.

Creating a Slide Show

If you're like me, you like to shoot video and still-image shots of your events and travels, and it's fun to combine them into a single movie. Fortunately, Adobe Premiere Elements makes this very simple. Though you can add images in both the Sceneline and Timeline views, let's work in the former because it's more visual.

1 On the top left of the My Project panel, click Sceneline (Sceneline) (if necessary) to switch to the Sceneline view.

2 Press the End key on your keyboard to move to the end of the movie.

3 In the Organize workspace, click the Get Media ( ) icon, and then click the PC Files and Folders button ( ). Adobe Premiere Elements opens the Add Media panel.

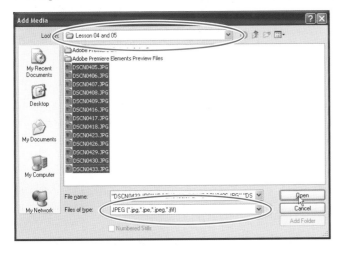

4 Navigate to the Lesson04 and 05 folder.

5 To display only the pictures in the folder, click the Files of type list box on the bottom of the Add Media panel, and choose JPEG. The dialog displays only files of the selected type.

6 Select all JPEG files in the folder.

7   Click Open to import the files.

8   Click the Media icon (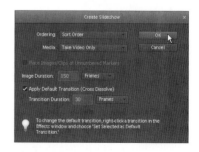) to enter Media view.

9   Ctrl-click the photos in the order you want them to appear in the slide show (in this project, I'm selecting them in the order that they appear in the Media view). Drag the selected group to the first open scene in the Sceneline, release the mouse button, and choose Add as Grouped Slideshow, which opens the Create Slideshow dialog.

10 In the Create Slideshow dialog, leave all options at their default settings, and click OK. Adobe Premiere Elements adds each photo to the project with a duration of 150 frames and a transition between each photo of 30 frames.

11 In the Save Project dialog, name the file *Lesson05_Final* and save it in your Lesson04 and 05 folder.

Wonderful! You've finished another lesson and learned how to cut, trim, split, and arrange your raw video into a cohesive movie. Over the next few chapters, you'll polish it into a fine-tuned production.

Review Questions

1 What are the key differences between the Timeline and Sceneline?

2 What is an In point and what is an Out point, and what can you do with each?

3 What are two methods of shortening your video clips?

4 How does Adobe Premiere Elements combine video tracks at the same position on the Timeline?

5 What are the two criteria assessed by Adobe Premiere Elements in Smart Trim mode?

Review Answers

1 Adobe Premiere Elements offers two views in the My Project panel: Sceneline and Timeline. The Sceneline shows each clip as a separate thumbnail without regard to duration and doesn't show all available video tracks. The Timeline graphically represents your movie project as video and audio clips arranged in vertically stacked tracks with clip duration represented by the length. There are many common activities that you can perform in both views, including arranging clips, trimming frames from the beginning or end of a clip, splitting and deleting clips, and adding titles and effects. Many producers use both views in the course of a project: for example, adding and sequencing content in the Sceneline, and then switching over to the Timeline to add background music, titles, and other clips. Once you start working with multiple video clips at the same location, the Timeline becomes the superior view.

2 The In point is the first frame of your clip as seen in the Sceneline or Timeline, and the Out point is the last frame. Both the In and Out points can be moved to create a shorter or longer clip.

3 You can shorten your clips by trimming their In points and Out points or by splitting the clip and deleting unwanted portions.

4 Adobe Premiere Elements renders the tracks from the top down. Any opaque areas of the clip in the Video 2 track will cover the view on the clip in the Video 1 track. Conversely, the clip in the Video 1 track will show through any transparent areas of the clip in the Video 2 track or if you reduce the Opacity of the clip in the Video 2 track.

5 Quality Level and Interest Level. The former concerns Adobe Premiere Elements' assessment of picture and audio quality on a technical level; the latter assesses multiple qualities such as dialogue and motion that tend to indicate whether or not a clip is interesting.

6 WORKING WITH EFFECTS

In this lesson, you'll learn how to apply effects to the clips of a vacation in London that you already know from previous lessons, and you'll also apply these effects to several new clips. Specifically, you'll learn how to do the following:

- Apply video effects to single and multiple clips
- Change effects and settings
- Copy effects and settings from one clip to another
- Create a pan over a still image with preset effects
- Control visual effects with keyframes
- Create a Picture-in-Picture effect
- Composite one video over another with Videomerge
- Apply Motion Tracking to a clip
- Apply Effect Masking to a clip

 This lesson will take approximately two hours.

Applying the Shadow/Highlight effect to brighten a
gloomy image.

Getting Started

Before you begin the exercises in this lesson, make sure that you have correctly copied the Lesson06 folder from the DVD in the back of this book onto your computer's hard drive. For more information, see "Copying the Classroom in a Book files" in the "Getting Started" section at the start of this book.

Now you're ready to begin working with the Lesson06 project file.

1 Launch Adobe Premiere Elements.

2 In the Welcome screen, click the Open Project button, and then click the Open folder.

3 In the Open Project dialog, navigate to the Lesson06 folder you copied to your hard drive. Within that folder, select the file Lesson06_Start.prel, and then click Open. If a dialog appears asking for the location of rendered files, click the Skip Previews button.

    Your project file opens with the Monitor, Tasks, and My Project panels open.

4 Choose Window > Restore Workspace to ensure that you start the lesson with the default panel layout.

Viewing the Completed Movie Before You Start

To see what you'll be creating in this lesson, you can play the completed movie.

1 In the Organize tab of the Tasks panel, click Project (▣).

2 In Project view, locate the file Lesson06_Movie.wmv, and then double-click it to open the video into the Preview window.

3 In the Preview window, click the Play button (▶) to watch the video about a visit to London, which you will build in this lesson.

4 When done, close the Preview window by clicking the Close button (✖) in the upper-right corner of the window.

> ● **Note:** Adobe Premiere Elements offers a large selection of diversified effects. It's a good idea to look up the gallery of video effects in your Adobe Premiere Elements Help file, which gives you a quick overview of all those effects actually applied to an image.

Using Effects

Effects (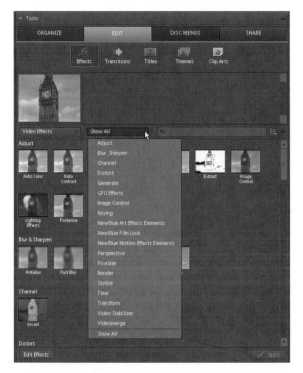) are located in the Edit tab of the Tasks panel. All effects are stored in either the Audio Effects folder or the Video Effects folder and are organized by type. For example, all video effects that create a blur are grouped within the Blur & Sharpen folder inside the Video Effects folder.

Note: One cool new feature in Adobe Premiere Elements 8 is that you preview the effects using the clip you have selected in the Timeline or Sceneline. That's why Big Ben is showing up in all the effect previews.

It's helpful to think about effects in the following categories:

- **Curative effects:** Curative effects correct problems in your video footage, including footage that's too bright or too dark, backlighted video, video that's too shaky because it was shot without a tripod, and even video that's a bit blurry. You can find curative effects in the Adjust folder (Auto Color, Auto Contrast, Auto Levels, and Shadow/Highlight), Blur Sharpen folder (Sharpen), Image Control folder (Black & White, Color Balance HLS, Color Balance RGB, Gamma Correction, Tint), and Video Stabilizer folder (Stabilizer).

- **Overlay effects:** Overlay effects allow you to composite one image over another. You can find overlay effects in the Keying and Videomerge folders.

- **Artistic effects:** Most other effects are artistic effects that let you create a different look or feel from the original clip. These artistic effects can be quite powerful, like the Old Film effect in the NewBlue Film Look folder that can make your video look like old film by adding details like scratches and graininess. Other artistic effects let you add lightning to a clip (Lightning effect in the Render folder), add earthquake-like effects (Earthquake effect in the NewBlue Motion Effects Elements folder), place a spotlight on a subject (Lighting effects in the Adjust folder), and apply many other looks and characteristics.

- **Speed controls:** You can speed up, slow down, or reverse your clips in the Timeline of the My Project panel by right-clicking the clip and choosing Time Stretch, or by choosing Clip > Time Stretch in the Adobe Premiere Elements menu.

- **Motion effects:** Motion effects allow you to zoom into and around your original video clip or still image, and are used to adjust the framing of a video or create a pan-and-zoom effect. You adjust these parameters using the Motion controls found in the fixed effects that are automatically available for every clip in the My Project panel. Other fixed effects include:

A. Properties button. **B.** Fixed effects. **C.** Properties view.

- **Image control:** With image control you can control the brightness, contrast, hue, and saturation of clips.

- **Opacity:** The Opacity effect lets you make a clip transparent and, by using keyframes, create fades and dissolves.

- **Volume:** Volume lets you control the volume of audio clips.

- **Balance:** Balance lets you adjust the balance of audio clips.

Note that once you apply an effect from the Effects panel to a clip, you can also adjust its parameters and set keyframes in the Effects Properties view. All effects that you add to a clip appear in the order in which you add them.

Though you can apply any and all of these effects at any time during the course of a project, the recommended workflow is to apply curative filters first, then adjust speed and motion, and then add other artistic effects. You can add an effect to any clip in the My Project panel, and even apply the same effect numerous times to the same clip, but with different settings. By default, when you add an effect to a clip, it applies to the entire clip. If you want to apply an effect to only part of a clip, split it first using the Split Clip icon beneath the Monitor panel, and then apply the effect to the desired clip segment.

> ● **Note:** clicking the Properties (▤) button in the upper left of the My Project panel. This opens the Edit workspace in Properties view. There you'll find the functions of all fixed effects, which you open by clicking the twirl-down triangles to the left of each effect.

Working with SmartFix

Unless you disable the application of the Auto Analyzer in the Organizer, at some point Adobe Premiere Elements will analyze your clips, either in the background while you're performing other edits or after capture or import. While analyzing the clips, Adobe Premiere Elements looks for problems in the video.

As you saw with SmartTrim in the previous chapter, Adobe Premiere Elements uses some of this information to recommend which clips to trim away. In addition, you can instruct the application to use some of this information to fix common problems like shakiness and poor exposure. This is how you do it.

1 If necessary, click the Timeline icon (Timeline) on the top left of the My Project panel. Then press the End key on your keyboard to move to the end of the project.

2 In the Organizer workspace, click the Media icon (Media) to enter Media view.

3 Scroll down until you find Trafalgar Square.avi. If you haven't previously run the Auto-Analyzer, click the clip to select it, right-click and choose Run Auto-Analyzer. Click and drag that clip into the Video 1 track on the Timeline. Adobe Premiere Elements opens the SmartFix window.

(See illustration on next page.)

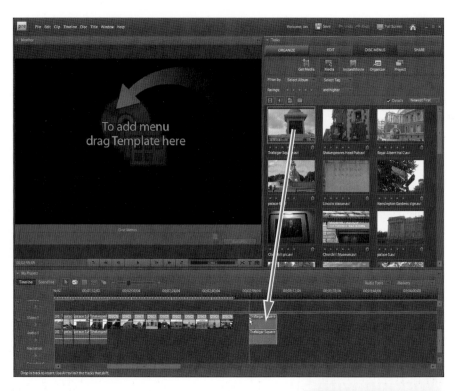

4 In the SmartFix window, click Yes to fix the
   quality problem in the clip.

5 In the Timeline, click the Trafalgar Square.avi
   clip to select it, and then click the Properties
   button (▥) on the top left of the Timeline.
   This opens the Task panel into Properties view.

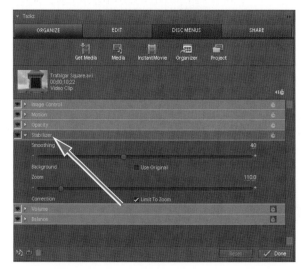

In the Properties view, you'll note that Adobe Premiere Elements applied the Stabilizer effect to minimize the shakiness in the clip. If the clip was too dark or exposure was poor, Adobe Premiere Elements would apply the excellent Shadow/Highlight effect.

6   Back in Media view, find the picture of the tree-lined road (DSCN0417.jpg). If you haven't previously run the Auto-Analyzer, click the picture to select it, right- click and choose Run Auto-Analyzer. Then drag it to the Timeline, clicking Yes in the SmartFix window.

7   Click the Properties button to open the Properties view (if necessary). You'll see that Adobe Premiere Elements applied the Shadow/Highlight effect to the clip.

If you click the eye icon next to the effect (officially called the "toggle the effect on or off" button), you'll see that the Shadow/Highlight effect does a marvelous job of brightening the shadows without "blowing out" the lighter regions.

Note that you can adjust the setting of any effect applied by Adobe Premiere Elements or disable or delete it. Unless you have a strong reason not to do so, it's generally a good idea to allow Adobe Premiere Elements to apply SmartFix whenever you add your clips to the My Project panel. It's not a panacea, but it's a great start towards improving clip quality.

8   To return to the correct starting point for the rest of the chapter, either delete the two clips you just added to the project, or reopen Lesson06_Start.prel as described in the "Getting Started" section earlier in this chapter.

9   When Adobe Premiere Elements asks if you want to save your changes, click No.

● **Note:** If you haven't completed Lesson 04, it's possible that neither Trafalgar Square.avi or DSCN0417.jpg are in your Media view. If not, click Get Media, PC Files and Folders, and locate and input the files in the Lesson06 folder. Then, select both files in Media view, right-click and choose Auto Analyze.

Perfecting Your Clips

All projects are unique, and all source clips present their own unique issues. Outdoor projects, such as this walk through London, are generally fairly simple to perfect. To optimize the video in this shoot, you'll correct backlighting in several clips, boost the color saturation in another, apply the Sharpen and Stabilizer effects, and reframe a shot using the Motion controls.

However, indoor shoots typically present a completely different range of problems since lighting is often inadequate and camcorders sometimes have problems producing accurate colors when shooting under fluorescent or incandescent lighting. When your personal projects involve indoor shoots, you should experiment with the Brightness, Contrast, Hue, and Saturation adjustments in the Image Control fixed effect, and the Auto Color, Auto Contrast, and Auto Levels controls in the Adjust folder. Often, applying the latter three—either individually or in concert—can produce quite remarkable improvements in minimal time and with little effort.

Applying and Resetting Fixed Effects

It's usually most convenient to start by adjusting the Brightness, Contrast, and Saturation of a clip using the Image Control adjustments. Here's the procedure.

1   In either the Sceneline or Timeline, click Royal Albert Hall2.avi, which is the twelfth clip in the movie. I remember the brick color being a little richer. Let's fix that. To make sure you're seeing what I'm seeing, drag the current-time indicator to about 1;10;01.

2   Click the Properties button on the upper left of the My Project panel.

3   In Properties view, click the twirl-down triangle to the left of the Image Control effect to open the parameter settings.

4   Drag the Brightness slider to the right until it reaches the value of 5 (or click the numeric entry to make it active, type 5, and then press Enter).

5   Drag the Contrast slider to the right until it reaches the value of 104 (or click the numeric entry to make it active, type 104, and then press Enter).

6   Drag the Saturation slider to the right until it reaches the value of 150 (or click the numeric entry to make it active, type 150, and then press Enter). There's that lovely color that I remember.

7   In Properties view, adjacent to the twirl-down triangle, find the eye icon () on the left side of the Image Control effect. As mentioned previously, the eye icon toggles the effect on or off so you can compare the clip with and without the adjustments. Toggle the eye icon on and off a few times.

8   Click the eye icon again to toggle the effect on. Note that the eye icon isn't simply for preview; if you don't toggle the effect back on, Adobe Premiere Elements will ignore the effect when rendering the final movie.

9   If you're satisfied with the results, click Done in the lower right of Properties view to return to the Organize workspace.

10 To reset the Image Control parameters to their default values, click the Image Control effect to select it, and then click Reset in the lower right of Properties view. This technique works for any effect, whether embedded or otherwise. Choose Edit > Undo to undo the reset and keep the adjusted values.

11 Choose File > Save As and save your project as *Lesson06_Work.prel*.

Reframing a Clip Using Motion Controls

The other fixed effects that you'll use frequently are the Motion controls. In this exercise, you'll learn how to use these effects to reframe a shot; later in the lesson, you'll learn how to use these controls to create a pan-and-zoom effect within an image.

Note: You don't have to click Done to "set" the effect; you could have simply clicked another clip and continued to edit. Once you apply and configure an effect, it remains applied until you reset or delete the effect.

The clip you'll edit is the fifth clip of the project, Churchill pic.avi, which is a shot of Winston Churchill in his museum. Unfortunately, the shot is poorly framed, a bit far away, and slightly crooked—I must have had jet lag when I shot it. In this lesson, you'll use Motion controls to reframe and straighten the shot.

1 In either the Sceneline or Timeline, click Churchill pic.avi, which is the fifth clip in the movie.

2 If you're not already in the Properties view, click the Properties button in the upper left of the My Project panel.

3 In Properties view, click the twirl-down triangle to the left of the Motion effect to open the parameter settings.

4 Let's straighten the picture first. Find the Rotation control in the middle of the Motion effect, click the numeric entry to make it active, type 2, and then press Enter.

5 Now let's zoom into the video and make it larger. Drag the Scale slider to the right until it reaches the value of 120 (or click the numeric entry to make it active, type 120, and then press Enter).

6 Now let's reframe the image. In the Monitor panel, click the frame to make the center crosshair active. Then drag the frame around until the picture is positioned to your liking. As you drag the frame around, note that the numeric Position parameters on the right are updated as you move it. You can position the frame either by dragging it directly as you just did or by typing in new numeric parameters. I used 400 and 215.

7   In the Monitor panel, right-click the frame, and choose Magnification > 100%. This sets your preview at a pixel-for-pixel preview, which is helpful when previewing Motion control adjustments.

8   Click the Play button in the Monitor panel to preview the effect.

You may notice that the frame looks fuzzy while it's playing and then gets sharper once it stops. That's because Adobe Premiere Elements shows an approximation of the applied effect during preview to maximize preview smoothness. If the image looks blurry after the preview stops, you probably zoomed in a bit too far, which you want to assess before finalizing the effect. To accomplish this, you'll render the effect and then preview again.

Rendering Effects

You don't have to render your effects to preview them, since Adobe Premiere Elements will show a very close approximation of the effect when you preview in the Monitor panel without rendering. If you render the effect, however, you'll see exactly what the final video will look like when you actually render your project, which is valuable in some instances, such as when you use the Motion controls to reframe and zoom into the video.

In Adobe Premiere Elements version 8, Adobe introduced background rendering, where the application renders all effects behind the scenes while you're perform- ing other edits. Adobe Premiere Elements lets you know when you need to render for an accurate preview by placing a red line in the time ruler of the Timeline. When Background Rendering is enabled, Adobe Premiere Elements automatically starts rendering each effect after it's applied, dis- playing rendering progress on the bottom right of the interface. When the process is complete, the red line in the time ruler turns to green.

You enable or disable Background Rendering in the General Preferences win- dow, which you can access by choosing Edit > Preferences > General. Note that Background Rendering is enabled by default. I recommend disabling the feature if you notice an irritating lag while editing or if operation becomes unstable.

▶ **Tip:** If you disable Background Rendering and want to manually preview a section of the Timeline, search the Adobe Premiere Elements Help file for "Render an area for preview."

Otherwise, Background Rendering is a great way to ensure that your project is always available for accurate preview.

Choosing and Applying Effects

You've finished working with the fixed effects for the moment. Next, you'll select and apply a standard effect from the Effects view. You can apply standard effects in either the Sceneline or Timeline; use the view that you feel most comfortable using. Let's sharpen the Churchill pic.avi clip that became a bit blurry when we zoomed it in the previous exercise.

1   If Churchill pic.avi isn't still selected, click to select it. Then, select Effects (𝑓𝑥 Effects) in the Edit tab of the Tasks panel.

2   In the list box next to Video Effects, click and select Blur & Sharpen.

3   To apply the effect, drag the Sharpen effect from Effects view and drop it onto the fifth clip in your Sceneline, Churchill pic.avi. Adobe Premiere Elements applies the effect immediately, and you should see a slight sharpening in the clip.

4 Click the Properties button in the upper left of the My Project panel or the Edit Effects button in Effects view to open Properties view.

5 In Properties view, click the twirl-down triangle to the left of the Sharpen effect to open the parameter settings.

6 Drag the Sharpen Amount slider to the right until it reaches the value of 20. Or, click the numeric entry to make it active, type *20*, and then press Enter.

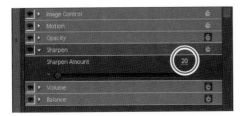

7 In the Properties panel, toggle the effect on and off using the eye icon to gauge the impact of the effect. Make sure that you leave the eye showing (toggled on) so that the effect is engaged.

8 Press the Enter key on your keyboard to render the effect and preview again.

9 If you're satisfied with the results, click Done in the lower right of Properties view to return to the Organize workspace. If not, repeat steps 6–9 to apply additional sharpening to the clip.

10 Save your project.

● **Note:** If you zoom in too far using the Motion controls, your image won't be sharp even if you apply the Sharpen effect. In that case, you must find the best balance between image position and sharpness.

● **Note:** Pressing the Enter key renders all effects in the project in chronological order. To render a specific area in the Timeline, use this technique detailed in the Adobe Premiere Elements Help file (search the Help file for "Render an area for preview").

Deleting Effects

You can't delete fixed effects, but to delete any other effect, right-click to select it in the Properties panel, and then choose either Delete Selected Effect or Delete All Effects from Clip.

Fixing Backlighted Video

If you shoot video against a bright background with automatic exposure set on your camcorder, the background will usually be bright, but the foreground objects may be very dark. This is a very common condition called *backlighting*. In this exercise, you'll learn to apply and configure Adobe Premiere Elements' Shadow/Highlight filter to correct this problem.

1   In either the Timeline or Sceneline, click the seventh clip (Lincoln statue.avi) to select it, and then drag the current-time indicator to 00;00;53;23.

2   Click the Properties button in the upper left of the My Project panel, and then click the Edit tab to enter Effects view (if necessary).

3   In the list box next to Video Effects, click and select Adjust.

4   Drag the Shadow/Highlight effect from the Effects view onto Lincoln statue.avi.

5   Use the playback controls to preview the effect, and then drag the current-time indicator back to 00;00;53;23.

● **Note:** The Shadow/Highlight effect divides each video frame into three regions based on the original brightness of the pixels in the frame, Shadows (darkest regions), Highlights (brightest regions), and Midtones (all other regions). The Shadow and Highlight sliders let you customize the adjustments to these respective regions, but the effect doesn't modify the Midtone values.

6   Click the Properties button on the top left of the My Project panel or the Edit Effects button at the lower left of the Effects view to open the Effects Properties view.

7   In Properties view, click the twirl-down triangle to the left of the Shadow/Highlight effect to open the parameter settings.

8   The default parameters are too conservative with this clip. Let's see if we can improve the results. To adjust the effect manually, deselect the Auto Amounts check box.

9   To adjust the darker regions, drag the Shadow Amount to the right to increase the brightness of pixels in the Shadows (including the faces in this clip) and to the left to decrease the brightness. Try to increase brightness as much as you can without fading the video. Try a setting of around 50.

10 To adjust the brightest regions, drag the Highlight Amount slider to the right to darken the brightness of Highlight pixels. Try a setting of around 50 here as well. Click the eye icon to the left of the Shadow/Highlight effect to toggle the effect on and off. Note how you've brightened the right side of President Lincoln's face and body.

These are the most important manual controls; to learn about the others, check the Adobe Premiere Elements Help file.

11 Save your project as *Lesson06_Work.prel*.

Working with Multiple Clips Simultaneously

The Shadow/Highlight effect is as close to a panacea as I've seen in any video editor. Although only the first photo in the slide show at the end of the movie was dark enough to trigger SmartFix's application of the Shadow/Highlight effect, they all could use some brightening.

One great new feature in Adobe Premiere Elements 8 is the ability to apply any effect—including Shadow/Highlight—to multiple clips. To try this, in Timeline mode, select the final nine photos on the Timeline, and then drag the Shadow/Highlight effect onto any one of them. Adobe Premiere Elements applies the effect to all selected clips.

If you change your mind, you can delete the effect from all clips simultaneously as well. Again, just click and select all clips, right-click, and choose Remove Effects > Video Effects, and Adobe Premiere Elements will remove all effects from all video clips. Give both operations a try—you'll find they are real time-savers.

Stabilizing Shaky Footage

One common problem with home video footage is excessive shakiness, which can occur when you walk while shooting or if you shoot from a moving car or bus. Via the SmartFix function, Adobe Premiere Elements has stabilized the worst of the clips, but the eighth clip in the project, Kensington Gardens sign.avi, could use some improvement. Play the clip and you'll notice the shakiness. In this exercise, you'll apply the Adobe Premiere Elements Stabilize filter to correct this problem.

1 In the list box next to Video Effects, click and select Video Stabilizer.

2 Drag the Stabilizer effect from Effects view and drop it onto the eighth clip in the project, Kensington Gardens sign.avi.

3 Click the Properties button in the upper left of the My Project panel or the Edit Effects button in Effects view to open the Effects Properties view.

4 In Properties view, click the twirl-down triangle to the left of the Stabilizer effect to open the parameter settings.

5 Preview the clip. There's no problem with this application of the Stabilizer effect, but sometimes you'll notice a black bar on the top, bottom, or sides of the clip where the adjustment was too strong and extended beyond the frame's edge. To correct this, in Properties view, drag the Zoom slider to the right until the bar disappears.

6 Drag through the rest of the clip to see if any other bars appear. If not, click Done on the lower right in Properties view to return to the Organizer or move on to your next edit.

● **Note:** As you've seen, the Stabilize effect works, in part, by zooming into the video, which can cause some softness. Consider applying the Sharpen effect to counteract this softness.

Play the clip, using the eye icon to the left of the Stabilizer effect to toggle it on and off. The clip is definitely easier to watch with the Stabilizer effect applied.

Changing Playback Speed

Speed changes are a commonly used effect, and Adobe Premiere Elements offers two techniques for speeding up or slowing down your video. In this exercise, you'll learn how to adjust the speed of clips bounded by others in the Timeline. In a subsequent exercise, you'll learn how to adjust the speed of a clip that doesn't have a clip immediately after it on the timeline.

Specifically, in this exercise, you'll adjust the speed of the eighth clip in the project, Kensington Gardens sign.avi. I like using local signs to introduce upcoming content, but at about two seconds, the shot isn't long enough. Let's extend it to about four seconds. Note that you can implement this effect only in the Timeline, so step 1 will send your clip to the Timeline of the My Project panel.

1 If you're currently working in the Sceneline, in the My Project panel, click the Timeline button to switch to Timeline. If necessary, zoom into the Timeline so you can easily see the individual clips.

2 Right-click Kensington Gardens sign.avi, the eighth clip in the project, and choose Time Stretch. Adobe Premiere Elements opens the Time Stretch panel.

3 Type *50* in the Speed box (where it will appear as 50.00%), and select the Maintain Audio Pitch check box.

4 Click OK to close the panel. Adobe Premiere Elements extends the clip to its new duration and pushes back all subsequent files.

5 Save your project as *Lesson06_Work.prel*.

Reversing Playback

Sharp-eyed readers (and that includes you, of course) will have noticed the Reverse Speed check box in the Time Stretch panel. This can serve a very useful function, as you'll see in a moment.

1 Still in Timeline view, move the current-time indicator to the start of the second clip on the Timeline, Big Ben 1.avi, and press the spacebar to preview through to the end of the next clip, Big Ben 2.avi.

I'm not sure what I was thinking when I shot the video, but the two clips would work better together if the first clip ended with a shot of Big Ben instead of starting with that shot.

No problem; Adobe Premiere Elements has my back.

2 Following the instructions in steps 3–5 of the previous exercise, apply the Time Stretch effect to Big Ben 1.avi, but don't change speed—simply select the Reverse Speed check box and click OK.

The preview appears again. As you'll see, you've reversed the pan to *end* with a quick glimpse of Big Ben, setting up the subsequent close-up.

Working with Keyframes

Every clip in the Timeline, and most effects that you apply to them, can be modified over time. This involves a concept called *keyframing*. Essentially, a keyframe is a location in the Timeline where you specify a value for a specific property. When you set two keyframes, Adobe Premiere Elements interpolates the value of that property over all frames between the two keyframes, effecting a change gradually over time, basically creating an animated effect.

For example, in the next exercise, you'll use keyframes to create an image pan, in effect simulating the movement of a camera over a still image. Or you can use keyframes to animate the appearance of an effect, which you'll do in a subsequent exercise.

Using keyframes effectively gives you significant flexibility and creativity in your projects. Although they sound challenging at first, if you work through the next few exercises, you'll quickly grasp their operation and utility.

Creating an Image Pan with Keyframes

The image pan is a popular effect in many documentaries and films. An image pan is defined as a movement of the camera, usually from left to right, although it can be from top to bottom and also zooming in or out. In traditional production, an image pan would actually involve the physical movement of a camcorder over an image; however, if you're working with footage from a stationary camera, Adobe Premiere Elements enables you to simulate camera movement using the Motion controls.

In this exercise, you'll use a horizontal image pan to animate the first photo in your slide show.

● **Note:** In Properties view, note that this image is 3,264 pixels wide and 2,248 pixels high. Though it's not critical that the original image's resolution exceed that of the project (720x480 in this instance), when it does, it ensures that you can zoom (up to a point) into regions in the video without causing blurriness. In general, when adding still images to a project, it's best to use images with a resolution larger than that of the project.

1   In Project view, right-click the DSCN0430.jpg image and choose Properties. Properties view enables you to—among other things—identify the size of the digital image you have imported. Close the Properties window.

Properties: DSCN0430.JPG

File Path: D:\PRE8\Lesson 06\DSCN0430.JPG
Type: JPEG
File Size: 1.8 MB
Image Size: 3264 x 2448
Pixel Depth: 32
Pixel Aspect Ratio: 1.0

2   If necessary, click the Timeline button to switch to the Timeline in the My Project panel.

3   Click to select the DSCN0430.jpg image on the Timeline (it's the second to last image). Click the time ruler above the image to move the current-time indicator to within the image, and then press the Page Up key to move the current-time indicator to the start of the image.

4   The image has been automatically scaled to fit entirely into the Monitor panel. Although the original image was 2,448 pixels high, Adobe Premiere Elements automatically scaled down the image to 480 pixels high. To return the image to its original size, right-click the image in the Timeline and choose Scale to Frame Size to deselect this option. The image zooms out to its full resolution, and you'll see only a small section of the image in the Monitor.

5 Click the Properties button in the upper left of the My Project panel or the Edit Effects button in Effects view to open the Effects Properties view.

6 In Properties view, click the twirl-down triangle to the left of the Motion effect to open the parameter settings.

7 In the upper right of Properties view, click the Show Keyframes ( ) button. You may need to expand the size of Properties view to better view the keyframes.

8 Note the mini-timeline at the top of Properties view, which has the same values as the Timeline in the My Project panel for the selected clip and has a matching current-time indicator. In the mini-timeline, the current-time indicator should be on the left in the middle of a dissolve transition with the previous image. Recall that Adobe Premiere Elements inserted the transition when you created the slide show in Chapter 5. If the current time indicator isn't in the middle of the dissolve transition, click the Page Up key to move it there.

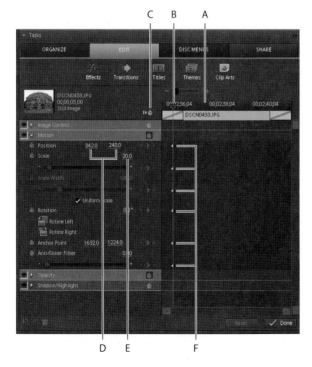

A. Mini-timeline.
B. Current-time indicator. **C.** Toggle Animation button (enables keyframes).
D. Horizontal and vertical position values.
E. Scale values (as a percentage of total size). **F.** Keyframes.

9   To the right of the Motion property is a small stopwatch. Click it and notice that a small diamond appears in the mini-timeline within Properties view to the right of each property in the Motion control. Each of these is a keyframe; next, you'll adjust the top two.

10   Click the Position values to make them active and type *342* and *240,* as shown in the previous screen.

11   Drag the Scale slider to the left until it reaches the value of 20. Or, click the numeric entry to make it active, type *20*, and then press Enter.

You've set the keyframes for the initial position to the desired values. Now you'll create and set the values for the second keyframe.

12   Click the My Project panel to make it active, then press the Page Down key to move the current-time indicator to the last frame of the image, which is in the middle of a dissolve transition with the next image.

13   Click the Position values to make them active and type *400* and *-159,* as shown. After you change the values, Adobe Premiere Elements automatically inserts a keyframe.

14   Drag the Scale slider to the left until it reaches the value of 80. Or, click the numeric entry to make it active, type *80*, and then press Enter.

After you change the values, Adobe Premiere Elements automatically inserts a keyframe.

15   Drag the current-time indicator to the beginning of the DSCN0430.jpg clip, and then press the spacebar to play the clip. You'll see a slow zoom into the picture that will play more smoothly after rendering. If you don't have background rendering enabled, you might want to render the effect using the technique detailed in the Adobe Premiere Elements Help file (search the Help file for "Render an area for preview"). Press the spacebar again to stop playback.

16   Save your project as *Lesson06_Work.prel.*

● **Note:** When adding pan and zoom effects to images like this one, sometimes it's easiest to delete the transition by clicking it, pressing the Delete key, and then adding the pan/zoom effect and reapplying the transition, which you'll learn how to do in Lesson 7.

Creating a Fade-out Using Keyframes

You can control keyframes in two locations in Adobe Premiere Elements: Properties view and the Timeline. In this exercise, you'll adjust the opacity keyframes of a video clip in the Timeline.

1   Click to select the DSCN0429.jpg image, which is the last image in the Timeline. You may need to scroll to the right in the Timeline to fully see the image.

● **Note:** The current-time indicators in Properties view and in the Timeline of the My Project panel are actually the same. You can use either one to navigate through your clip. However, the Timeline in Properties view enables you to navigate through only the currently selected clip and is used primarily for working with keyframes.

2 Let's make the video tracks as large as possible to provide some working space. To the right of the DSCN0429.jpg clip, right-click a blank area on the Timeline and choose Track Size > Large. You may have to adjust the scroll bars on the right of the Timeline to see the clip after adjusting the track size.

3 Drag the current-time indicator to about 2;49;00 in the Timeline. For precision, you can check the timecode on the bottom left of the Monitor panel. Or, to get there quickly and precisely, click the timecode on the bottom left of the Monitor to make it active, type the numbers *2 4 9 0 0* on your keyboard, and press Enter. Don't type in the semicolons, just the numbers, and the current-time indicator will move to that location when you press Enter.

4 Click the Zoom In tool (![+]) in the Timeline to increase your view of the clip.

When working with clip keyframes, it's often helpful to increase the magnification. The orange line spanning horizontally across the clip is the connector line (or graph) between keyframes. By default, all clips have the Opacity property enabled.

5 Working with DSCN0429.jpg, place your pointer over the orange connector line at the location of the current-time indicator. The pointer changes to a double-arrow icon (![double-arrow]).

6 Drag the connector line down towards the bottom of the clip. As you drag, you'll see a small window with changing numbers. The numbers represent the opacity values. Drag the connector line down to approximately the 50% level. Don't worry if you can't get an exact number. When you release the pointer, you'll see that the clip now has an opacity value of only 50% and is much darker than before.

7 Drag the connector line back up towards the top of the clip to restore the clip's opacity to 100%.

Now you'll add keyframes to help Adobe Premiere Elements create a fade to black at the end of the movie.

8 The current-time indicator should be positioned at 2;49;00; if not, drag it there. Then position your pointer on the orange connector line where it intersects with the current-time indicator line, and the pointer should change to the double-arrow icon (![icon]).

9 With the double-arrow icon as your pointer, hold down the Ctrl key on your keyboard, and click the connector line once. You should see a small yellow diamond added to the orange connector line at the beginning of the clip, representing your first keyframe.

10 Press the Page Down key to move the current-time indicator to the end of the movie. Using the same procedure, create a keyframe at that location.

11 Click the keyframe at the end of the movie clip and drag it down to the bottom of the track. The number on the right of the yellow box next to the pointer is the Opacity value; drag it until that value equals 0.00.

12 To view the Opacity fade-out, move your current-time indicator to the beginning of the DSCN0429.jpg clip, and then press the spacebar.

13 Save your project as *Lesson06_Work.prel*.

In Lesson 7, you'll learn how to create a similar effect using the Cross Dissolve transition. Although the visual effect is similar, working with keyframes lets you customize the effect to a much greater degree.

Working with Keyframes

Once you've set a keyframe, you can modify it by dragging it to a new location or value. To delete a keyframe, right-click it and choose Delete.

The other keyframe-related controls shown in the context menu are advanced options that control the rate and smoothness of change applied by Adobe Premiere Elements. For more on these options, search the Help file for "Controlling change between keyframes."

Finally, you can access all keyframes inserted on the Timeline in Properties view. Select the clip DSCN0429.jpg, and then click the Properties (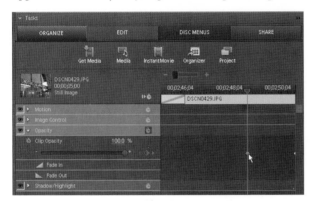) button in the upper left of the My Project panel. This opens Properties view.

If necessary, click the Show Keyframes ( ) button on the top right in Properties view to view the keyframes. Then click the twirl-down triangle to the left of the Opacity effect to open the parameter settings and view the keyframes that you created in the Timeline.

You can set and modify opacity-related keyframes in either or both locations. In general, the Timeline is best for fast and simple adjustments, like the fade-out that you just applied, whereas Properties view is a better choice for complicated, more precise adjustments.

Using Keyframes to Animate Effects

You've learned how to apply effects and how to create and modify keyframes. Now you'll animate an effect using keyframes. This is a very powerful capability: Essentially, it lets you create custom transitions using any Adobe Premiere Elements effect.

One word of caution: This section is more advanced than some users of Adobe Premiere Elements may need, so feel free to skip to the next lesson if you wish. However, you should know that such keyframing is the basis of animation in programs such as Adobe Premiere Pro and Adobe After Effects, which means this could be a useful introduction to using those tools, and the exercise is not difficult to complete. If you do choose to skip it, you can always revisit it later if you wish.

In this exercise, you'll be animating the NewBlue Old Film effect to create a unique transition that you'll apply to the start of each major section of the project.

1   Select Effects () in the Edit tab of the Tasks panel, and in the list box next to Video Effects, click and select NewBlue Film Look.

2   Locate the Westminster Abbey.avi clip (the first clip in the Timeline) and click the clip to select it.

3   Press the Home key to move your current-time indicator to the first frame of the Westminster Abbey.avi clip. Increase the magnification of the Timeline if needed.

4   Drag the Old Film effect from Effects view and drop it onto the Westminster Abbey.avi clip to apply it. You'll see the effect applied in the Monitor panel.

5   Click the Edit Effects button in Effects view, and then click the twirl-down triangle next to Old Film to reveal the controls.

6   If keyframes are not showing, in the top right of Properties view, click the Show keyframes ( ) button. You may need to expand the size of Properties view to better view the keyframes.

7   With the current-time indicator at the start of the clip, click the small stopwatch to the right of the Old Film controls to enable animation for this property. After you click the stopwatch, a small diamond appears in the mini-timeline within Properties view to the right of all configurable properties in the Old Film control. These are the initial keyframes.

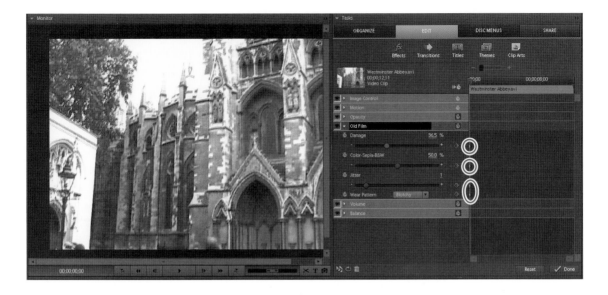

8 When producing your own movies, you might want to adjust the effect settings to customize them for your video. Let's keep things simple here and accept the default values.

9 Now you'll set the second set of keyframes. In the mini-timeline in Properties view, click and drag the current-time indicator to the right to 00;00;02;00 (which you can see on the bottom left of the Monitor panel).

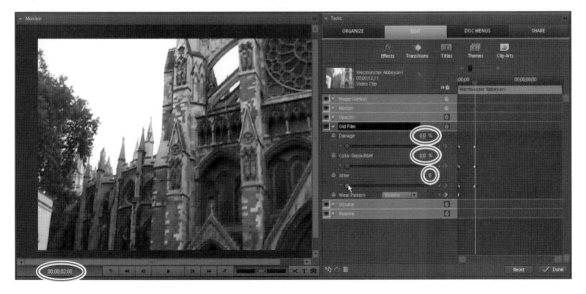

10 Drag the Damage, Color-Sepia-BW, and Jitter sliders to the left until they reach 0 (or 0.0 as the case may be). Or, click each numeric entry to make it active, type *0*, and then click Enter. This tells Adobe Premiere Elements to set each effect parameter at zero value, which essentially turns the effect off.

Changing the value automatically adds a second keyframe, which is represented as a second diamond in the Timeline in Properties view. Once animation has been turned on, Adobe Premiere Elements automatically animates the effect between the two values.

● **Note:** If you hadn't set the second set of keyframes, the Old Film effect would have continued without change through the end of the clip but wouldn't continue on to subsequent clips.

11 Click the Home key to return to the beginning of the move, and then press the spacebar to play the clip and the effect. The clip starts out with the Old Film in full effect and returns to normal appearance at the 00;00;02;00 mark. Press the spacebar again to stop playback.

12 Save your project as *Lesson06_Work.prel*.

Copying Effects from One Clip to Another

Because effects are customized a single clip at a time, it would be quite time-consuming to place the same effect across numerous clips, especially if you had to drag and drop the effect on each clip. Fortunately, Adobe Premiere Elements provides a simple way to copy effects and their settings from one clip to another.

1 Click the first clip, Westminster Abbey.avi, in either the Sceneline or Timeline, to select it.

2 Click the Properties button in the upper left of the My Project panel to open the Effects Properties view.

3 Click the Old Film effect in Properties view.

● **Note:** You can also right-click in Properties view and choose Copy or press Cntrl+C to copy the selected effects.

4 Choose Edit > Copy.

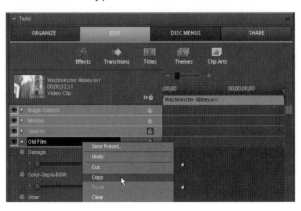

5   In either the Sceneline or Timeline, click to select the palace 1.avi clip (the thirteenth clip from the start of the movie), and click the Properties button on the upper left of the My Project panel to open the Properties view.

6   Right-click in the blank gray area beneath the fixed and standard effects in Properties view, and then choose Paste. Adobe Premiere Elements applies the Old Film effect to this clip with the same properties and keyframes.

7   Repeat this procedure and paste the effect (you shouldn't have to copy again; just continue to paste) onto the first image in the slide show that you added to the back of the movie, which should be DSCN0417.jpg.

8   Click the top of the My Project panel to make it active. Press the Home key to place the current-time indicator at the beginning of the project, and then press the spacebar to begin playback. When reviewing the movie, note the effects you have applied to the clips.

9   Choose File > Save As and save your project as *Lesson06_End.prel*.

This concludes the main lesson. Next, you'll learn how to implement several additional effects using other source clips in a separate project file.

Creating a Picture-in-Picture Overlay

Adobe Premiere Elements can superimpose multiple tracks of video. In this exercise, you will superimpose one video clip in a small frame over your preexisting background clip that covers the entire screen. This effect is called a Picture-in-Picture (PiP) overlay.

1   To load the project file containing the new content, click File > Open Project, and then navigate to the Lesson06 folder you copied to your hard drive.

2   Within that folder, select the file Greenscreen.prel, and then click Open. If a dialog appears asking for the location of rendered files, click the Skip Previews button.

3   Choose Window > Restore Workspace to ensure that you start the lesson with the default panel layout.

4   In the Timeline, click Rockshow.avi, the only clip. The selected clip appears in the Monitor panel.

5   In the Organize tab of the Tasks panel, click the Project button.

6   In Project view, locate the Gina_guitar.avi clip. Click once to select the clip, hold down the Shift key, and drag the clip towards the upper-left corner of the Rockshow.avi clip in the Monitor panel.

7 Release the pointer and choose Picture-in-Picture from the menu that appears.

● **Note:** If the superimposed clip is longer than the background clip, it appears over successive clips in the Sceneline for its entire duration and appears superimposed over those clips during playback.

8 Click No in the Videomerge panel.

9 Click to select the superimposed clip and notice that the clip changes appearance. There are now handles on the edges, indicating that the clip is active.

10 Select Window > Properties to open Properties view.

11 In Properties view, click the arrow to the left of Motion to reveal its properties. Make sure the Uniform Scale check box is selected.

12 Place your pointer over the value for Scale, and then drag the value to 40. As you change the scale, the Gina_guitar.avi clip shrinks to 40 percent of its original size.

13 If necessary, you can reposition the clip using the Position controls. Or simply drag the clip to the desired position in the Monitor panel.

14 Press the Home key on your keyboard to go to the start of your project, and then click the Play button ( ) to review your work.

15 Save your project as *Lesson06_pip.prel*.

Compositing Two Clips Using Videomerge

Compositing is the process of merging two clips together, one atop the other, while removing the background color of the top clip to reveal the second. This allows you to place your subject in a variety of environments, both real and simulated.

Adobe Premiere Elements' Videomerge effect makes compositing as easy as drag and drop. Videomerge automatically determines the background of the top clip and makes it transparent. Video or image clips on the tracks below it become visible through the transparent areas. You'll get the best results with Videomerge if you shoot the clip to be composited using the following rules:

- Create a strong (preferably dark or saturated), solid, uniform color background to shoot against.

- Make sure that the background is brightly and uniformly lit to avoid shadows.

- When choosing a background color, avoid skin tones and colors that are similar to the subject's clothing or hair color. (Otherwise, the skin, clothes, or hair will become transparent, too). Bright green and blue are the best choices.

With this information as background, reload the Greenscreen.prel project file (you should have already saved the first project as Lesson06_pip.prel) and follow this procedure.

1 In the Timeline, click Rockshow.avi, the only clip. The selected clip appears in your Monitor panel.

2 In the Organize tab of the Tasks panel, click the Project button.

3 In Project view, locate the Gina_guitar.avi clip. Click once to select the clip, hold down the Shift key, and drag the clip onto the Rockshow.avi clip in the Monitor panel.

4 Release the pointer and choose Place on Top and click Yes to apply Videomerge.

Adobe Premiere Elements inserts Gina_guitar.avi in the Video 2 track over Rockshow.avi, automatically detects the blue background, and makes it transparent.

(See illustration on next page.)

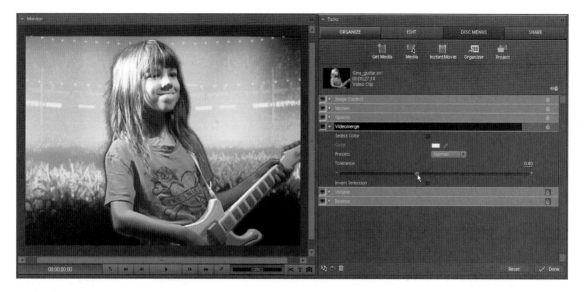

5 In the Timeline, click Gina_guitar.avi to select it, and then click the Properties
   (⊞) button on the upper left of the My Project panel.

6 In Properties view, click the twirl-down triangle to the left of the Videomerge
   effect to open the parameter settings.

Most of the time, Videomerge automatically produces optimal results without
adjustment. Should you need to customize your Videomerge settings, search for
"Videomerge" in the Adobe Premiere Elements Help file.

Changing Speed Using the Time Stretch Tool

Previously, you learned how to change the speed of clips bounded in the Timeline
by other clips on both sides. Now you'll learn how to use the Time Stretch tool to
accomplish the same task but in a more visual way.

Here's the problem you'll solve. The Rockshow.avi clip used as a background in
the previous two exercises is 31 seconds long, and the Gina_guitar.avi clip is about
27 seconds long. You could just trim the Rockshow clip to the same duration, but
that would delete content at the end of that clip.

A more elegant solution is to use Adobe Premiere Elements' Time Stretch feature
to speed up the Rockshow.avi clip so that it's the same duration as Gina_guitar.avi.

1 In the Timeline, click the Time Stretch icon (⊙) on the upper left of the My
   Project panel.

2 Hover your pointer over the right edge of the Rockshow.avi clip until the Time
   Stretch icon (▐▙▸) appears.

3 Drag the right edge of the Rockshow.avi clip to the left until it aligns with the end of the Gina_guitar.avi clip.

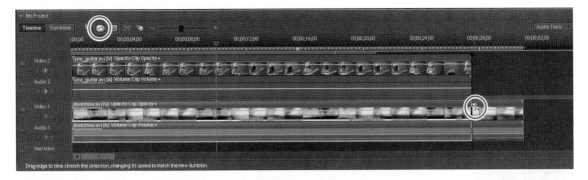

4 Click the Selection tool () on the upper left of the My Project panel to restore the normal pointer.

5 Right-click Rockshow.avi and choose Time Stretch. Adobe Premiere Elements opens the Time Stretch panel. Note that the speed should have increased to 112.86, which is precisely the correction needed to make Rockshow.avi the same duration as Gina_guitar.avi. In most instances, you would click Maintain Audio Pitch to maintain the pitch of the clip, but since Rockshow.avi has no audio, that isn't necessary in this case.

6 Save your project as *Lesson06_videomerge.prel*.

Working with Motion Tracking

Motion tracking gives you the ability to automatically track moving objects in a project so you can add labels, thought bubbles, or other effects to the moving object. This exercise teaches you how to use this function.

1 To load the project file containing the new content, click File > Open Project, and then navigate to the Lesson06 folder you copied to your hard drive.

2 Within the Lesson06 folder, select the file Motion tracking.prel, and then click Open. If a dialog appears asking for the location of rendered files, click the Skip Previews button.

3 Click to select the clip in the My Project panel, MotionTrack1.avi.

4 Select the Motion Tracking icon ( ) on the upper left of the Timeline to turn on Motion Tracking mode. If the dialog opens, click Yes in the Motion Tracking window to enable Adobe Premiere Elements to track moving objects in the clip. The Auto Analyzer starts to run.

5 Drag the current-time indicator to 00;00;15 where the girl enters the box.

● **Note:** In addition to clip art, you can use motion tracking with titles, graphics, and picture-in-picture effects.

6 Click the Edit tab, and then click the Clip Art icon. Make sure that Show All is selected in the drop-down list. Click Butterfly02 and drag it to any point over the girl's head.

7 Press the Home key to move to the start of your project, and then click the Play button (▶) to review your work. Watch how the butterfly moves with the girl.

8 Save your project as *Lesson06_butterfly.prel*.

Fine-tuning Motion Tracking Effects

● **Note:** In my version of Adobe Premiere Elements, this exercise ran correctly only one time, which was the first time Adobe Premiere Elements analyzed MotionTrack1.avi. After then, the rectangle won't reappear.

If you want to run the exercise again, go to the Elements Organizer and delete MotionTrack1. avi. The next time you run the project, Adobe Premiere Elements will have to reanalyze the clip, and the exercise should work as detailed.

Motion tracking tracks the largest object moving in the video. Suppose you want to track additional objects. Here's the workflow.

1 To load the project file containing the new content, click File > Open Project, and then navigate to the Lesson06 folder you copied to your hard drive.

2 Within that folder, select the file Motion tracking.prel, and then click Open. If a dialog appears asking for the location of rendered files, click the Skip Previews button.

3 Click to select the clip in the My Project panel, MotionTrack1.avi.

4 Select the Motion Tracking icon (⬤) on the upper left of the Timeline to turn on Motion Tracking mode. If the dialog opens, click Yes in the Motion Tracking window to enable Adobe Premiere Elements to track moving objects in the clip. The Auto Analyzer starts to run.

5 Drag the current-time indicator to 00;00;15 where the girl enters the box.

6 On the upper right of the Monitor panel, click the Add Object button (Add Object). Adobe Premiere Elements adds a scalable box to the Monitor panel.

7   Drag the box over the object that you'd like to track, and then drag the edges to fit the object. In the upper-right corner of the Monitor panel, click Track Object (Track Object). Adobe Premiere Elements analyzes the clip to track the moving object.

8   Drag the current-time indicator to the right.

You'll notice that Adobe Premiere Elements only tracks the object about halfway through the clip. When the girl turns her head, the detail needed to track the object is lost. In this regard, Adobe Premiere Elements will do the best job tracking objects with clear edges and strong contrast with other objects in the video. Once Adobe Premiere Elements loses the detail necessary to track the selected object, the program will simply stop tracking, and any effects applied via the Motion Tracking control will also stop.

9   As before, you can drag a clip art object into the box, and it will follow the girl across the screen. Or, you can create an effect "mask" as detailed in the next section.

Working with Effect Masking

Effect masking gives you the ability to constrain an effect to a certain section of an image, and if that section is moving, to track it around the frame. For example, reload the project file from the previous exercise (without saving the project you just created), and work through steps 1–8 again. Then follow these steps.

1 Select Effects () in the Edit tab of the Tasks panel, and in the list box next to Video Effects, click and select Blur & Sharpen.

2 Drag the Gaussian Blur effect from Effects view and drop it onto the little box you created in the MotionTrack1.avi clip. Then, click any open area in the Timeline to set the effect. You should see the Monitor panel flash briefly.

● **Note:** You can apply a static mask to any clip by right-clicking the clip and choosing Effects Mask > Apply.

3 Click MotionTrack1.avi to select it, then click the Edit Effects button in Effects view, and then click the twirl-down triangle next to Gaussian Blur to reveal the controls. Set the Blurriness setting to 25 by dragging the slider to the right (or click the numeric entry to make it active, type 25, and then press Enter).

Adobe Premiere Elements applies the effect only within the box (called a mask), and the box follows the girl's motion in the video until motion tracking is lost.

Exploring on Your Own

Congratulations! Now you understand how to apply video settings, change effects and settings, copy effects from one clip to another, create an image pan, animate an effect with keyframes, create a Picture-in-Picture effect, and composite one video over another with Videomerge. You also know how to use Motion Tracking and how to "mask" an effect. Here are some effects that you can experiment with on your own:

1 Create a PiP effect using two or more clips on the same screen.

2 Experiment with alternative effects such as Adjust > Brightness & Contrast, or Distort > Bend. To get a sense of the different effects available in Adobe Premiere Elements, choose Help > Premiere Elements Help, or press F1 to access the Help guide. The Applying Effects section includes a gallery of video effects.

3 Experiment with the various effects presets located in the Effects panel—specifically, the Horizontal and Vertical image pans.

Review Questions

1 What are curative effects, and when should you apply them?

2 What's the quickest way to apply identical effects and settings to multiple clips?

3 What are fixed effects, and what is their purpose?

4 What is a keyframe, and what does it contain?

5 How do you modify keyframes once they've been added to a clip?

6 How do you apply the same effect to multiple clips on the Timeline?

Review Answers

1 Curative effects improve one or more aspects of a clip, such as exposure, backlighting, or excessive shakiness. You should apply curative effects to a clip before applying artistic and other effects.

2 After selecting the clip that contains the effect or effects that you want to copy, click an effect to select it in the Properties panel, or Shift-click to select multiple effects. Copy your selection by choosing Edit > Copy. Then select the clip to which you want to transfer the effects and choose Edit > Paste.

3 Fixed effects are the Property parameters that every clip in Adobe Premiere Elements has enabled by default. These effects are Motion, Opacity, and Volume. Within the Motion effect, Scale, Position, Rotation, and Anchor Point are all properties that can be adjusted to create, for example, a PiP effect.

4 A keyframe contains the values for all the controls in an effect and applies those values to the clip at the specific time.

5 Once keyframes have been added to a clip, they can be adjusted by clicking and dragging them along the connector line. If there are two keyframes, moving one keyframe farther away from the other extends the duration of the effect; moving a keyframe closer to another keyframe shortens the effect.

6 Select all target clips in the My Project panel and apply the effect to any single clip.

7
CREATING TRANSITIONS

If you've followed the lessons in this book in order, you should now feel comfortable adding and deleting footage in your project, and trimming clips to improve the pacing of the movie you're producing. In this lesson, you'll learn how to take a project in which your clips have already been sequenced and trimmed and add nuance and dimension using transitions between the clips. You'll learn how to do the following:

- Apply a transition using Transitions view

- Preview transitions

- Modify transition settings

- Apply the default transition to multiple clips

- Copy and paste transitions

- Create fade-ins and fade-outs

- Render transitions

 This lesson will take approximately one hour.

Inserting a Dip to Black transition at the start
of the movie.

Getting Started

You'll modify scenes in this lesson's project by adding transitions in stages. But first you'll open the Lesson07 project and prepare your Adobe Premiere Elements workspace.

1 Make sure that you have correctly copied the Lesson07 folder from the DVD in the back of this book onto your computer's hard drive. See "Copying the Classroom in a Book files" in the Getting Started section at the start of this book.

2 Launch Adobe Premiere Elements.

3 In the Welcome screen, click the Open Project button, and then click the Open folder.

4 In the Open Project dialog, navigate to the Lesson07 folder.

5 Within that folder, select the file Lesson07_Start.prel, and then click Open. If a dialog appears asking for the location of rendered files, click the Skip Previews button.

Your project file opens with the Monitor, Tasks, and My Project panels open.

6 Choose Window > Restore Workspace to ensure that you start the lesson in the default panel layout.

Viewing the Completed Movie Before You Start

To see what you'll be creating in this lesson, you can play the completed movie.

1 In the Organize tab of the Tasks panel, click Project ( ). In the Project view, locate the file Lesson07_Movie.wmv, and then double-click it to open the video in the Preview window.

2 In the Preview window, click the Play button ( ) to watch the video about a walk around London, which you will build in this lesson.

3 When done, close the Preview window by clicking the Close button ( ) in the upper-right corner of the window.

Working with Transitions

Transitions phase out one clip while phasing in the next. The simplest form of a transition is the cut. A cut occurs when the last frame of one clip is followed by the first frame of the next. The cut is the most frequently used transition in video and film, and the one you will use most of the time. However, you can also use other types of transitions to achieve effects between scenes.

Transitions

Using transitions, you can phase out one clip while phasing in the next, or you can stylize the beginning or end of a single clip. A transition can be as subtle as a cross-dissolve, or emphatic, such as a page turn or spinning pinwheel. You generally place transitions on a cut between two clips, creating a double-sided transition. However, you can also apply a transition to just the beginning or end of a clip, creating a single-sided transition, such as a fade to black.

When a transition shifts from one clip to the next, it overlaps frames from both clips. The overlapped frames can be either frames previously trimmed from the clips (frames just past the In or Out point at the cut) or existing frames repeated on either side of the cut. It's important to remember that when you trim a clip, you don't delete frames; instead, the resulting In and Out points frame a window over the original clip. A transition uses the trimmed frames to create the transition effect, or if the clips don't have trimmed frames, the transition repeats frames.

—*From Adobe Premiere Elements Help*

Using Transitions View in the Tasks Panel

Adobe Premiere Elements includes a wide range of transitions, including 3D motion, dissolves, wipes, and zooms. The animated thumbnail view that appears when you click on a specific transition gives you a good idea of how it might be applied to your project. Transitions are grouped into two main folders in Transitions view: Audio Transitions and Video Transitions.

1   To access Adobe Premiere Elements transitions, click the Transitions button ( ) in the Edit tab of the Tasks panel. Hover over or select a transition to see an animated preview.

(See illustration on next page.)

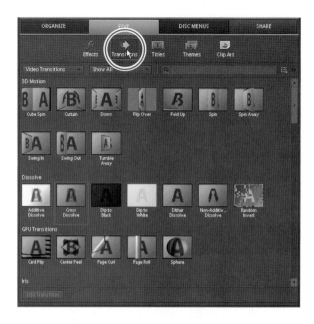

2   Select Video Transitions (if it's not already selected) from the category menu in the upper-left corner of Transitions view. Then select NewBlue 3D Transformations Elements from the menu next to it to see only the different types of transitions in Transitions view.

3   Adobe Premiere Elements includes a Favorites category to which you can add your most frequently used transitions. Right-click the Checker Board transition in Transitions view, and then select Add to Favorites from the context menu.

4 To view the content of your Favorites category, select Favorites from the category menu in the upper-left corner of Transitions view. You'll see the Checker Board transition added to the Favorites category.

Applying a Transition

Understanding how transitions work is essential to using them successfully. For a transition to shift from one clip to another, the transition must overlap frames from both clips for a certain amount of time.

1 In the Monitor panel, position your current-time indicator at the 00;01;22;00 mark, the edit point between the Royal Albert Hall2.avi clip and the palace 1.avi clip. You'll be placing a transition between these two clips.

2 If Sceneline is not already selected in the My Project panel, switch to it now.

3 From Transitions view, which should still be showing the content of the Favorites category, drag the Checker Board transition to the rectangle between the Royal Albert Hall2.avi clip and the palace 1.avi clip in the Sceneline. You'll know the transition has been added because its icon is visible in the rectangle between the two clips in the Sceneline.

Note: You do not have to reposition the current-time indicator to place transitions between clips. However, it's often helpful in locating the correct point in your project.

4 In the Sceneline, double-click the rectangle between the two clips to preview the Checker Board transition. After the transition ends, press the spacebar to stop playback.

Note: To delete a transition, right-click it and choose Clear (in the Timeline) or click to select it and press the Delete key (in the Sceneline).

Viewing Transition Properties

When you add a transition to a clip, the default length of the transition is determined by your preferences. You can change the length of transitions after applying them. Additionally, there are several other attributes of transitions that you can adjust. These include alignment, start and end values, border, and softness.

In this exercise, you'll add a Push transition that pushes one image offscreen to replace it with the next clip. You will then modify the various attributes of the transition in Properties view.

1   In Transitions view of the Edit tab, choose Video Transitions from the category menu. Make sure Show All is selected in the menu next to it. Then click in the text search box to the right of the magnifying glass icon (🔍) and type the word *push*. Adobe Premiere Elements automatically searches the list of video transitions and locates the Push transition.

2   If necessary, scroll to the right in the My Project panel until you can see the third and fourth clips of the movie, Big Ben 2.avi and Churchill Museum.avi. Drag the Push transition from Transitions view to the rectangle between these two clips in the Sceneline.

3   In the Monitor panel, position the current-time indicator a few frames before the transition. Press the spacebar to view the transition. The Push transition will push the first clip off to the side. After the transition ends, press the spacebar to stop playback.

4 Select the Push transition in the Sceneline, and then click the Edit Transition button (Edit Transition) in the lower-left corner of Transitions view. This will load the transition's parameters into Properties view where you can edit them.

5 Click the Show Keyframes button (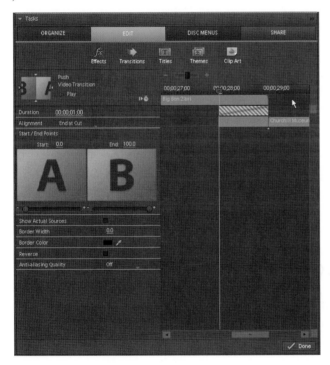) at the top of Properties view to view a magnified version of your Timeline. This enables you to view the transition as it is applied between your two clips. If necessary, resize the Properties panel or just its Timeline to better see this Timeline.

6 In the Timeline of Properties view, drag the current-time indicator back and forth over the transition to preview your transition effect.

Stay in this window. You will now modify your transition's settings.

Modifying Transition Settings

All transitions have default settings. To achieve specific results, you can customize the settings in Properties view. Modifying the length of a transition is easy, as you will see in this exercise.

1 To change the length of a transition in Properties view, place your pointer over the Duration value, and then drag to the left to change the Duration to 00;00;00;15 (15 frames). Remember that there are 30 frames in one second of NTSC video; therefore, 15 frames represent a half second of time.

● **Note:** If you don't see all the controls in the Transition Properties panel, expand the panel to make it wider.

2 Drag the current-time indicator—in either the Monitor panel or Properties view—to a position before the Push transition, and press the spacebar to preview the transition. After the transition ends, press the spacebar to stop playback. If you should accidentally click the track area of your Sceneline, you will deselect the transition and its parameters will vanish from Properties view. Don't worry; just click the transition in your Sceneline to select it again and display its parameters in Properties view.

3 In Properties view, select the check box marked Reverse. This reverses the transition so that the second clip now pushes the first clip to the left. Depending on the size of your monitor, you may need to scroll down and resize Properties view or its Timeline to see this check box.

4 Click the Timeline button on the upper-left corner of the My Project panel to shift into Timeline mode. Zoom into the Timeline, if necessary, to see the transition.

5 Drag your current-time indicator to approximately halfway through the transition, at roughly the 00;00;28;17 mark.

Because you're in the middle of the transition, your screen will be split in half. This makes it easier to preview the modifications you'll apply in the next steps.

6 If necessary, scroll down Properties view to view the additional controls. Click the value for Border Width, type the number *10*, and then press Enter.

This creates a 10-pixel border on the edge of your transition. The default color of the border is black, but you can modify this as well.

7 Click the black color swatch next to the Border Color. This opens the Color Picker dialog.

8 In the color slider, which displays the spectrum of colors in a vertical strip, click in the blue hues.

9 Then, inside the larger color spectrum, click in the lower-right corner to select a medium blue.

10 Click OK to close the Color Picker dialog. The border of your transition is now 10 pixels wide and blue.

11 Drag your current-time indicator to a position before the transition, and then press the spacebar to play your modified transition. After the transition ends, press the spacebar to stop playback.

12 Choose File > Save As, name the file *Lesson07_Work* in the Save Project dialog, and then click Save to save it in your Lesson07 folder.

Replacing a Transition

Replacing an existing transition between two clips is done in essentially the same way as adding a new transition: Simply drag the transition from the Media panel onto the existing transition in the Sceneline. You can do this repeatedly to compare the effects of different transitions.

To practice adding and replacing transitions—this time using the Timeline—you will now apply an Iris Box transition between the final video clip on the Timeline, Shakespeares Head Pub.avi, and the first image, DSCN0417.JPG, and then replace it with an Iris Round transition.

1 In the My Project panel, click the Timeline button. If necessary, use the zoom controls and scroll your view so that the aforementioned clips are visible.

2 Press the Page Up and Page Down keys to position the current-time indicator at the edit line between the two clips. You might want to click the Zoom In tool ( ) to magnify the view at this edit line.

3 If necessary, click the Transitions button to open Transitions view in the Edit tab, click in the text search box to the right of the magnifying glass icon (), select the word "push," and then type *iris* to automatically list all the Iris transitions.

4 In the following steps, do not release the pointer until instructed. Drag the Iris Box transition over the edit line between Shakespeares Head Pub.avi and DSCN0417.JPG; do not release the pointer. Pay careful attention to the appearance of your pointer.

5 Move your pointer on top of the edit line between the two clips. Notice how your pointer changes to the Center at Cut icon ( ). Release the pointer to center the transition over the cut.

▶ **Tip:** For more information about transition alignment, search for "transition alignment options" in Adobe Premiere Elements Help.

6 Preview the Iris Box transition by dragging your current-time indicator before the transition and then pressing the spacebar. When the transition is over, press the spacebar to stop playback. Notice how the transition is represented by a gray box with two arrows above the cut between the clips in the Timeline.

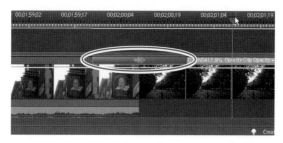

7 In Transitions view, select the Iris Round transition and drag it on top of the Iris Box transition in the Timeline to replace it. You can have only one transition between two clips.

8 Preview the new transition by dragging the current-time indicator before the transition and pressing the spacebar to start playback. After the transition ends, press the spacebar to stop playback.

Note: Anytime you insert a transition with diagonal lines, ovals, or other edges that aren't exactly vertical or horizontal, jagged edges can appear. Smooth them out with the Anti-aliasing Quality control used in this exercise.

9 Select the Iris Round transition in the Sceneline, and then click the Edit Transition button (Edit Transition) in the lower-left corner of Transitions view.

This transition's parameters are loaded into Properties view where you can edit them.

10 Find the Anti-aliasing Quality control on the bottom of the Transition Properties view. Click the list box, and choose High, which will smooth rough edges in some regions of the oval.

Adding a Single-sided Transition to Create a Fade-in

Transitions do not necessarily need to be located between two clips. For example, you can quickly add a fade-in and fade-out to the beginning and end of your movie.

1   If you're not already in Timeline view, in the My Project panel, click the Timeline button. Press the Home key to position the current-time indicator at the beginning of the first clip.

2   In the Transitions view of the Edit tab, select the word "iris" in the text search box to the right of the magnifying glass icon (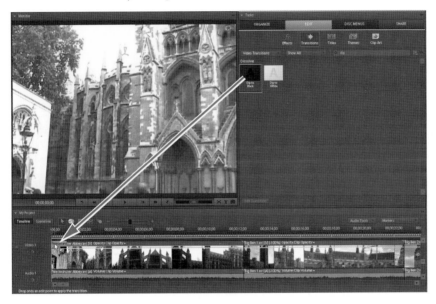), and then type the word *dip*. Two Dip transitions will automatically be located in the Dissolve folder.

3   Drag the Dip to Black transition from the Transitions view to the beginning of the Westminster Abbey.avi clip on the Video 1 track.

4   Press the spacebar to play the transition. The beginning of the transition starts at black and then fades in to the video. After the transition ends, press the spacebar to stop playback.

5 To extend the duration of these transitions by a half second, grab the right edge of each transition box one at a time, and drag it to the right until the text box next to the drag pointer indicates that you've added 00;00;00;15. Release the pointer.

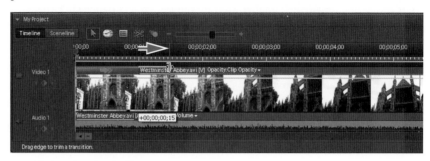

6 Save your project as *Lesson07_End.prel*.

GPU (Graphics Processing Unit) transition effects

Adobe Premiere Elements comes with many GPU-accelerated transitions including Card Flip, Center Peel, Page Curl, Page Roll, and Sphere. These transitions take advantage of the added video processing capabilities offered by video display cards that have Graphics Processing Unit (GPU) chips. These display cards help with graphics acceleration, so transitions can be previewed and rendered more quickly than by the CPU alone. If you have a display card that supports DirectX 9.x, Pixel Shader (PS) 1.3 or later, and Vertex Shader 1.1 or later, you can use the GPU-accelerated transitions. They are visible only if you have a card with a GPU and they reside in the Video Transitions view.

—From Adobe Premiere Elements Help

Applying the Default Transition to Multiple Clips

There's no rule that says you need to use transitions between all clips in your movies. However, rather than use cuts between clips, many producers insert very short cross-dissolve transitions between clips to smooth out any visual jarring between the clips. A new feature in Adobe Premiere Elements makes this very simple to do. In this exercise, you'll start by changing the duration of the default transition and then applying it to multiple clips simultaneously.

1 Choose Edit > Preferences > General to open the Preferences panel.

2 Highlight the number in the Video Transition Default Duration to make it active, type in 5, and press Enter.

3   Click OK to close the Preferences panel.

4   If you're not already in Timeline view, in the My Project panel, click the Timeline button. Press the Backslash (\) key to display the entire contents of the project in the Timeline.

5   Click and drag to select all video clips on the Timeline.

6   In the Adobe Premiere Elements menu, choose Timeline > Apply Default Transition.

7   Click OK if the "Insufficient media" error message appears. This appears because we're using short, mostly untrimmed clips in this exercise; you shouldn't see this too often in your own projects.

Note: You can also copy and paste a transition to multiple clips by copying the transition, selecting the target clips, and pasting the transition on the selected clips.

8 Adobe Premiere Elements applies the default transition between all selected clips, replacing any previously inserted transitions. However, Adobe Premiere Elements doesn't change the duration of the previously inserted transitions, which you'll have to adjust manually if you want them to match that of the newly inserted clips.

9 Drag the current-time indicator around the project and preview the transitions. You'll notice that the effect is subtle but smoothes the flow from clip to clip.

Making Transitions Work in Your Movie

Now that you know the how of transitions, let's spend a bit of time discussing the when and why. While there are few absolutes about the art of transitions, your productions will benefit by incorporating these two concepts into your creative decisions.

But recognize that you don't need to include a transition between each and every clip in your movies. If you watch a Hollywood movie, for example, you'll see that noticeable transitions (that is, those longer than four or five frames) are seldom used between clips *within a scene* but are often used *between scenes.*

Why? Because the transition lets the viewer know that there's been a change in time or location. That is, if a scene jumped from a kitchen at night to the backyard the next day, simply jumping from scene to scene would confuse the viewer. You can imagine the viewer saying, "Hey, what happened here? One second they were in the kitchen drinking milkshakes at night, and the next second they were playing dodgeball in the yard in sunlight." However, if the editor had inserted a fade to black between the two scenes, the viewer would understand that there was a change.

Within the context of the London project, there are three distinct scenes—the initial walk downtown, the visit to Buckingham Palace, and the slide show. These would be the natural locations for noticeable transitions within this project. In fact, in the project going forward, you'll notice that the Checker Board transition has been inserted at these locations. These transitions are all one-second long, whereas the dissolves between movie clips are all five frames. You may recall that the transitions we inserted in our slide show back in Lesson 5 were all one-second long as well, which worked because each slide was like a separate scene.

Of course, with family videos, your goal is to produce smiles, not to win an Academy Award. If you'd like to use transitions as content rather than in their traditional role, feel free to add as many as you'd like, anywhere you'd like. Just be sure to consider the following rule.

When using transitions, you should match the tone of the transition to the tone of the movie. In a fun, family video like a trip to the zoo or other vacation, you could use any transition that Adobe Premiere Elements offers—in some cases, the zanier the better. This is why highly noticeable transitions are used frequently in children's shows like *Barney & Friends* or *The Wiggles*.

On the other hand, when shooting a solemn event—say, a wedding or graduation—the tone is usually much more serious. In these instances, you'd probably want to use only Cross Dissolves or the occasional Fade to Black transition to maintain that tone.

Exploring on Your Own

My compliments, that's another lesson well done! You've discovered how transitions can make your projects more professional looking by adding continuity between clips. You've learned about placing, previewing, modifying, and rendering different transitions, as well as applying them en masse.

As you continue to edit with transitions, you'll get a better idea of how to use them to enhance the tone or style of your project. The best way to develop that style is by trying different transitions and discovering how they affect your movie. So here's your task list for further experimentation.

1   Make the changes to your project discussed in "Making Transitions Work in Your Movie."

2   Experiment with different transitions; preview their animated icons in Transitions view. Remember that dragging a transition onto an existing transition will replace it.

3   Be sure that you're comfortable modifying the default parameters of your transitions. One by one, select the transitions you have added and explore their settings in Properties view.

Review Questions

1   Where are Video Transitions located, and what are two ways to locate specific transitions?

2   How do you modify transitions?

3   How can you extend the duration of a transition?

4   How can you apply a transition to multiple clips simultaneously?

Review Answers

1   Video transitions are located in Transitions view, which you can access at anytime from your Edit workspace. You can browse for individual transitions, which are organized in categories and by transition type. Additionally, you can find a specific transition by typing its name or part of its name into the search field in Transitions view.

2   Click the transition you want to modify to select it, and choose Edit Transition in Properties view.

3   One method of extending the duration of a transition is to change its length in Properties view. Select the transition in the Sceneline to access its properties. You can also change the duration of a transition by dragging its edges in the Timeline of the My Project panel.

4   Two techniques can be used: One is to select multiple clips on the Timeline and choose Timeline > Apply Default Transition. Adobe Premiere Elements will insert the default transition between all selected clips. You can also copy a previously applied transition, select multiple clips on the Timeline, and then paste the transition onto any selected clip.

8 TITLES AND CREDITS

In this lesson, you'll learn how to create original titles and rolling credits for a movie about a walk through London. You'll be adding still titles and rolling titles, placing images, and using the drawing tools in the Monitor panel. Specifically, you'll learn how to do the following:

- Add and stylize text
- Superimpose titles and graphics over video
- Create and customize rolling titles
- Use title templates

 This lesson will take approximately two hours.

Creating a full-screen opening title in Adobe
Premiere Elements.

Working with Titles and Title-editing Mode

Within Adobe Premiere Elements, you can create custom graphics and titles. When you add a title over one of your video clips, it's also added to your Project view as a new clip. As such, it's treated much like any other clip in your project. It can be edited, moved, deleted, and have transitions and effects applied to it.

Adobe Premiere Elements allows you to create original titles using text, drawing tools, and imported graphics. However, to help you quickly and easily add high-quality titles to your project, Adobe Premiere Elements also provides a number of templates based on common themes such as Sports, Travel, and Weddings.

Getting Started

To begin, you'll launch Adobe Premiere Elements and open the Lesson08 project file. Then you'll review a final version of the project you'll be creating.

1 Before you begin, make sure that you have correctly copied the Lesson08 folder from the DVD in the back of this book onto your computer's hard drive. See "Copying the Classroom in a Book files" in the Getting Started section at the beginning of this book.

2 Launch Adobe Premiere Elements and click the Open Project button in the Welcome screen. If necessary, click Open in the menu that appears. If Adobe Premiere Elements is already open, choose File > Open Project.

3 Navigate to your Lesson08 folder and select the project file Lesson08_Start.prel. Click the Open button to open your project. If a dialog appears asking for the location of rendered files, click the Skip Previews button. The Adobe Premiere Elements work area appears with the Edit workspace selected in the Tasks panel.

4 The project file opens with the Properties view and the Media, Monitor, and My Project panels in view. Choose Window > Restore Workspace to ensure that you start the lesson with the default panel layout.

Viewing the Completed Movie Before You Start

To see what you'll be creating as your first project in this lesson, you can play the completed movie.

1 In the Organize tab of the Tasks panel, click the Project button ( ). In Project view, locate the file Lesson08_Movie.wmv, and then double-click it to open the video into the Preview window.

2 In the Preview window, click the Play () to watch the video about a walk through London, which you'll build in this lesson.

3 After watching the complete movie, close the Preview window by clicking the Close button (✕) in the upper-right corner of the window.

Creating a Simple Title

You can add titles to your movie—whether simple still titles, advanced titles with added graphics, or styled text scrolling across the screen horizontally or vertically—directly in the Monitor panel of Adobe Premiere Elements. To begin, you'll create a basic still title. Working with the London project, you'll add a title clip at the beginning of the movie. But first you'll add a few seconds of black video over which you can then type the title text.

1 In the Sceneline of the My Project panel, click the first clip to select it. In the upper-right corner of Project view, click the New Item button (▣), and then choose Black Video from the menu that appears.

2 Adobe Premiere Elements inserts a 5-second black video clip after the first clip in the Sceneline. To move the black video clip to the beginning of the movie, click and drag it to the left of the first clip in the Sceneline.

3 With the black video still selected in the Sceneline, choose Title > New Title > Default Still. Adobe Premiere Elements places the default title text over the black video in the Monitor panel and switches to title-editing mode. In the mini-timeline of the Monitor panel, notice the bluish-gray-colored clip representation for the new title clip that's placed on top of the lavender-colored clip representation for the black video clip. Also, notice the text and drawing tools now visible on the right side of the Monitor panel, and the text options, text styles, and text animation choices accessible from Properties view.

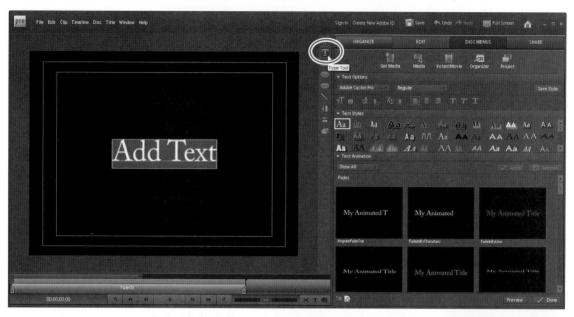

● **Note:** In the Type Tool button, the Horizontal Type tool is grouped with the Vertical Type tool. To switch between the two, click and hold the Tool button, and then choose from the menu that appears.

4 The Horizontal Type tool should be selected by default. If it's not, click the Type Tool button () to the right of the Monitor panel to select it now.

5 Click in the text box and drag your pointer over the default text to select it, type the words *A walk through*, and then press the Return key to create a new line. Next, type the word *LONDON*.

6 To reposition your text, click the Selection tool (⬉) in the upper-right corner of the Monitor panel, and then click anywhere inside the text to select the text block. Drag to reposition the text so it appears centered in the upper third of your title window. Two white margins display in the title window: These are referred to as the title-safe and action-safe margins. Stay within the inner margin (title-safe) while repositioning your text. Don't worry about the exact position for now; you'll reposition the text later in this lesson.

▶ **Tip:** You can add multiple text entries to a single title, or you can create multiple titles, each containing unique text strings.

7 Choose File > Save As, name the file *Lesson08_Work* in the Save As dialog, and then click Save to save it in your Lesson08 folder.

Adobe Premiere Elements treats basic titles, such as the one you just created, like still image files. After you've created a title, an image file is automatically added to your Project view. In this case, the new title was superimposed over the black video clip at the beginning of the movie, but as you'll see, you can also place it over any other clip in your movie. After creating and adding a title to the project, you can change text or its appearance at any time.

Modifying Text

After entering your title text, you can adjust text appearance, much like in a word processor or page layout program. In this exercise, you'll learn how to adjust the alignment of your type as well as its style, size, and color.

Changing the Text Alignment, Style, and Size

To begin, let's switch over to the Timeline, so you can see how Adobe Premiere Elements displays titles in that view.

Title-safe and Action-safe Margins

The title-safe and action-safe margins visible in the Monitor panel when you're in title-editing mode designate the title's visible safe zones. These margins are visible by default.

Safe zones are useful when producing DVDs or other video that will be viewed on a traditional TV set rather than on your computer. That's because when displaying video, most consumer TV sets cut off a portion of the outer edges of the picture, which is called *overscan*. The amount of overscan is not consistent across TVs, so to ensure that everything fits within the area that most TVs display, keep text within the title-safe margins and keep all other important elements within the action-safe margins.

If you're creating content for computer-screen viewing only, the title-safe and action-safe margins are irrelevant because computer screens display the entire image.

A. Safe Action margin. **B.** Safe Title margin.

To turn title-safe and action-safe margins on or off, choose Window > Show Docking Headers if the docking headers are not currently visible, and then choose Safe Title Margin or Safe Action Margin from the Monitor panel menu. Or right-click in the Monitor panel, and then choose View > Safe Title Margin or View > Safe Action Margin. The margin is visible if a check mark appears beside its name.

1   Click Timeline in the upper-left portion of the My Project panel. In the Timeline, double-click the new title (Title 01), which should be on the Video 2 track.

2   To center the text in its text box, use the Selection tool (↖) to select the title text box, and then click the Center Text button (▤) located under Text Options in Properties view.

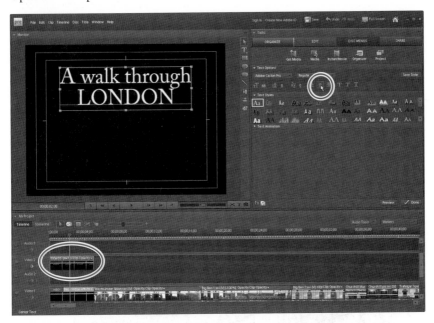

3   In the Monitor panel, choose the Type tool and drag it in the text box to select the first line of text. Under Text Options in Properties view, choose Calligraph421 BT from the font menu and Roman from the style menu next to it. Choose another font and style if you don't have this font on your system.

4   With the first line of text still selected, to change the font size, *do the following*:

   •   Under Text Options in Properties view, place the pointer over the Size value (▥). The pointer will change to a hand with two black arrows (▨).

   •   Drag to change the Size value to 50. If you have difficulties getting a precise value by dragging, click the size value once, and then type *50* into the text field.

(See illustration on next page.)

5 Select the second line of text—the word "LONDON"—with the Type tool, and choose Lithos Pro White 94 from the list of predefined text styles under Text Styles in Properties view. This changes the text font and applies a drop shadow.

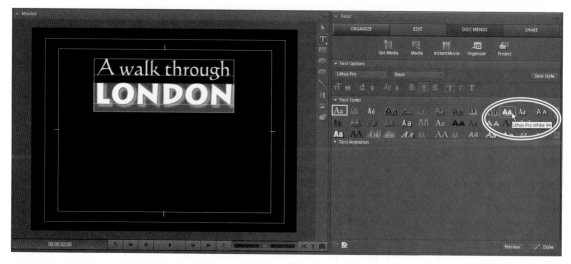

▶ **Tip:** You can also change the size of text by selecting its text box, and then dragging one of the anchor points. Hold down the Shift key as you are dragging to maintain a proportional height and width of the text box and the type therein.

6 Next, you'll spread the letters in the bottom line of text. Select the bottom line of text with the Text tool, and *do the following*:

- Under Text Options in Properties view, locate the Kerning value next to the Kerning icon ( ). Position the pointer over the numerical value, and it will change to a hand with two black arrows ( ).

- Drag the size value to 10. If you have difficulties getting a precise value by dragging, click the size value once, and then type *10* into the text field.

7 Now you'll increase the spacing between the two lines of text. Select both lines of text with the Text tool, and *do the following*:

- Under Text Options in Properties view, place the pointer over the Leading value ( ). The pointer changes to a hand with two black arrows ( ).

- Drag the size value to 20. If you have difficulties getting a precise value by dragging, click the size value once, and then type *20* into the text field.

8 Choose File > Save to save your work.

Centering Elements in the Monitor Panel

At this point, your title probably isn't precisely centered horizontally within the frame. You can fix this manually, or you can let Adobe Premiere Elements do the work for you.

1 Using the Selection tool, click the text box to select it.

2 Choose Title > Position > Horizontal Center. Or, right-click the text box, and then choose Position > Horizontal Center. Adobe Premiere Elements centers the text box horizontally within the frame. Depending on how you positioned the box earlier in this lesson, you might see little or no change.

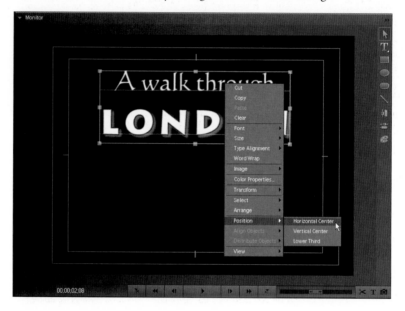

3 Choose File > Save to save your work.

Changing the Color of Your Type

As you've seen, changing the style and size of your type is easy. You can change all text within a text box equally by first selecting the text box using the Selection tool, and then applying the change. Or, you can restrict the change to portions of the text by selecting them using the Type tool. You will now change the color of the word "LONDON."

1 Select the Horizontal Type tool ( ), and then drag over the word "LONDON" to highlight the text.

Next, you'll change the color of the type from white to an orange-yellow. Note that any changes you make will apply to only the selected type.

2 Click the Color Properties button (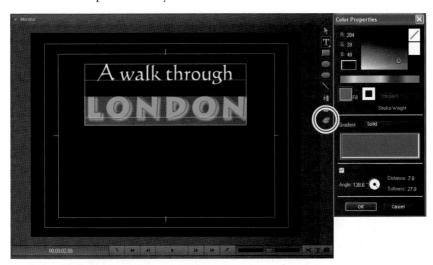) at the bottom of the tool buttons in the Monitor panel to open the Color Properties dialog. Set the RGB values to R: *204*, G: *39*, and B: *38*. Notice that Drop Shadow is selected. This is part of the definition of the predefined style Lithos Pro White 94.

3 Click OK to close the Color Properties dialog. Use the Selection tool and click outside the text box in the Monitor panel to deselect the text and review your work.

4 Choose File > Save to save your work.

Adding an Image to Your Title Files

To add an extra element of depth and fun to your titles, you can import and insert images from any number of sources. For instance, you can use photos from your digital still camera as elements in your title file. In this exercise, you'll use an arrangement of still images taken from the video clips and place it in the lower half of the title image.

1 With the Monitor panel still in title-editing mode, choose Title > Image > Add Image, or right-click the Monitor panel, and then choose Image > Add Image.

The file Open dialog appears. By default, the dialog may point you to the list of files in Adobe Premiere Elements Logos folder. These are the default images that were installed with the application. Feel free to use these in your other projects, whether from this book or otherwise.

2   In the Open dialog, navigate to the Lesson08 folder. Within that folder, select the file title_London.psd, and then click Open to import the image into your title.

▶ **Tip:** If you have overlapping frames, you can change the stacking order by right-clicking on a selected frame, and then using one of the Arrange commands from the context menu. To align multiple frames, select the frames you want to align, right-click, and then choose any of the Align Objects commands.

3   The image of three ovals appears stacked in front of the text box in your title. Use the selection tool to drag the placed image downwards, making sure that the bottom of the image stays above the title-safe area.

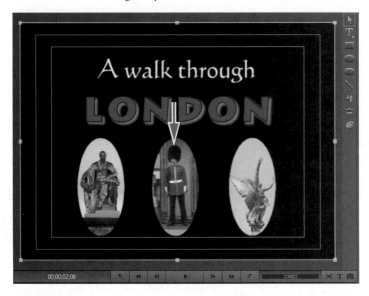

4   If you're unhappy with the size of the image you've inserted, drag any anchor point to resize the placed image. Hold down the Shift key while dragging to maintain the height and width proportions of the image.

5   Right-click the image and choose Position > Horizontal Center.

6   Choose File > Save to save your work.

Creating Fade-in and Fade-out Effects

Any transition that you use on video clips can also be added to title clips. In this exercise, you'll add a fade-in and fade-out effect to the title clip.

1   In the Timeline view of the My Project panel, click Title 01, which should be on the Video 2 track. Click the Zoom In button to zoom into approximately the amount of detail shown in the following figure.

2 On the upper left of the My Project panel, click the Properties button (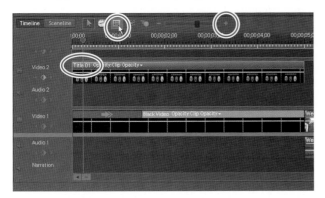).

3 In Properties view, click the twirl-down triangle next to Opacity to see the
Opacity controls.

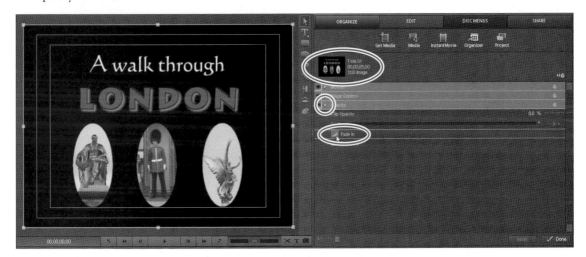

4 Under Opacity in Properties view, click the Fade In button once. The title image
seems to disappear from the Monitor panel. Drag the current-time indicator
in the Timeline to the right to see the image fade in. If you adjusted the default
transition duration to five frames as detailed in Chapter 7, after five frames the
clip's opacity is at 100 percent and fully visible again. While five frames is an
appropriate length for interscene dissolves, fade ins should be a full one second.
Let's fix that.

5 In the Timeline, drag the second keyframe in Video 2 to the 01;00 second mark. That extends the fade-in from five frames to one full second.

Animate a Still Title

You can easily apply a preset animation to any still title that contains only a single line of text. Text animation presets quickly and easily animate the characters in your title so that they fade or pop characters into view, or fly in from the top or bottom of the screen. For example, using the Fade In By Characters preset instantly makes each character in your title fade into view until the title is complete.

To preview an animation, position the pointer on the animation thumbnail in the Text Animation section of the Tasks panel. (To see the Text Animation section, you must select a title so that the Tasks panel is in title-editing mode.)

1 To begin, do *one of the following*:

- Create a new still title.

- In the Timeline, double-click the title clip.

- In the Sceneline, select the superimposed clip. In the Monitor panel, click the clip, and then double-click the title text.

The Tasks panel changes to Title Editor view, displaying the text options.

2 Under Text Animation, select an animation preset. Click the Preview button in the lower-right corner of the Tasks panel to see how the animation looks on your title text.

3 To apply the animation to the title, *do one of the following*:

- Click the Apply button in the upper-right corner of the Text Animation section in the Tasks panel.

- Drag the animation preset to the Monitor panel and drop it on top of the title text.

4 Click Done at the bottom of the Tasks panel to close out of Title Editor view.

5 Back in Properties view, click the Fade Out button once to add a fade-out effect for the clip.

6   Review your work by playing the movie from the beginning, and then choose
    File > Save to save your project.

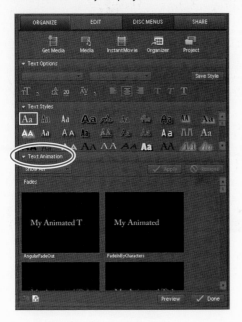

▶ **Tip:** Since the video on Video 1 is pure black, there's no reason to fade-in that video. If the video on Video 1 was any other color, you would have to fade in both tracks comprising the title to achieve the desired effect.

Note: To remove an animation from a title, select the title text and click the Remove button in the upper-right corner of the Text Animation section in the Tasks panel.

—*From Adobe Premiere Elements Help*

Superimposing a Title over Video Clips

Inserting titles over a black background video works well for opening titles, but Adobe Premiere Elements also lets you superimpose titles directly over video clips. Though you can add titles in both the Timeline and Sceneline, in this exercise, you'll work in the former, adding titles to three locations in your movie.

1   With Timeline selected in the My Project panel, press the Home key on your keyboard to move to the start of the movie. Then click the Page Down key to move to the start of the Westminster Abbey.avi clip.

2   Choose Title > New Title > Default Still. With the Text tool, select the default text and type *Around Westminster.*

3 Drag the text to select it and change the font size to 50.

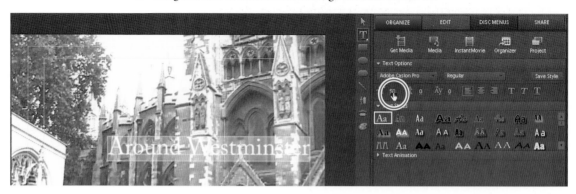

4 Use the Selection tool to position the title in the lower-left corner of the title-safe area.

To improve the readability of the text, you can try to change the text color or apply a style with a drop shadow. Or, you can add a colored rectangle behind the text, as explained in the following steps.

5 Select the Rectangle tool ( ) from the tools on the right side of the Monitor panel, and the cursor changes to a cross-hair. Drag to create a rectangle over the text you just created. Don't worry about obscuring the text; in a moment, you'll position the rectangle behind the text.

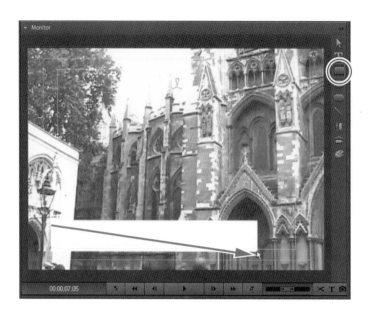

6 Click the Color Properties button () at the bottom of the tool buttons in
   the Monitor panel to open the Color Properties dialog. Set the color to black
   by clicking the large black rectangle near the upper-right corner of the dialog.
   Click OK to apply the color to the rectangle you created and close the Color
   Properties dialog.

7 Let's soften the black color by making the background slightly transparent. Right-click the rectangle, and choose Transform > Opacity. Adobe Premiere Elements opens the Opacity panel. Type *60.00* into the Opacity % field and click OK to close the panel.

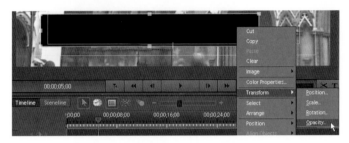

8 Now you'll shift the new rectangle behind the text. Right-click the rectangle and choose Arrange > Send to Back to place your rectangle behind your white type. The white text is now clearly visible over the rectangle. If necessary, you can edit the size of the rectangle by clicking it to make it active and then dragging any edge to a new location.

When you add multiple elements, such as text, squares, or circles to a title, you create a stacking order. The most recent items added (in this case, the rectangle) are placed at the top of the stacking order. You can control the stacking order—as you did here—using the Arrange commands from the context menu or the Title menu.

To quickly add matching titles at the same position in other clips, you can use the Copy and Paste commands.

9 Using the Selection tool, click to select the rectangle, and then Shift-click to also select the text frame. Choose Edit > Copy.

10 Drag the current-time indicator to around 00;01;27;01, which should be around the start of the palace 1.avi clip.

11 Choose Title > New Title > Default Still to switch to title-editing mode. Use the Selection tool to select the default text that was added, and then choose Edit > Clear.

12 Choose Edit > Paste to add the black rectangle with the words "Around Westminster" at the same position as in the original clip. Using the Type tool, select the words "Around Westminster" and replace them by typing *Buckingham Palace*.

13 Use the Selection tool to select the black rectangle, and adjust its width to the new text length by dragging the right-center anchor point to the left.

14 Repeat steps 11–13 to add the title *Pix from around town* at the start of the slide show at about 00:02:05;10, and then adjust the size of the rectangle.

15 Following the procedure discussed earlier in the "Creating Fade-in and Fade-out Effects" section of this lesson, fade each title in and out. For these fades, the new 5-frame default transition duration should be fine.

16 Review your movie, and then save your project.

Creating a Rolling Credit

The titles you have created to this point have been static, but Adobe Premiere Elements can create animated titles as well. There are two types of animated titles: rolls and crawls. A rolling credit is defined as text that moves vertically up the screen, like the end credits of a movie. A crawl is defined as text that moves horizontally across the screen, like a news ticker. In this exercise, you will create a rolling credit at the end of the project.

1 Press the End key on your keyboard to move to the end of the project.

2 Choose Title > New Title > Default Roll. Adobe Premiere Elements switches to title-editing mode and inserts a new rolling title.

3 Using the Type tool, select the text Main Title at the top of the Monitor panel, and then type *The End*.

4 Right-click the title text box, and choose Position > Horizontal Center.

5 Click the other text box, and press Ctrl-A on your keyboard to select all text. Then type *Starring:* and press Enter to move to the next line. On the next line, type *Albert Memorial*, press Enter, type *Big Ben*, press Enter, type *Buckingham Palace*, press Enter, type *Churchill Museum*, press Enter, type *Kensington Gardens*, press Enter, type *Lincoln Statue*, press Enter, type *Royal Albert Hall*, press Enter, type *Trafalgar Square*, press Enter, type *Westminster Abbey* and press Enter once more.

(See illustration on next page.)

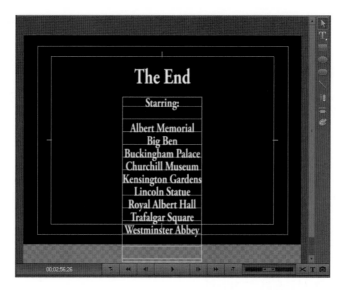

6 To center the text, click the Center Text button (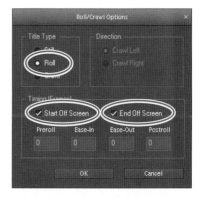) under Text Options in Properties view.

7 Right-click the text box and choose Position > Horizontal Center.

8 Choose Title > Roll/Crawl Options.

● **Note:** The Roll/Crawl Options command is also accessible from the Monitor panel menu.

9 In the Roll/Crawl Options dialog, make sure Roll is selected for Title type and that both Start Off Screen and End Off Screen options are also selected. Finally, make sure that Preroll, Ease-In, Ease-Out, and Postroll values are all set to 0. Click OK to close the dialog.

When you play the clip, the text box with the credits will move—in the 5-second default length of the title— from bottom to top across the monitor.

10 Place your current-time indicator just before the beginning of the rolling credits. Press the spacebar to play the rolling credits clip and then save your project.

Changing the Speed of a Rolling Title

When Adobe Premiere Elements creates a rolling title, it spreads the text evenly over the duration of the title. The only way to change the speed of a rolling title is to increase or decrease the length of the title clip. The default duration for titles is five seconds. If you want to have the text move more slowly across the screen, you need to increase the clip length.

1 In the Timeline, place your pointer over the end of the Title 06 rolling title clip. When the pointer changes to a red bracket pointing to the left (), drag the clip to the right. Note that as you drag there is a small, yellow context menu that shows you how much time you are adding to the clip. Add about five seconds to the length of the clip, and then release the pointer.

● **Note:** If your titles do not display smoothly, they may need to be rendered. Pressing the Enter key on your keyboard will render all effects, transitions, and titles in a project.

2 Place your current-time indicator just before the beginning of the rolling credits. Press the spacebar to play the rolling credits clip. Notice how your titles are now moving more slowly on the monitor.

3 Save your project as *Lesson08_End.prel*.

Using Title Templates

Creating your own titles, as you have done in the exercises in this lesson, will give you the most flexibility and options when it comes to customized titles. However, this involves performing a considerable number of steps from start to finish. To help you get started designing your titles, Adobe Premiere Elements ships with numerous templates for different types of projects, including the cool European Travel template that looks like it was custom designed for our DVD. There's also a matching DVD template, which creates a very polished look for your production. All you need to do is customize the text, replace an image, or do both to create a great-looking title.

1 Select Titles ( ) in the Edit tab of the Tasks panel. Choose a category of title templates from the menu on the left, and then choose a template name from the menu on the right. If necessary, scroll down to see all available templates within the chosen theme, such as rolling titles and alternative title graphics.

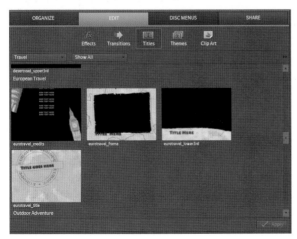

2 To superimpose a title template over a video clip, select the clip in the Sceneline, and then drag the template from Titles view onto the Monitor panel. If you're working in the Timeline, drag it to a track above the target video clip.

3 Use the Type tool to select the default text and replace it with your own text. Use the Selection tool to reposition or resize text and image frames. Add or delete text and image frames as necessary.

Exploring on Your Own

Experiment with the different templates Adobe Premiere Elements provides. Keep in mind that elements like the color of text and the position of graphics can be modified. Here are a few steps to follow as you discover what's available:

1 Replace the custom title you created with a title created from a template.

2 Explore the drawing tools available to you when in title-editing mode.

3 Change the font for the titles that you added to Calligraph421 BT to match the opening title.

4 Create an animated title, choosing from the available options under Text Animation in Properties view.

5 Place different transitions between your title clips and your video clips to view the different effects you can achieve.

Congratulations, you have completed the lesson. You've learned how to create a simple still title with text and graphics. You changed the style, size, alignment, and color of text. You've positioned and aligned text and graphic frames in the Monitor panel, and you've used one of the Arrange commands to change the stacking order of overlapping frames. You added black video to your project and applied fade-in and fade-out effects to your title clip. You know how to create rolling credits and how to use and customize title templates. It's time for a well-earned break. But before you stop, review the questions and answers on the next page.

Review Questions

1 How do you create a new title?

2 How do you exit title-editing mode, and how can you reenter it to make adjustments to a title clip?

3 How do you change the color of title text?

4 How do you add a fade-in or fade-out effect to a superimposed title clip?

5 What is a rolling credit, and how do you speed it up or slow it down?

Review Answers

1 With a video clip selected in the My Project panel, choose Title > New Title > Default Still. A title clip will be created and superimposed over the selected video clip.

2 To exit title-editing mode, click Done in the lower-right corner of Properties view, or click to select any clip in the My Project panel. To reenter title-editing mode, click to select the superimposed title text image in the Monitor panel, and then double-click it.

3 Switch to title-editing mode in the Monitor panel. Select the text using the Type tool. Then click the Color Properties button, and pick a new color in the Color Properties dialog.

4 In the Monitor panel, right-click the scene, and then select the title clip from the context menu. Under Opacity in Properties, click the Fade In or Fade Out button.

5 A rolling credit is text that scrolls vertically across your screen. The only way to make a rolling credit change speed is by selecting the clip in the Timeline of the My Project panel, and then extending the length of the clip to slow it down or shortening the clip to speed it up.

9 WORKING WITH SOUND

The sound you use has a big impact on your movies. Adobe Premiere Elements provides you with the tools to narrate clips while previewing them in real time; create, add, and modify soundtracks; and control the volume levels within clips. The project in this lesson helps you explore the basics of working with audio. You'll create a background music track, adjust the volume of an audio clip, add sound effects, add a narration clip, and mix the audio for maximum effect. Specifically, you'll learn how to do the following:

- Create a custom-length background music track with SmartSound

- Add narration

- Use SmartMix to automatically optimize the volume of your background music track and narration

- Adjust the volume of an audio track with and without keyframes

- Use the Audio Mixer

- Use audio effects

 This lesson will take approximately 1.5 hours.

Applying SmartMix to your project.

Getting Started

To begin, you'll launch Adobe Premiere Elements and open the project used for this lesson. Then you'll review a final version of the project you'll be creating.

1 Before you begin, make sure that you have correctly copied the Lesson09 folder from the DVD in the back of this book onto your computer's hard drive. For more information, see "Copying the Classroom in a Book files" in the Getting Started section at the beginning of this book.

2 Launch Adobe Premiere Elements and click the Open Project button in the Welcome screen. If Adobe Premiere Elements is already open, choose File > Open Project, and click the Open folder.

3 Navigate to your Lesson09 folder and select the project file Lesson09_Start.prel. Click the Open button to open your project. If a dialog appears asking for the location of rendered files, click the Skip Previews button. The Adobe Premiere Elements work area appears with the Organize workspace selected in the Tasks panel.

4 The project file opens with the Properties view and the Media, Monitor, and My Project panels. Choose Window > Restore Workspace to ensure that you start the lesson with the default panel layout.

Viewing the Completed Movie for the First Exercise

To see what you'll be creating as your first project in this lesson, a video about a walk through London, you can play the completed movie.

1 In the Edit tab of the Tasks panel, click Project ( ). In Project view, locate the file Lesson09_Movie.wmv, and then double-click it to open the video into the Preview window.

2 In the Preview window, click the Play button ( ) to watch the video that you will build in this lesson.

3 When you're finished watching the completed video, close the Preview window by clicking the Close button ( ) in the upper-right corner of the window.

Creating Background Music with SmartSound

Adobe has partnered with SmartSound to provide you with a library of musical soundtracks to match your project, as well as easy access to a complete library of background music that you can purchase directly from SmartSound (www. smartsound.com). As you'll learn in this exercise, using SmartSound Quicktracks for Adobe Premiere Elements, you can quickly choose and create a custom-length soundtrack that matches the mood of your production. You can create SmartSound music tracks in either the Sceneline or Timeline of the My Project panel; in this exercise, you'll work in the Timeline.

1   If necessary, switch to the Timeline by clicking the Timeline button in the upper-left corner of the My Project panel.

2   Press the End key on your keyboard to move the current-time indicator to the end of the project. Note the timecode in the bottom left of the Monitor panel, which should be 00;03;06;27. You'll use this duration in a later step to choose the duration of the background music track.

3   Press the Home key on your keyboard to return the current-time indicator to the start of the project.

4   In the upper-right corner of the My Project panel, click the Audio Tools drop-down list, and choose SmartSound. Adobe Premiere Elements opens the SmartSound Quicktracks for Adobe Premiere Elements panel. If this is the first time you use SmartSound, you'll have to click through a license agreement, registration window and search screen. Choose the desired options and move to Step 5.

5   Click the "Click here to select music!" link. Adobe Premiere Elements opens SmartSound Maestro. As you can see in the Find Music column, you can select On My Computer to search for tracks you already own, or select All to search for music on the SmartSound website. Once you choose the library, you can further search by style and intensity to narrow your choices in the Results area.

6 In the Find Music column, choose On My Computer.

7 In the Style list box, choose Classical.

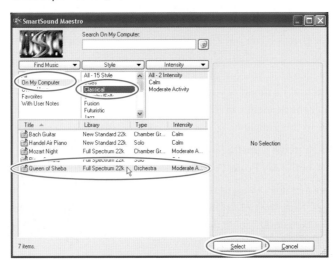

8 In the results area that displays the tracks your search criteria returned, choose Queen of Sheba, which is the track you'll add to this project. Click the Select button; SmartSound Maestro closes, and the SmartSound Quicktracks for Adobe Premiere Elements dialog opens.

9 In the Length box, type *03;06;27*. Note that you'll have to enter each two-digit number separately into the Length duration box, starting with those on the left, which is different from other similar numeric fields within Adobe Premiere Elements.

10 Click the Preview button to preview the song; you may also choose another variation from the Variation list box and preview again.

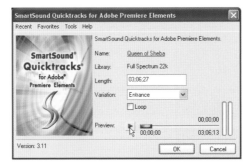

11 When you're satisfied with your selection, click OK. Adobe Premiere Elements opens the Exporting SmartSound Soundtrack dialog.

12 Make sure that you'll be saving the background music track to the Lesson09 folder.

13 Leave the name as selected by SmartSound and click Save to save the file.

14 SmartSound saves the file, briefly displaying an export window, and inserts it into the Soundtrack track in the project starting at the location of the current-time indicator. If you can't see your Soundtrack track in the Timeline, use the scrollbar on the right to scroll down and view it.

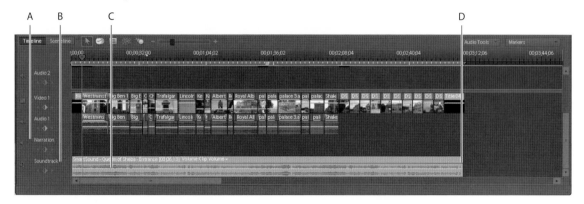

A. Narration track. **B.** Soundtrack track. **C.** New SmartSound audio track. **D.** End of SmartSound audio track.

15 Choose File > Save As, name the file *Lesson09_Work* in the Save As dialog, and then save it in your Lesson09 folder.

You can play the new sound file by pressing the spacebar. If you drag your current-time indicator to a few seconds before the end of the movie, and then press the spacebar again to play the last few bars, you'll note that the soundtrack ends naturally, not abruptly, demonstrating that SmartSound really does deliver theme-specific, custom-length soundtracks.

Adding Narration

Now let's add narration to the project.

1 Make sure you have Timeline selected in the My Project panel.

2 Choose File > Get Media from > PC Files and Folders, select the file Lesson09_Narration.wav, and click Open.

3 Drag the Lesson09_Narration.wav clip from Project view and drop it onto the Narration track in the Timeline, making sure to align it to the start of the first video clip, Westminster Abbey.avi, rather than the start of the movie.

(See illustration on next page.)

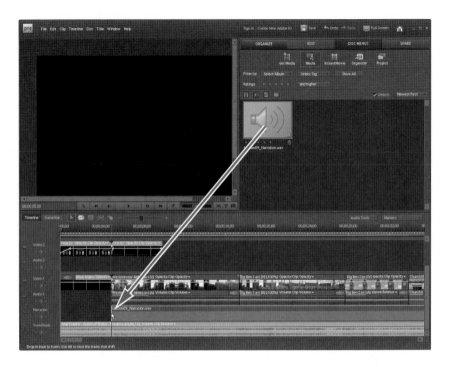

4   Click the Play button ( ) to hear the voiceover added to the project. Between the traffic noise included with the video clips and the background music, you can barely hear the narration track. Let's fix that.

Adjusting Project Volume with SmartMix

Now you have three audio tracks: one included with the videos, the background music from SmartSound, and the narration that you just added. All tracks add value: The traffic noise adds valuable context to the video, the background music supplies a nice flow, and the narration provides your take on the walk through London. The problem is, the three tracks drown each other out.

Intuitively, when present, the narration takes precedence and needs to be heard over the other two tracks. Fortunately, there's a tool that can do just that: SmartMix, which you'll learn how to apply in this exercise.

1   Make sure you have Timeline selected in the My Project panel.

2   Click the Backslash (\) key to show the entire project. Adjust the interface so that you can see all three audio tracks.

Narrating a Clip

In this exercise, you're working with a narration that I supplied, but at some point, you may want to create your own narration. For best results, confirm that your microphone is working correctly with your computer and Adobe Premiere Elements before narrating a clip.

Using your computer's microphone, you can narrate clips while previewing them in the Monitor panel. Your narration is then added to the Narration soundtrack visible in either the Timeline or Sceneline.

1 If you're working in the Timeline, drag the current-time indicator to the point where you want the narration to begin. If you're working in the Sceneline, select the clip you want to narrate. Then, in the Monitor panel, drag the current-time indicator to the point where you want the narration to begin.

2 In the Timeline or Sceneline, click the Audio Tools list box on the upper right side of the My Project panel, and choose Add Narration.

3 In the Record Voice Narration panel, click the Mic Source button and select your sound device from the menu.

4 For best results, turn off your computer speakers to prevent feedback. To monitor sound while you narrate, plug headphones into your computer and deselect Mute Audio While Recording. If your speakers are turned on, move as close to the microphone as possible, and keep the microphone as far away from the speakers as possible to prevent feedback.

5 Speak into the microphone at a conversational volume, and raise or lower the Input Volume Level slider until your loudest words light up the orange part of the meters.

6 Click the Record Narration button.

7 Near the top of the Record Voice Narration panel, a timer appears next to Start Recording In. When Start Recording In changes to Recording, speak your narration as the selected clip plays.

8 When you finish narrating, click the Stop button. (If you don't click the Stop button, recording automatically stops at the beginning of the next file in the Narration track or 30 seconds past the end of the last clip in the Timeline or Sceneline.)

9 To preview your recording, click the Go To Previous Narration button. Then click the Play Present Narration button.

10 To continue recording from the point at which you stopped, click the Record button again to overwrite any narrations that are already in the Narration track.

11 Click the Pause button at any time to stop the preview.

An audio clip containing your narration is added to the Media panel and to the Narration track in the Timeline or Sceneline (below the selected clip). In the Sceneline, a microphone icon appears in the upper-right corner of the clip you've narrated.

—*From Adobe Premiere Elements Help*

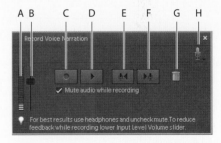

Record voice narration: **A.** Volume indicator.
B. Input Volume Level slider. **C.** Record.
D. Play. **E.** Go To Previous Narration Clip.
F. Go To Next Narration Clip. **G.** Delete.
H. Microphone source.

3 In the upper-right corner of the My Project panel, click the Audio Tools drop-down list, and choose SmartMix > Options. Adobe Premiere Elements opens the Mixer Options dialog.

4 Here's where you tell Adobe Premiere Elements which audio tracks to prioritize and which to place in the background. Adobe Premiere Elements assumes that Audio 1—the audio shot with the video—should be in the foreground, which in many instances it should be. Here, however, it should not, so click the Audio 1 list box and choose Background. Then click Apply. Adobe Premiere Elements analyzes all audio tracks and applies the SmartMix.

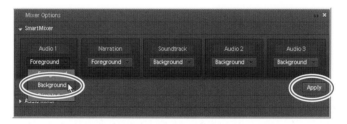

5 Adobe Premiere Elements prioritizes the narration by reducing the volume of Audio 1 and the Soundtrack with keyframes in the audio file (which you'll learn to insert and adjust next).

6 Press the spacebar to play the first few moments of the video. Overall, the audio is much better, but the narration is still a bit indistinct, and the traffic noise might still be a bit too loud. You'll have to fix that manually by undoing the first application of SmartMix, applying it again, disabling any adjustment to the Audio 1 track, and then adjusting the Audio 1 track and Narration tracks manually as described below.

7 Click the Undo key (↶ Undo) on the upper right of the Adobe Premiere Elements interface to undo SmartMix.

8 If you closed the Mixer Options dialog, in the upper-right corner of the My Project panel, click the Audio Tools drop-down list, and choose SmartMix > Options. The Mixer Options dialog opens.

9 Click the Backslash (\) key to show the entire project. Adjust the interface so that you can see all three audio tracks.

10 Click the Audio 1 list box and choose Disabled, then click Apply, and then close the Mixer Options dialog. This tells SmartMix to ignore this track during the SmartMix analysis and to leave it untouched. This gives you the result that you want with the Soundtrack, which would be the time-consuming component of the audio mix if you had to correct for this manually.

Adjusting the Volume of an Audio Track

The background music track is set; now you need to adjust the volume of the Video 1 and Narration tracks.

Adjusting Clip Volume with Gain Controls

Adobe Premiere Elements offers two basic ways to adjust the volume of your audio tracks. You can adjust "gain," which is the level of volume within a clip, or "volume," which is the level of audio output of a particular clip within a sequence. The difference is pretty subtle—and in most instances, you can use one or the other control to get the desired volume.

There is a key implementation difference, however, when working with multiple clips, as you are here. Specifically, you can adjust the gain levels, but not the volume levels, of multiple clips simultaneously. So, to control the volume of the traffic and other noise in the Video 1 track, you'll apply a group gain adjustment to all clips in the track. Here's how.

1   Drag along the Audio 1 track to select all files in that track.

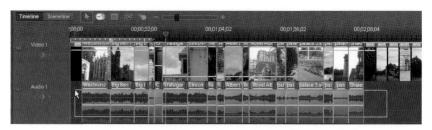

2   Right-click any audio clip in Audio 1 and choose Audio Gain. Adobe Premiere Elements opens the Clip Gain panel.

● **Note:** In Adobe Premiere Elements, volume is measured in decibels. A level of 0.0 dB is a track's original volume, not silence. Changing the levels to a negative number reduces the volume (but not necessarily to silence). Changing the volume to a positive number increases the volume.

3   Click the Gain level text box to make it active, and type *-25*. Or, click on the number and drag it to the left to about the same level.

4   Click OK to apply the gain adjustment and close the Clip Gain panel. You'll see the levels in the waveform on the Audio 1 track decrease substantially.

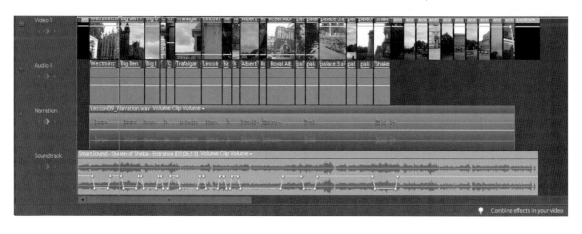

5 Shift the current-time indicator to the start of the Westminster Abbey clip, and press the spacebar to play the movie again. While you can still hear the traffic noise faintly, it's much less prominent, and the complete audio mix is coming together quite nicely. Now let's boost the volume of the narration.

Adjusting Clip Volume with the Volume Graph

In Lesson 6, you learned how to adjust clip opacity on the Timeline by dragging the Opacity graph upwards and downwards. You can adjust the volume of any audio clip the same way. Let's adjust the volume of the Narration track using this technique.

1 Working with the Lesson09_Narration.wav clip on the Narration track, place your pointer over the yellow volume graph line. You can do this at any location in the clip. The pointer changes to a double-arrow icon ( ).

2 Drag the volume graph upwards to the limit, which should be about 6.02.

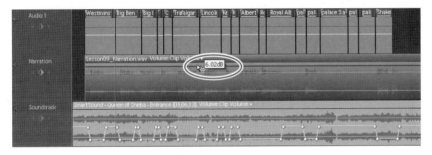

3 Shift the current-time indicator to the start of the Westminster Abbey clip, and press the spacebar to play the movie again. While you can still hear the traffic noise faintly, it's much less prominent, and the complete audio mix is definitely in great shape. Cut it, print it, let's move on.

4 Choose File > Save to save your work.

● **Note:** If 6 dB isn't sufficient to boost your audio to the desired level, you can also adjust the Gain control as detailed in the previous exercise. In fact, try boosting the Gain of the Lesson09_Narration. wav clip by about 5 dB, preview again, and decide if that sounds even better.

● **Note:** Adjusting the volume line doesn't change the waveform display. However, as you'll see in the next exercise, adjusting gain directly does change the waveform. Though adjusting the volume line is easier and more accessible than adjusting gain directly, if you overboost volume, you can produce distortion without being able to view the clipping in the waveform. For an explanation of waveform and clipping, see the sidebar "About Waveforms."

About Waveforms

By default, Adobe Premiere Elements' audio tracks display the file as a waveform, which is a graphic representation of the volume of audio in the file. When volume is low, the bushy line representing the waveform narrowly surrounds the centerline. As volume increases, the bushy line extends farther away from the centerline. Volume is optimal when the peaks in the individual waveform approach, but just barely touch, the outer edges of the graph area. I've reset the gain values of the clips on Audio 1 to illustrate this concept.

The audio on the narration track and Soundtrack are both healthy—just about approaching the outer edges of the graph area but never touching for long. The Trafalgar Square clip, because that was shot on a noisy London intersection, is also healthy, whereas the two Churchill Museum clips—particularly the second clip shot in the museum—are both too low.

If these tracks contained audio that you wanted to hear, you would have to boost the volume using either the Volume or Gain controls. Try the Gain control first, and when you open the Clip Gain panel, click the Normalize button. Normalization boosts the volume of the entire audio file to a level just below that which would produce distortion at any point in the clip. When you click the Normalize but-

ton, Adobe Premiere Elements analyzes the clip and chooses the optimal gain value–in this case, 15 dB for the first Churchill Museum clip. Click OK to accept that value, and you've boosted volume as far as you can go without distorting the audio.

The only problem with normalization comes when you have a single long clip with extreme low and high volumes. Let's say you were shooting a wedding and didn't get close enough (or mic the bride or groom) to capture the vows at sufficient volume. So the levels are very low when the bride and groom are speaking. However, when the crowd starts applauding, the levels are quite high. If you apply normalization to this clip, Adobe Premiere Elements won't boost the volume of the applause beyond the point of causing distortion, which often means that it won't boost the volume of the vows at all. Your best option in this case is to split the clip into low- and high-volume regions—vows in one, applause in another—and apply normalization separately or only to the vows audio.

If you boost Gain excessively, you'll see the top of the waveform pressing against the outer border of the graph area. This is a condition called "clipping," where the outer edges of the waveform are truncated because volume is too high. In severe cases, clipping causes noticeable distortion that can make the clip unusable. If you see this when boosting the gain of an audio clip, reset the gain to a lower level. If you see clipping in narrations that you've recorded, you may need to rerecord.

Note that whenever you boost audio volume, you also increase the background noise present in the clip. In these instances, you can try Adobe Premiere Elements' DeNoiser filter, but like all noise reduction filters, it isn't a panacea and may not resolve the problem.

Note that several of these waveforms were adjusted for demonstration purposes and won't look the same on your project Timeline.

Raising and Lowering Volume with Keyframes

You learned about working with keyframes in video in Lesson 6 in a section titled (appropriately enough) "Working with Keyframes." Audio keyframes operate identically to the video-related keyframes discussed in that lesson. To refresh your memory, a keyframe is a point in the Timeline where you specify a value for a specific property—in this case, audio volume. When you set two keyframes, Adobe Premiere Elements interpolates the value of that property over all frames between the two keyframes.

For some properties, including opacity for video and volume for audio, you can create keyframes in the Timeline by pressing the Ctrl key, and then clicking the associated graph with your pointer. Next, drag the keyframe upwards or downwards to adjust its value, or to the left or right to adjust its location. To delete keyframes in the Timeline, click to select them, right-click, and then choose Delete.

Alternatively, you can create and modify keyframes in Properties view. This exercise will review these procedures and reinforce the relationship between keyframes in the Timeline and keyframes in Properties view. Specifically, in this exercise, you'll add keyframes to fade in the volume of the music track at the beginning of your movie.

1   Using the My Project panel in the Timeline, place the current-time indicator near the start of the project, around the 00;00;01;00 mark.

2   Click to select the SmartSound-Queen of Sheba – Entrance[03;06;13] clip in the Timeline's Soundtrack.

3   Select Window > Properties, and then click the Show Keyframes button ( ) in the upper-right corner of Properties view.

4   Use the Zoom slider to zoom into the mini-timeline until you can see the 00;00;01;00 timecode in the mini-timeline.

5   Click the Toggle Animation button ( ) for the Volume effect to activate keyframes. This will set the first keyframe at the current-time indicator. If the Toggle Animation button is already activated, click to disable it (and delete all keyframes), and then click again to activate keyframes.

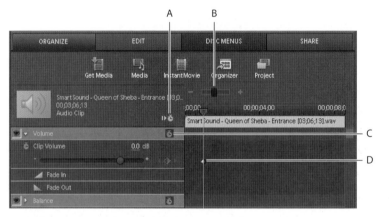

A. Show Keyframes button. **B.** Zoom slider. **C.** Toggle Animation button.
D. Keyframe.

You'll set the next keyframe in the Timeline.

6   Press the Page Up key to move the current-time indicator to the beginning of the movie. If necessary, use the Zoom slider on top of the Timeline to zoom in for more detail.

7   In the Timeline of the My Project panel, position the pointer over the orange volume graph of the SmartSound-Queen of Sheba – Entrance[03;06;13] clip at the current-time indicator. Make sure not to position the pointer too far to the left. The pointer needs to change to a white arrow with double arrows ( ), not the Trim Out tool ( ). Press the Ctrl key on your keyboard, and the pointer changes to the insert keyframe pointer ( ). Click the volume graph to add a second keyframe.

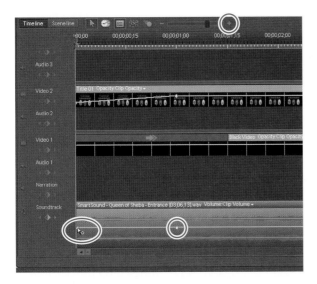

8 Drag the new keyframe all the way down to create the start of the fade in.
   You can check Properties view: The Clip Volume reads -oo to resemble the
   mathematical symbol –∞ for negative infinity.

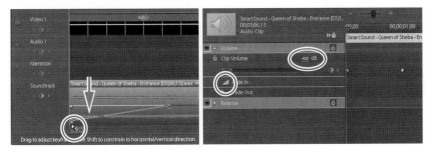

9 To hear this change, press the Page Up key, and then press the spacebar to play.
   You'll hear the soundtrack fade in over the first second of the production rather
   than starting at full strength.

10 Save your project as *Lesson09_work.prel*.

Working with the Audio Mixer

If for some reason SmartMix doesn't produce the result that you want, you have
another alternative—Adobe Premiere Elements' Audio Mixer. Using the Audio
Mixer, you can adjust the volume and balance of the different audio tracks as the
audio plays, so you can make sure your audience hears what you want it to hear.
For example, you can lower the volume for the Soundtrack while people are talking
and increase it again when they are silent.

● **Note:** This exercise
was designed to help
show the relationship
between audio
keyframes in the
Timeline and Properties
view. However, a
faster way to produce
a fade-in effect is
to click the Fade In
icon (Fade In) for
the audio clip in the
Properties view, as
shown in the preceding
figure.

Let's start fresh by reloading Lesson09_Start and then narration and background music clips.

1 Navigate to your Lesson09 folder and select the project file Lesson09_Start.prel. Click the Open button to open your project.

2 Choose File > Get Media from > PC Files and Folders, select the file Lesson09_Narration.wav, and click Open.

3 Press the Home key to move the current-time indicator to the start of the clip. Then drag the Lesson09_Narration.wav clip from Project view and drop it onto the Narration track in the Timeline, making sure to align it to the start of the first video clip, Westminster Abbey.avi, not the start of the movie.

4 Choose File > Get Media from > PC Files and Folders, select the file SmartSound-Queen of Sheba – Entrance[03;06;13], and click Open.

5 Press the Home key to move the current-time indicator to the start of the clip. Then drag the SmartSound-Queen of Sheba – Entrance[03;06;13] clip from Project view and drop it onto the Soundtrack track in the Timeline at the start of the movie.

6 Press the Home key to place the current-time indicator at the beginning of the movie. Press the spacebar to begin playing your video. Same familiar mess that we started with.

7 When you're finished previewing the movie, press the Home key again to set the current-time indicator right at the beginning of the video, which is where you want to start mixing audio.

8 In the upper-right corner of the My Project panel, click the Audio Tools drop-down list, and choose Audio Mix. The Audio Mixer panel opens.

9 Your Audio Mixer panel shows five audio tracks, but only three—Audio 1, Narration, and Soundtrack—contain audio. You can ignore the last two.

10 Press the Home key to place the current-time indicator at the beginning of the project, and then press the spacebar to begin playback.

11 Grab the levels handles for Audio 1, Narration, and Soundtrack and adjust them as desired. Good luck. Note that all adjustments made via the Audio Mixer will be reflected as keyframes on the audio track and in its respective Properties view but will become visible only after you stop playback.

Creating a Split Edit

At times, you may want the audio to begin before the video or to extend after the video into the next clip (or vice versa). Trimming linked audio and video separately is called a split edit. Usually, when you create a split edit in one clip, you must create one in the adjacent clip so they don't overlap each other. You can create two kinds of split edits:

- A J-cut, or audio lead, in which audio starts before linked video or video continues after the audio.

- An L-cut, or video lead, in which video starts before linked audio or audio continues after the video.

—From Adobe Premiere Elements Help

Edit to the Beat of Your Favorite Song

You can use Detect Beats () in the Sceneline or Timeline to automatically add markers at the beats of your musical soundtrack. Beat detection makes it easy to synchronize slide shows or video edits to your music.

1   Add an audio clip or a video clip that includes audio to the soundtrack in the Timeline or Sceneline.

2   In the upper-right corner of the My Project panel, click the Audio Tools drop-down list, and choose Detect Beats. Adobe Premiere Elements opens the Audio Mixer panel.

3   In the Beat Detect Settings dialog, specify settings as desired and click OK.

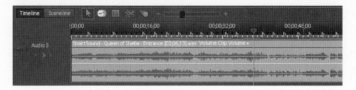

4   Markers appear in the Timeline corresponding to the beats in the soundtrack.

Working with Sound Effects

In most projects, the primary audio-related variable that you'll adjust is volume, and you've explored a number of techniques to accomplish that here. In addition, Adobe Premiere Elements has multiple audio effects to further enhance your projects, including controlling the volumes and frequencies of the different channels in your audio files, detecting and removing tape noise, eliminating background noise, and adding the reverberation of sounds to give ambience and warmth to the audio clip.

You can find the audio effects in Effects view by choosing Audio Effects in the effect type list box. You apply audio effects by dragging them onto the target audio clip, and then configure them in Properties view. If any of the effects look particularly interesting, you can search the Adobe Premiere Elements Help file for more details.

Exploring on Your Own

Great news: You've finished another lesson and learned the basics of working with sound. Specifically, you learned to create a custom-length soundtrack with SmartSound, how to add narration to your projects, how to use SmartMix, how to adjust audio gain directly and how to create and adjust keyframes in the Timeline and Properties view.

But you're not finished yet. The best way to master the audio tools in Adobe Premiere Elements is to continue to explore them.

1   Experiment with different songs available in SmartSound. Think of some upcoming projects (birthdays, holidays, vacations) and try to find the appropriate tracks for those videos.

2   Experiment with various audio effects such as Delay and Dynamics. A description of Adobe Premiere Elements audio effects can be found in the "Audio Effects" section of Adobe Premiere Elements Help.

3   As you did for the fade-in of the soundtrack, try to create a fade-out for the end of your project.

Review Questions

1   What is SmartMix, and when should you use it?

2   What is the Audio Mixer, and how do you access it?

3   How would you change the volume of a clip over time using keyframes?

4   How do you change the presets of an audio effect?

5   What is normalization and how is it different from adjusting audio volume directly?

Review Answers

1   SmartMix is a feature that lets you identify which audio track(s) you want in the foreground and which ones you want in the background. It automatically adjusts the volume of the background clips to ensure that the foreground clip—usually speech or narration—is clearly audible. You should use SmartMix whenever you're trying to mix two audio tracks, especially when one contains narration or other dialogue.

2   Using the Audio Mixer, you can easily adjust the audio balance and volume for different tracks in your project. You can refine the settings while listening to audio tracks and viewing video tracks. Each track in the Audio Mixer corresponds to an audio track in the Timeline or Sceneline and is named accordingly. You can access the Audio Mixer by clicking the Mix Audio button (Mix Audio) or choosing Window > Audio Mixer.

3   Each clip in the Adobe Premiere Elements Timeline has a yellow volume graph that controls the keyframes of the clip. To add keyframes, Ctrl-click the line. You must have at least two keyframes with different values to automatically change the volume level of an audio clip. You can also use the Audio Mixer to set keyframes to change the volume of your audio clip over time.

4   First, select the clip that contains the effect you want to adjust in the Timeline. Second, in the Effects view, click the Edit Effects button. In Properties view, expand the property by clicking the triangle next to the property name (if available), and then drag the slider or angle control.

5   Normalization boosts the audio volume of all samples of an audio clip the same amount, stopping when further volume increases would produce distortion in the loudest sections of the clip. When you adjust volume manually, you run the risk of causing distortion if you boost volume.

10 WORKING WITH MOVIE THEMES

In the previous six chapters, you learned how to produce a completely customized movie from your source clips. In this chapter, you'll learn how to apply a Movie theme to your source clips to produce an engaging, stylized movie in a matter of moments.

Movie themes are collections of professionally created, theme-specific titles, effects, transitions, and background music. Before applying a theme, Adobe Premiere Elements analyzes your video footage for content, and then edits your content to best fit the tone of the theme.

As with InstantMovies, you can apply an entire theme or just parts of it to perfectly fit your creative concept. In this lesson, you'll learn how to do the following:

- Select a Movie theme
- Choose some Movie theme properties and apply them to your clip
- Edit your movie after applying a Movie theme

 This lesson will take approximately 30 minutes.

Choosing a Movie theme.

Getting Started

To begin, you'll launch Adobe Premiere Elements, open the Lesson10 project, and review a final version of the movie you'll be creating.

1 Before you start the project, make sure that you have correctly copied the Lesson10 folder from the DVD in the back of this book onto your computer's hard drive. See "Copying the Classroom in a Book files" in the Getting Started section at the beginning of this book.

2 Launch Adobe Premiere Elements.

3 In the Welcome screen, click the Open Project button. If necessary, click Open in the pop-up menu. The Open Project dialog opens.

4 In the Open Project dialog, navigate to the Lesson10 folder you copied to your hard drive. Within that folder, select the file Lesson10_Start.prel, and then click Open. If a dialog appears asking for the location of rendered files, click the Skip Previews button.

Your project file opens with the Monitor, Tasks, and My Project panels open.

5 Choose Window > Restore Workspace to ensure that you start the lesson with the default panel layout.

Viewing the Completed Movie Before You Start

To see what you'll be creating in this lesson, take a look at the completed movie.

1 In the Organize tab of the Tasks panel, click Project ( ). In Project view, locate the file Lesson10_Movie.wmv, and then double-click it to open the video into the Preview window.

2 In the Preview window, click the Play button ( ) to watch the video about a walk through London, which you'll build in this lesson.

3 When finished, close the Preview window by clicking the Close button ( ) in the upper-right corner of the window.

About Movie Themes

You first had a glimpse of Movie themes back in Lesson 4, when you learned how to create an InstantMovie from the Organizer. As you recall, an InstantMovie is a Movie theme applied to clips in the Organizer. In this lesson, you'll learn how to apply a Movie theme to clips in the Timeline.

When should you use each approach? When you create an InstantMovie, you can choose your content via tagging and apply Smart Tagging to your source clips, which is fast and effective when attempting to identify the best three or four minutes of video from a mass of source clips.

Note that creating an InstantMovie in the Organizer differs from working in the Timeline in one fundamental way: You can't edit source clips before applying an InstantMovie. This makes applying Movie themes in the Timeline a better option if there's source footage that you don't want included in the final movie.

Movie themes enable you to quickly create videos with a specific look and feel. The Wedding Doves theme, for example, adds an elegant, animated introduction, an overlay of flying white doves, wedding background music, and closing credits for a wedding video. In contrast, the Comic Book theme provides more funky effects and fonts along with Picture-in-Picture overlays that might be more appropriate for a kids' party video.

You can apply all the properties in a theme, choose to add only a subset, or even just modify some parts. Likewise, you can add a theme to an entire movie or to only a single clip.

You access Movie themes via the Themes button (⊞) in the Edit tab of the Tasks panel. The different themes use animated thumbnails that give you a good idea of the overall feel of the theme.

> **Note:** When you apply a theme, all the effects and transitions that you've previously applied to a project are deleted and replaced by the theme. Before applying a theme, choose File > Save to save your project. If you apply a theme and then decide you don't like it, choose Edit > Undo to return to your original version.

Applying a Movie Theme

In the exercises that follow, you'll apply a Movie theme to the London clips that you've edited throughout the book. You'll apply the theme to clips in the My Project panel, using either the Timeline or Sceneline, so you should edit out any undesired scenes before applying a theme.

However, don't spend a lot of time ordering the clips on the Timeline: If you choose, Adobe Premiere Elements will either arrange the clips to best fit the Movie theme or display them in chronological order. In addition, don't correct brightness, contrast, or stabilization issues before applying a theme, because in order for Adobe Premiere Elements to apply the theme-specific effects, it will have to remove all the effects you've previously applied. Don't worry; as with InstantMovies, you can edit your movie after applying the Movie theme and correct any color, brightness, or stabilization issues then.

When you have all the desired clips in the Timeline, follow this procedure to apply a Movie theme.

1 Click the Themes button ( ) in the Edit tab of the Tasks panel.

Note: The Smart Tagging check box is active only when you're applying an InstantMovie in the Organize panel.

2 Click the European Travel Style to select it, and then click Next.

3 Customize the theme as described here. *Do the following*:

- Customize the Opening and Closing Titles. Keep the Opening Title relatively short or your text may not fit in the title box used by many themes.

- Select the Auto Edit check box to have Adobe Premiere Elements analyze your clips and edit them to fit the selected theme. If you don't select Auto Edit, Adobe Premiere Elements uses the clips as is and doesn't edit them.

- Select the Entire Movie radio button to apply the theme to all clips on the Timeline.

- In the Music box, select the My Music radio button, and then click the Browse button to choose the target song. Navigate to the Lesson10 folder and choose SmartSound-Queen of Sheba – Entrance[03;06;13].wav.

- Drag the Music/Sound FX slider to the left as shown in the previous figure to prioritize background audio over the traffic noise in the original clips.

- If you have dialogue in your project (which this clip doesn't), select the SmartMix check box and Adobe Premiere Elements will reduce the volume of the music track when it detects dialogue.

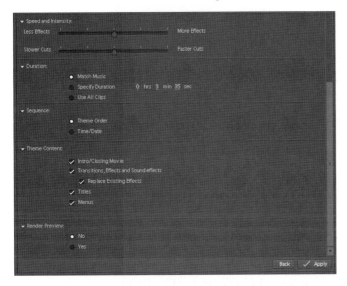

- In the Speed and Intensity dialog, adjust the Effects and Cuts sliders as desired.

- In the Duration box, select Match Music, which produces a movie that matches the duration of the selected music. This is the approach I recommend in most instances. Or, you can specify a duration or select Use All Clips, which uses all clips at their original duration with no background music.

- In the Sequence box, select Theme Order, which allows Adobe Premiere Elements to use clips as they best match the theme. Your other option, Time/Date, uses the clips in the order that they were shot.

- In the Theme Content box, leave all check boxes selected.

- In the Render Preview box, leave No selected.

4   After selecting your options, click Apply to create the InstantMovie. Click No when the InstantMovie dialog asks if you want to add more clips. Click Yes when another dialog warns that user-applied effects will be replaced.

5   Adobe Premiere Elements creates the InstantMovie and inserts it into the My Project panel.

6   Use the playback controls in the Monitor panel to preview the InstantMovie. If a dialog box appears that asks if you want to render before previewing, click No.

7   Adobe Premiere Elements adds the InstantMovie to the My Project panel in consolidated form. To break apart the InstantMovie into its components to edit them, click to select the new InstantMovie, right-click, and choose Break Apart InstantMovie.

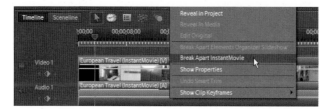

8   Choose File > Save As, name the file *Lesson10_End* in the Save As dialog, and then save it in your Lesson 10 folder.

Exploring on Your Own

Experiment with the different Movie themes provided with your copy of Adobe Premiere Elements. Keep in mind that you can apply an entire theme or pick and choose parts of it.

Apply a Movie theme to selected clips in the My Project panel to become familiar with this option.

Well done—you've completed this lesson. You've learned how to apply a Movie theme and how to customize its properties.

Review Questions

1 What is a Movie theme?

2 How is a Movie theme different from an InstantMovie?

3 When are InstantMovies a better option than applying Movie themes to clips in the Timeline?

4 How do you edit a movie after applying a Movie theme?

Review Answers

1 Movie themes are templates that enable you to quickly turn your clips into a professional-looking movie. You can choose from event-based themes like Birthday or more style-based themes like Silent Film. A Movie theme includes coordinated transitions, effects, and music, as well as layouts for titles and credits. You can apply an entire theme or choose to select only parts of it.

2 InstantMovies are Movie themes applied to clips in the Organizer.

3 InstantMovies are a better option when you'd like to use tagging and Smart Tagging to help choose videos included in the movie. Applying Movie themes in the My Project panel is preferred when you have to edit content before applying the Movie theme.

4 Right-click the finished movie and choose Break Apart InstantMovie.

11 CREATING MENUS

In this lesson, you'll create a menu for a movie to be recorded on a DVD or Blu-ray Disc. You can follow along with most of this lesson even if your system does not have a DVD or Blu-ray Disc burner, although it will be helpful if it does. You'll learn how to add menu markers that allow your viewers direct access to scenes in your movies and how to create and customize disc menus. You'll also learn how to preview a menu and then burn a DVD or Blu-ray Disc for playback on a standard DVD or Blu-ray Disc player. Specifically, you'll learn how to do the following:

- Add menu markers to your movie
- Create an auto-play disc
- Use templates to create disc menus
- Customize the look of the menus
- Preview a disc menu
- Record a DVD or Blu-ray Disc

 This lesson will take approximately two hours.

Creating a DVD with menus.

Getting Started

To begin, you'll launch Adobe Premiere Elements, open the Lesson11 project, and review a final version of that project.

1 Before you begin, make sure that you have correctly copied the Lesson11 folder from the DVD in the back of this book onto your computer's hard drive. See "Copying the Classroom in a Book files" in the Getting Started section at the beginning of this book.

2 Launch Adobe Premiere Elements.

3 In the Welcome screen, click the Open Project button and then click Open in the pop-up menu. In the Open Project dialog, navigate to the Lesson11 folder, select the file Lesson11_End.prel, and then click Open. If a dialog appears asking for the location of rendered files, click the Skip Previews button.

A finished version of the project file you will create in this lesson opens with the Monitor, Tasks, and My Project panels open. You may review it now or at any point during the lesson to get a sense of what your project should look like.

4 Select Disc Menus in the Tasks panel to switch to the Disc Menus workspace. In the Disc Layout panel, click Preview to open the Preview Disc window.

The Preview Disc window allows you to view and test your menus as they will appear when played on a DVD or Blu-ray player.

5 In the Preview Disc window, click the Scene Selection button in the main menu to switch to the Scene Selection menu. Click the Westminster button to begin playing this section.

6 Press the spacebar to stop the playback, and then close the Preview Disc window by clicking the Close button (✖) in the upper-right corner of the window.

7 After reviewing the finished file, choose File > Close. In the dialog, click No so that you do not save any changes made to the project. Then click the Open Project button, click Open, select the file Lesson11_Start.prel, and click Open. If a dialog appears asking for the location of rendered files, click the Skip Previews button.

8 Choose Window > Restore Workspace to ensure that you start the lesson with the default panel layout.

Understanding DVDs and Blu-ray Discs

DVD is a generic term that encompasses a few different formats. The format you will work with in Adobe Premiere Elements is commonly referred to as DVD-Video. In terms of disc content and playability, this is the same type of DVD that you can purchase or rent and play on a DVD player connected to your TV set or on a computer fitted with the appropriate drive.

A Blu-ray Disc—often abbreviated as BD—is an optical disc format that can store 25 gigabytes (GB) on a single-layer disc or 50 GB on a dual-layer disc. It gets its name from the blue-violet laser a Blu-ray player uses to read it (as opposed to the red laser used by CD and DVD players and drives).

To make a DVD or Blu-ray Disc in Adobe Premiere Elements, you must have a compatible DVD or Blu-ray Disc burner. It's important to note that although your system may have a DVD or Blu-ray Disc player, it may not be a recordable drive, also known as a DVD or Blu-ray Disc writer or burner. A computer drive that's described as "DVD-ROM" or "BD-ROM" will only play DVDs or Blu-ray Discs, not record them. (But a "BD-ROM/DVD-R/CD-R drive" will play Blu-ray Discs, play and record DVDs, and play and record CDs.) Check the system specifications of your computer to see which drive (if any) you have. Drives capable of recording DVDs and Blu-ray Discs are also available as external hardware. Often, such external recordable drives are connected through your system's IEEE 1394 port, although some drives connect through the USB port.

Note that the process of authoring your projects, or creating menus and menu markers, is identical for Blu-ray Discs and DVDs. You'll designate which type of disc to record just before you burn the disc in the final exercise of this lesson.

Physical Media

The type of disc onto which you'll record your video is important. You should be aware of two basic formats: Recordable (DVD-R and DVD+R for DVDs, BD-R for Blu-ray Discs) and Rewritable (DVD-RW and DVD+RW for DVDs, BD-RE for Blu-ray Discs). Recordable discs are single-use discs; once you record data onto a recordable disc, you cannot erase the data. Rewritable discs can be used multiple times, much like the floppy disks of old.

Also available are dual-layer DVD-Recordable discs (DVD-R DL and DVD+R DL) that offer 8.5 GB of storage space instead of the 4.7 GB of standard DVD-R, DVD+R, DVD-RW, and DVD+RW discs. Dual-layer BD-R discs, featuring 50 GB of storage space, will come to market soon, but you don't need to be concerned with them at this point.

So which format should you choose? The first thing to note is that DVD-R and DVD+R discs are 100 percent interchangeable. Any drive that records one will record the other, and the same players and drives that play one will almost certainly play the other, at least with single-layer media. It's the same with DVD-RW and DVD+RW. In the very early days of DVD, there was a meaningful distinction between the – and + formats, but it's been irrelevant for close to a decade now.

Compatibility is one of the major issues with recordable disc formats. On the DVD side, there are many older DVD players that may not recognize some rewritable discs created on a newer DVD burner, for example. Compatibility is also more of a concern with dual-layer media than with single-layer discs. Another issue is that, as of this writing, the media for recordable discs is less expensive than the media for rewritable discs (usually much less than $1 per disc). However, if you make a mistake with a recordable disc, you must use another disc, whereas with a rewritable disc you can erase the content and use the disc again. For this reason, I suggest using rewritable discs for making your test discs, and then using recordable discs for final or extra copies.

On the Blu-ray Disc side, the technology is still fairly new and playback compatibility is at least a minor issue with all media. But because the BD-R and BD-RE formats were developed at the same time, BD-RE discs are just as likely to play in a given player as their BD-R counterparts. Generally, the cost of BD-R and BD-RE media is about the same, but because it is so high for both ($3–$5 per disc), you're better off using BD-RE discs for your projects so you can rerecord if you make a mistake.

Manually Adding Scene Markers

When watching a DVD or Blu-ray Disc movie, you normally have the option to jump to the beginning of the next chapter by clicking a button on the remote control. To specify the start of chapters or sections in your project, you must add scene markers.

Note: This project is only about two minutes long due to necessary limitations on the file size. Most projects would likely be longer, but the basic principles remain the same.

1   Scroll through the entire movie in the Timeline of the My Project panel.

    This project consists of three main sections, labeled Around Westminster, Buckingham Palace, and Pix from around town. Each section has a title superimposed for the first five seconds. You will place scene markers at the beginning of each section so your viewers can access these sections more easily during playback. You'll start by adding the marker for the Around Westminster section.

2   Press the Home key on your keyboard to move the current-time indicator to the start of the movie. Then press the Page Down key to move to the start of the Westminster Abbey.avi clip.

3   On the extreme right side of the My Project panel, click the Markers drop-down list box, and choose Menu Marker > Set Menu Marker. The Menu Marker panel opens.

4   You'll work more with this dialog later in this lesson; for now, just click OK to close the panel.

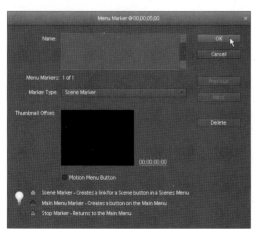

5 Notice the green scene marker icon added just below the previous marker on the time ruler.

6 In the My Project panel, click the Sceneline button to switch to Sceneline. If necessary, scroll to the right to view the Westminster Abbey clip. Notice the scene marker icon added to the clip in the Sceneline.

7 Click the Timeline button in the My Project panel to return to the Timeline.

8 Drag the current-time indicator to 01;28;17, which should be the location of the second overlay title and the start of the palace 1.avi clip.

9 Right-click the time ruler at the current-time indicator and choose Set Menu Marker. Click OK to close the Menu Marker panel.

10 Use either procedure to add another menu marker at 00;02;06;26, which is the start of the slide show. You should now have three markers in your project, one for each section of this short movie.

Creating an Auto-play Disc

Most professional DVDs and Blu-ray Discs have menus to help viewers navigate through the disc content. You will work with menus shortly, but there is a quick and easy way to produce a disc without menus: creating an auto-play disc. An auto-play disc is similar to videotape: When you place the disc into a player, it will begin playing automatically. There is no navigation, although viewers can jump from scene to scene—defined by the markers you just added—using a remote control.

Auto-play discs are convenient for short projects that don't require a menu or as a mechanism to share unfinished projects for review. For most longer or finished projects, you'll probably prefer to create a menu.

Note: The Auto-Play button should be dimmed and no template selected. Click the Auto-Play button if your Disc Layout panel looks different from the one shown here.

1   Select Disc Menus in the Tasks panel to switch to the Disc Menus workspace. The Disc Layout panel replaces the Monitor panel, and Templates view opens in the Disc Menus tab of the Tasks panel. If you want to see the panel names, choose Window > Show Docking Headers.

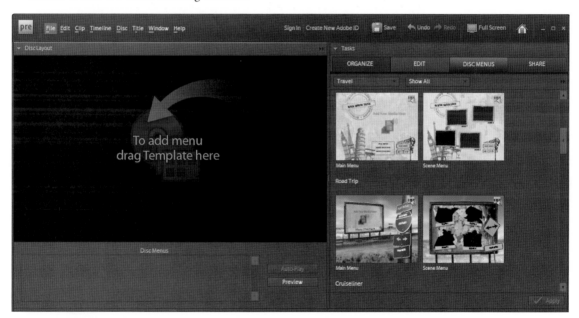

2   In the Disc Layout panel, click the Preview button to open the Preview Disc window. The Preview Disc window allows you to view and test your disc as it will appear when viewed on a DVD or Blu-ray Disc player.

3   In the Preview Disc window, click the Play button (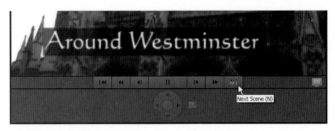) to begin playing your project. Once the first video clip begins playing, click the Next Scene button ( ), and the video will jump to the next scene. The scenes are defined by the scene markers you added to your project. When viewing this disc on a TV set, viewers can use a remote control to advance through the scenes.

4   Click the Close button () in the upper-right corner of the Preview Disc window to close it.

5   Choose File > Save As and save this project file into your Lesson11 folder as *Lesson11_Work.prel*.

Automatically Generating Scene Markers

Manually placing markers in the Timeline gives you ultimate control over the placement of your markers. For long videos, however, you may not want to place all the markers by hand. To make the process of placing markers easy, Adobe Premiere Elements can create markers automatically based on several configurable parameters.

1   Choose File > Save As and save this project file into your Lesson11 folder as *Lesson11_Markers.prel*. You'll return to the original project file after you finish exploring the automatic generation of scene markers.

2   In the Disc Layout panel, choose Auto-Generate Menu Markers from the panel menu. Or, right-click in the preview area of the Disc Layout panel, and then choose Auto-Generate Menu Markers.

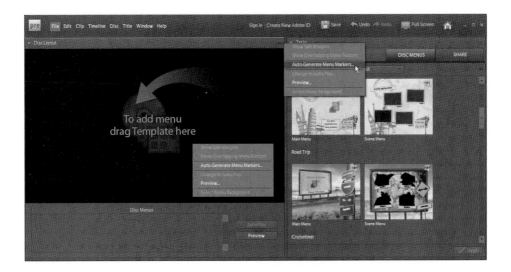

3 The Automatically Set Menu Scene Markers dialog appears. Keep the default option selected to set a scene marker At Each Scene, or to be more specific, at the beginning of every clip on the Video 1 track. The Clear Existing Menu Markers check box should remain deselected unless you want to erase existing markers. Click OK to close the dialog. Scene markers appear at the beginning of every clip.

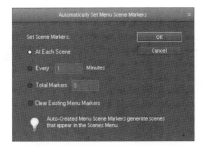

4 If you're not in the Timeline already, switch to the Timeline in the My Project panel to review the position of all the markers in your project.

5 Click the Preview button in the Disc Layout panel.

6 In the Preview Disc window, click the Play button (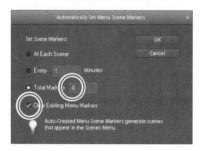) to begin playing your project. Once the first video clip begins playing, click the Next Scene button ( ) repeatedly and notice how the video jumps from scene to scene.

● **Note:** You can reposition markers in the Timeline by dragging them to the left or right.

7 Click the Close button ( ) in the upper-right corner of the Preview Disc window to close it.

8 Right-click in the preview area of the Disc Layout panel, and then choose Auto-Generate Menu Markers to again open the Automatically Set Menu Scene Markers dialog.

9 Choose the Total Markers option and type *4* into the number field. Select the Clear Existing Menu Markers check box, and then click OK.

Four markers are now evenly spread out across the Timeline.

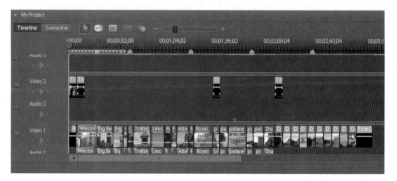

Using the Total Markers option may be preferable to creating a marker for every clip in order to reduce the number of scenes in your movie. As you'll see in the next exercise, when creating a disc with menus, Adobe Premiere Elements automatically creates buttons and menus based on the markers in your project. Too many markers might result in too many navigation buttons and screens for your movie.

10 Choose File > Save. Then choose File > Open Recent Project > Lesson11_Work.prel to return to the project file from the previous exercise.

Creating a Disc with Menus

Building an auto-play disc as you did in the previous exercise is the quickest way to go from an Adobe Premiere Elements project to an optical disc you can watch in your living room. However, auto-play discs lack the ability to jump directly to different scenes, as well as other navigational features that most users expect when watching a DVD or Blu-ray Disc. You can quickly create such navigation menus in Adobe Premiere Elements using a variety of templates designed for this purpose.

1 If you are not currently in the Disc Menus workspace, select Disc Menus in the Tasks panel to switch to it now.

2 Adobe Premiere Elements ships with many distinctive menu templates—predesigned and customizable menus that come in a variety of themes and styles. Select Travel from the category menu, and then select the template called European Travel from the menu next to it.

3 To apply the European Travel template to your project, click to select the template in Templates view, and then click the Apply button (✓ Apply) in the lower-right corner of Templates view. Or, drop the template from Templates view onto the Disc Layout panel.

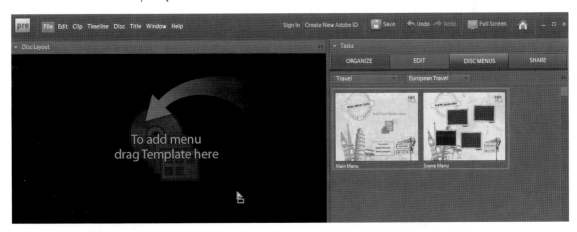

Each template contains a Main menu and a Scenes menu. The Main menu is the first screen that the viewer sees when the disc is played. The Scenes menu is a secondary panel accessed when the viewer clicks the Scene Selection button in the Main menu.

● **Note:** To replace the selected template, click another to select it, and then click Apply to apply it to the project, or drop it onto the Disc Layout panel. To delete all menus, right-click the Disc Layout window and choose Change to Auto-Play.

4 Under Disc Menus at the bottom of the Disc Layout panel, click to select Main Menu 1.

Two buttons are currently visible in this menu: Play and Scenes. Additionally, there is a generic text button called Movie Title Here. You'll now change the text of this generic button to something more appropriate for your project.

5 In the preview area of the Disc Layout panel, click the Main Movie Title text once. A thin, white rectangle appears around the button indicating that it is selected.

6 Double-click the Main Movie Title text to open the Change Text dialog. If the text under Change Text is not already highlighted, select it now, and then type *My London Walk.* Click the OK button to close the Change Text dialog and to commit the change.

7 Let's make the text *My London Walk* stand out a bit more. Click the text to make it active, and then on the right, click the Make Text Bold icon. Note that you could also change the font and font size, and italicize or underline the text.

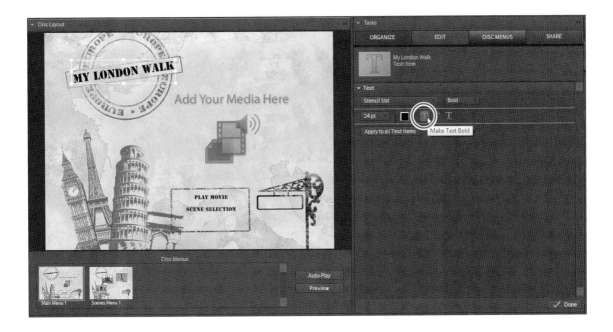

8   Click the Preview button to preview the main menu. Place your pointer over
    the Play Movie and Scenes Selection buttons, but don't click them yet. Notice
    the orange/red circles that appear in the text box when the pointer passes over
    them. This rollover effect is part of the menu template and shows viewers which
    button they're selecting. Click the Play Movie button and the movie begins
    to play.

The preview feature shows how your DVD will look after recording the project to disc. Note, however, that the quality of the previewed video may not be indicative of the final video. Because of the differences between computer monitors and TV sets, you may see noticeable horizontal lines as the video is playing on the computer monitor. These lines are referred to as interlacing and will not be visible in the final movie when played on a TV.

9   As the movie is playing, click the Main Menu button (▣) at the bottom of the Preview Disc window. Clicking this button at any point during playback returns you to the main menu, so you don't have to watch the whole movie if you're just testing your menus.

10 Click the Close button (✖) in the upper-right corner of the Preview Disc window to close it.

11 Choose File > Save to save your project file.

Modifying Scene Marker Buttons

One of the benefits of DVDs and Blu-ray Discs is the ability to jump quickly to specific scenes in a movie. For each scene marker you add in the Timeline, Adobe Premiere Elements automatically generates a Scene Marker button on the Scenes menu. If the template has image thumbnails on the Scenes menu, as the menu you're working with does, Adobe Premiere Elements automatically assigns an image thumbnail to it. You can customize the appearance of a Scene Marker button by providing a name for the label and changing the image thumbnail used to identify the scene. Note that if you have more scene markers than scenes on a Scene menu, Adobe Premiere Elements creates additional Scenes menu pages and navigational buttons to jump back and forth between the pages.

Changing Button Labels and Image Thumbnails

1   Click the Scenes Menu 1 thumbnail under Disc Menus in the Disc Layout panel to view the Scenes menu.

Adobe Premiere Elements has generated the three Scene Marker buttons and their image thumbnails based on the scene markers you added in the first exercise. By default, Adobe Premiere Elements named the Scene Marker buttons Scene 1, Scene 2, and Scene 3. You'll customize these for your content shortly.

In addition, by default, the thumbnail in the Scene Marker button is the first frame of the clip the button links to. This doesn't work well in this case because the clips are obscured either by a transition or the animated pastel sketch effect, so viewers can't easily discern the content of the scene. Let's change these thumbnails to more appropriate frames.

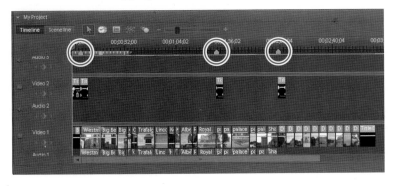

2 Double-click the first marker to open the Menu Marker dialog for the first marker. In the Name field, type *Westminster*.

● **Note:** When using menu templates, one- or two-word titles fit best into the text boxes.

3 In the Thumbnail Offset section, notice that the time counter is set to 00:00;00;00. Place your pointer over the time counter, drag to the right about 00;00;05;17, and then release the pointer to freeze the movie at that location. Or, click the time counter and enter the timecode directly. Click OK, and Adobe Premiere Elements updates the button name and image thumbnail in the Scenes menu.

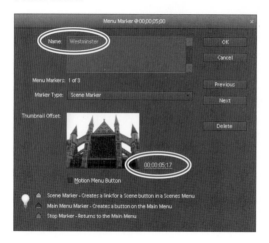

Next, you'll change the names of the remaining two buttons and their respective image thumbnails.

4 Double-click the second marker to open the Menu Marker dialog. In the Name field, type *Buckingham*.

5 Place your pointer over the time counter, drag to the right to about 00;00;24;11, and then release the pointer to freeze the movie at that location. Click OK. Adobe Premiere Elements updates the button name and image thumbnail in the Scenes menu.

6 Double-click the third marker, type *Slideshow* into the name field, and drag the time counter to about 00;00;17;00. Click OK. Adobe Premiere Elements updates the button name and image thumbnail in the Scenes menu.

7 When finished, click the Preview button to open the Preview Disc window. Click the Scenes button to navigate to the Scenes Selection menu. Notice that Adobe Premiere Elements has updated button names and thumbnails.

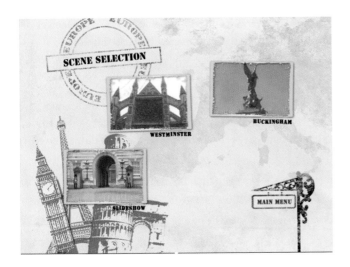

8   At the bottom of the Preview Disc window you can see a group of navigation buttons, which simulate the controls on a DVD remote control. Click any of the arrows to advance through the Scene Menu buttons, and click the center circle (the Enter button) to play that scene. Adobe Premiere Elements automatically controls the navigation of all menu buttons, so you should preview all scenes on the disc to ensure that you placed your markers logically. When done, close the Preview Disc window.

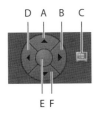

A. Up. **B.** Right. **C.** Main Menu button.
D. Left. **E.** Enter. **F.** Down.

9   Choose File > Save to save your project file.

Working with Submenus

Before you start customizing menu appearance, there are some other navigation and button placement options that you should be aware of. For example, many Hollywood movies have a link on the main menu to bonus or deleted clips sections. Adobe Premiere Elements lets you create a submenu button on your main menu by adding a special menu marker.

In addition, by default, once a viewer starts watching any portion of the movie, the video will continue on to the end, even if there are intervening scene markers. In the project you've been working on, this isn't a problem, but with other projects, you may want to stop playback after a scene completes and return the viewer to the menu. You can accomplish this using the stop marker discussed here.

In this exercise, you will add a button on the main menu linking to a bonus video clip.

1. Under Disc Menus in the Disc Layout panel, click to select Main Menu 1. Currently, two buttons are in this menu: the Play Movie and Scenes Selection buttons. The template design leaves space for more buttons below these two buttons, if needed.

2. Select the Timeline in the My Project panel. Press the End key on your keyboard to move the current-time indicator to the end of the last clip.

   You will now add a special marker to the end of your movie.

3. Right-click the time ruler at the current-time indicator and choose Set Menu Marker. The Menu Marker panel opens.

4. Choose Stop Marker from the Marker Type menu. When a stop marker is reached during playback, the viewer will return to the Main Menu.

5. Click OK to add the stop marker. In the Timeline, stop markers are colored red to help you differentiate them from the green scene markers and the blue main menu markers. You will learn more about main menu markers later in this lesson.

   Next, you'll add an additional clip named Downing Street.avi to the end of the Timeline. This clip will be a bonus clip that users can access from the Main menu but is not part of the main movie.

6   Select the Organize tab of the Tasks panel, and then click Project. In Project
    view, drag the Downing Street.avi clip into the Video 1 track after the Credit
    sequence at the end of your Timeline. Be sure to place the clip a few seconds
    from the last clip, leaving a gap between the clips.

7   Press the Page Down key to advance the current-time indicator to the beginning
    of the added Downing Street.avi clip, and then right-click and choose Set Menu
    Marker to open the Menu Marker dialog.

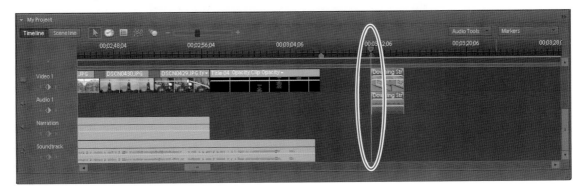

Three Types of Menu Markers

Scene markers ( **):** Adding a scene marker to your Timeline automatically adds a scene button to the scene menu of your disc. Scenes menus are secondary to the main menu, and there should be a Scenes button on the main menu that links to the Scenes menu.

Main menu markers (**):** Adding a main menu marker to your Timeline automatically adds a button to the main menu of your disc. Most templates have space for either three or four buttons on the first menu page. The Play Movie button and the Scenes button are present by default. This will leave you with space for one or two more buttons, depending on the template you have chosen. If you add additional main menu markers to your movie, Adobe Premiere Elements will create a secondary main menu.

Stop markers (**):** Adding a stop marker to your Timeline forces Adobe Premiere Elements to stop the playback of your Timeline and return the viewer to the main menu. Use stop markers to control the viewer's flow through the movie. For example, if you want the viewer to return to the main menu after each scene, insert a stop marker at the end of each scene. You can also use stop markers to add bonus or deleted scenes after the main movie, linking to this content using either scene or main menu markers.

● **Note:** You don't have to add a stop marker at the end of the bonus clip. When Adobe Premiere Elements reaches the end of the Timeline, it will automatically return the viewer to the main menu.

8　In the Menu Marker dialog, choose Main Menu Marker from the Marker Type menu. In the name field, type *Bonus Clip*, and then click OK to close the Menu Marker dialog.

Adobe Premiere Elements adds a button named Bonus Clip to the Main Menu 1 in the Disc Layout panel.

9　Click the Disc Menus tab and then the Preview button, and then click the Bonus Clip button to play the video associated with it. When the bonus clip has finished playing, the main menu appears. If you play the main movie from start to finish, you will not see the bonus clip because of the stop marker you added at the end of the last clip in the main movie.

10 Close the Preview Disc window.

11 Choose File > Save to save your project file.

Customizing Menus in Properties View

When you produce a disc in Adobe Premiere Elements, you have multiple customization options for your menu, including the ability to change fonts and font colors, to add a still image or video background, to add background music to the menu, and to animate the button thumbnails on your menus. You accomplish all these tasks in Properties view, which displays different options depending on the object you select. Let's take a quick tour.

1 Make sure you are in the Disc Menus workspace, and then choose Window > Restore Workspace to reset the location of your panels.

2 Under Disc Menus in the Disc Layout panel, click the Scenes Menu 1 thumbnail to make sure the Scenes Menu 1 menu is loaded.

3 Click in the Scenes Menu 1 menu near the bottom of the menu, being careful not to select any navigational or thumbnail buttons.

Properties view displays two sections: Menu Background and Motion Menu Buttons. You can expand and collapse these two sections by clicking the arrows to the left of the section. In the Menu Background section are subsections for Video or Still backgrounds and Audio backgrounds.

4   Click the Buckingham marker button. Adobe Premiere Elements displays a rectangle, referred to as the *bounding box*, around the button. There are eight selection points around the box that you'll work with in a moment.

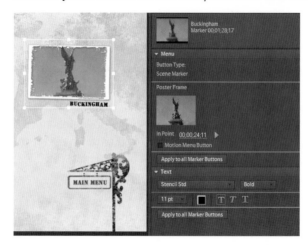

Note that Properties view now displays two sections: Menu options on top and Text options on the bottom. The Menu options are very similar to those selected in the Menu Marker panel. Some, such as the Poster Frame In Point, you can change directly in Properties view; others, such as the Button Type, you have to return to the Menu Marker panel to modify.

● **Note:** As always, in addition to clicking the menu to open Properties view, you can also choose Window > Properties from the Adobe Premiere Elements main menu to open Properties view.

5   Click the Scene Selection title in Scenes Menu 1. Adobe Premiere Elements displays a bounding box around the title and displays only the Text options in Properties view.

Those are the different control sets of Properties view. Fortunately, you don't have to remember what they are and what they do. Just click the menu component you'd like to edit, and Adobe Premiere Elements automatically opens the necessary controls.

Customizing Menus with Video, Still Images, and Audio

You can customize your menus in Adobe Premiere Elements by adding a still image, video, or audio to the menu. You can also combine multiple items, such as a still photo and an audio clip. Alternatively, you can add a video clip and replace the audio track with a separate audio clip.

Note that your customization options differ based on the menu template you select. If the menu has a drop zone, like the template you're working with in this lesson, still images or video inserted into the menu will display in the drop zone.

Otherwise, with templates that lack drop zones, the inserted still image or video will appear full screen in the menu background. You'll see an example of that in a moment.

Although Adobe Premiere Elements allows you to customize a disc menu, keep in mind that changes made will not be saved back to the template; they apply only to the current project. If you'd like to create custom templates to be used in multiple projects, you can create one in Adobe Photoshop Elements, and then add the template to Adobe Premiere Elements.

Adding a Still Image or Video Clip to Your Menu

You'll use the same procedure to add a still image or video clip to a menu. In this exercise, you'll insert a video clip into a menu. By default, when you insert a video, the audio plays with the video as well, though you can change this by inserting a separate audio file, as you will do later.

Follow this procedure to add a video clip to your menu.

1 Under Disc Menus in the Disc Layout panel, click to select Main Menu 1. Click in the main menu, being careful not to click one of the active buttons.

2 In Properties view, in the Menu Background box, click the Browse button, navigate to the Lesson11 folder, and choose the Big Ben 2.avi clip. Click Open to close the dialog and insert the clip into the menu.

● **Note:** You'd follow this same procedure to select a still image either to fit into the drop zone or to use as a full-screen background image.

3 Note the options available in the Menu Background box in Properties view. Specifically, you can do the following:

- Play the video by clicking the green play triangle ().

- Choose an In Point for the video to start, either by dragging the time counter or by typing in the timecode for the desired starting point.

- After choosing an In Point, you can select the Use Still Frame check box to use the current frame as the background or within the drop zone.

- Apply the default transition to the video clip before the menu starts to loop by selecting the Apply Default Transition before loop check box. Note that the maximum duration for video menus is 30 seconds, and that the menu will loop indefinitely after that time.

For this exercise, leave the options at their default settings, and click Preview to preview the menu. When finished, close the Preview window and return to the Disc Layout panel.

4 Choose File > Save to save your project file.

As mentioned, when you add a video to a menu with a drop zone, the video plays within that drop zone. When you add a video to a menu without a drop zone, the video plays in the background of the menu.

Accordingly, to create a menu with your own full-screen still image or video in the background, choose a template without a drop zone. If you opt to customize a menu with a full-screen background image or video, you'll have to manually insert it into each menu created by Adobe Premiere Elements. Note that you can insert a different still image or video clip as a background in each menu, or use the background image that came with the menu template.

Adding an Audio Clip to the Background

Let's substitute a separate audio clip for the audio included with the menu.avi video clip. Use this same procedure to add audio to any menu template, whether modified with a still image background or used as is.

1   Click Main Menu 1 in the Disc Layout panel to open its Properties view. If necessary, scroll down the Properties view to locate the Audio section.

2   Click the Browse button, select the soundtrack.wav clip in the Lesson11 folder, and then click Open.

3   If you'd like to add a fade-out so the audio loops nicely, select the Apply Default Transition before loop check box.

4   In the Disc Layout panel, click the Preview button. You can see the video or video frame and hear the audio track you selected for the Main menu background.

5   Close the Preview window.

6   If you'd like to remove the audio portion from the menu background, click the Reset button next to the speaker icon in the Audio section of Properties view.

7   Following this same procedure, select Scene Menu 1 from the Disc Layout panel and add the soundtrack.wav clip as the background audio file, making sure to enable the default transition.

8   Save your project.

Animating Buttons

If the menu template that you select uses thumbnail scene buttons, you can elect to animate the buttons. With an animated button, a designated duration of video from the linked scene will play within the thumbnail while the menu displays. The Main menu for this project does not include any buttons with image thumbnails. However, the Scene menu does have image thumbnails. Let's animate these thumbnails.

1   Select the Scenes Menu 1 thumbnail under Disc Menus in the Disc Layout panel.

2   Click the Westminster button to select it. Currently, this button displays a still frame extracted from the video clip at the 00;00;05;17 mark.

● **Note:** You can't set the Out Point or the end of clips in Properties view, but you can set all your motion menu buttons to be the same duration, as explained in the following steps.

3 In Properties view, in the Menu box, scroll down if necessary to see all of the Poster Frame section, and then select the Motion Menu Button check box. To animate all Marker buttons, click the Apply to all Marker Buttons button.

4 If you'd like to change the In Point of the video clip and play a different segment in the animated thumbnail, drag the time counter (which currently reads the 00;00;05;17) to the desired spot.

5 Click an empty area of your background menu. This deselects the current scene button, and Properties view switches to the Menu Background properties. Scroll down to the bottom of Properties view, if necessary, to locate the Motion Menu Buttons box.

6 Note that the default duration for the Motion Menu Buttons is 00;00;29;29, or just under 30 seconds. Leave this value at the default.

7 Click the Preview button in the Disc Layout panel. In the Main menu, click the Scenes Selection button to access the Scenes menu. All the buttons should now be animated.

8 Close the Preview Disc window.

9 If you'd like to pick a different In Point for your thumbnail video, select the Motion Menu Button option and choose suitable In Points for the two other scene buttons. If you didn't click the Apply to all Marker Buttons button in a step 3, you must individually activate scene buttons to animate them. All animated buttons share the same duration.

10 Save your project.

Customizing Button Size, Location, and Text Attributes

Beyond adding still images, video, and audio to your menu, you can also change the size, appearance, and location of buttons and text on your menus. In this exercise, you will make changes to your menu appearance and buttons.

1 Make sure you are in the Disc Menus workspace, and then choose Window > Restore Workspace to reset the location of your panels.

2 Under Disc Menus in the Disc Layout panel, click the Main Menu 1 thumbnail to make sure the main menu is loaded.

3 Click the Play Movie button to select it. The eight-point bounding box opens. Place your pointer on the upper-right corner, and then drag upward and outward to enlarge the text box.

Scaling text boxes in this manner can be tricky because the width and height do not scale proportionally. Text can easily become distorted.

4 Press Ctrl-Z on your keyboard to undo the changes. Adobe Premiere Elements allows you to undo multiple steps, so you can backtrack through your changes.

Overlapping Buttons

Buttons on a disc menu should not overlap each other. If two or more buttons overlap, there is a potential for confusion. Someone who is using a pointer to navigate and click the menu may not be able to access the correct button if another one is overlapping it. This can easily happen if button text is too long or if two buttons are placed too close to each other.

Overlapping buttons can sometimes be fixed by shortening the button name, or in general, by simply by moving the buttons so that there's more space between them. By default, overlapping buttons in Adobe Premiere Elements are outlined in red in the Disc Layout panel. This feature can be turned off or on by choosing Show Overlapping Menu Buttons from the Disc Layout panel menu at the right side of the docking header.

5   With the Play Movie button still selected, press the equals sign (=) on your keyboard and the text box size increases proportionally. Press the minus sign (-) on your keyboard to reduce the size of your text box proportionally. Using the keyboard commands to change the size avoids the risk of distorting the text.

6   Click the Scenes Selection button in the Disc Layout panel to select it, and then press the left arrow key on your keyboard to move it. Pressing the arrow keys on your keyboard allows you to move a button one pixel at a time in the direction of the arrow. Press the right arrow key to move the button back to its original location.

7   Save your project.

Note: All buttons and titles within Adobe Premiere Elements templates are within the title-safe zone. If you plan to resize or move buttons or text on the menu, you should enable Show Safe Margins in the Disc Layout panel menu at the right side of the docking header menu, as shown in the following figure, and make sure that all content is within the title-safe zone before recording your disc.

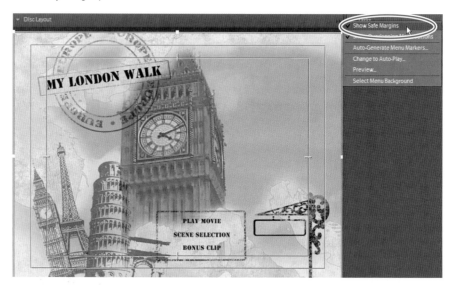

Changing Menu Button Text Properties

Properties view lets you modify the font, size, color, and style of your menu buttons, and you can automatically apply changes made to one button to similar buttons.

You can modify the text attributes of five types of objects: Menu Titles, which are text-only objects that aren't linked to clips or movies; Play buttons, which link to the beginning of your main movie; Scene Marker buttons, which link to the Scenes menu; Marker buttons, which directly link to a menu marker on the Timeline; and Navigational buttons, such as the link back to the main menu in the Scenes menu.

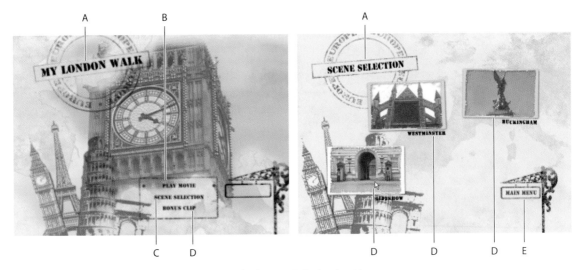

A. Menu title. B. Play button. C. Scene button. D. Marker button. E. Navigational button.

1   Under Disc Menus in the Disc Layout panel, click the Scenes Menu 1 thumbnail.

2   Click the Westminster marker button. Properties view updates automatically and shows that this is a marker button—specifically, a Scene Marker button. The Text subsection allows you to change the properties of the text. If necessary, scroll down in Properties view to see all of the Text subsection.

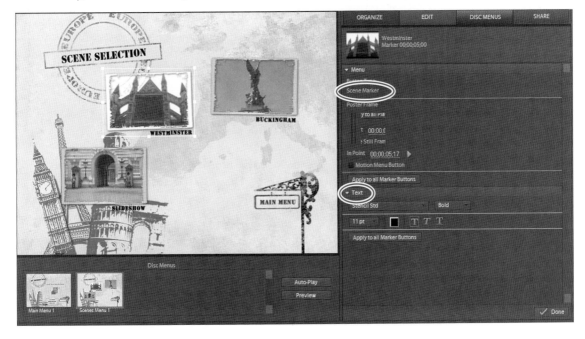

3 In the Text subsection, click the font menu, and note that you can change the font of this or any text in the menu. The Stencil Std. font looks best here, so let's leave that selected.

4 The next menu, the Text Size menu, allows you to change the text size to any of the preset sizes. Change the text size to 12pt.

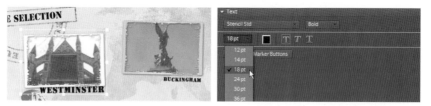

5 Next, let's change the color of the text to red, to match the coat of the guard in the Slideshow frame. To begin, click the black color swatch next to the Text Size menu to open the Color Picker dialog. Click once in the vertical color spectrum in the general range of red. Then click in the lower-right corner of the large color field to choose a bright red. The parameters of the color I selected are R: 195, G: 31, B: 40. Click OK to apply the color.

A. Click here to pick the specific shade within the selected range of colors. **B.** Click here to change the general range of colors.

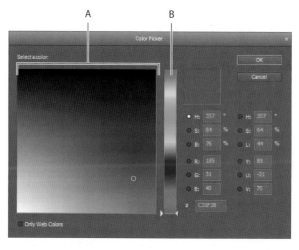

Notice that the other Scene Marker buttons have retained their original formatting. Normally, changes affect only the selected object. But Adobe Premiere Elements also gives you the option to change the text attributes of all buttons of the same type simultaneously.

6 In the Text subsection of Properties view, click the Apply to all Marker Buttons button. This applies the same text attributes to all three Scene Marker buttons.

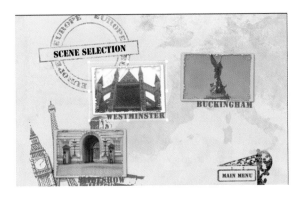

7   Under Disc Menus in the Disc Layout panel, click the Main Menu 1 thumbnail. Notice that the Bonus Clip marker has also changed its appearance. This is because the Marker Button category encompasses both Scene Marker and Main Menu Marker buttons.

8   Choose File > Save As and save this project file into your Lesson11 folder as *Lesson11_Final.prel*.

Burning DVDs or Blu-ray Discs

After you've previewed your disc and have checked the menus and button names, you're ready to record the project to a DVD or Blu-ray Disc. As noted at the beginning of the chapter, you must have either a DVD or a Blu-ray Disc writer to record a disc in that format.

When making a DVD or Blu-ray Disc, Adobe Premiere Elements converts your video and audio files into a compressed format. Briefly, compression shrinks your original video and audio files to fit it on a disc. For example, a 60-minute video in DV or HDV format requires approximately 13 GB of hard disk space. However, a DVD-Video holds only 4.7 GB of space. So how do you fit 13 GB of video into a 4.7 GB disc? Through compression!

The process of compression can be quite lengthy. In essence, Adobe Premiere Elements evaluates every frame of video in your project and attempts to reduce the file size without sacrificing the image quality. You should allow quite a bit of time for this process. For example, 60 minutes of video may take 4 to 6 hours to compress and record onto a DVD, and compressing and recording HD video onto a Blu-ray Disc can take even longer. For this reason, it may be a good idea to initiate the disc-burning process (which begins with compressing the video) at a time when you will not need your computer.

To maintain maximum quality, Adobe Premiere Elements compresses the movie only as much as is necessary to fit it on the disc. The shorter your movie, the less compression required and the higher the quality of the video on the disc.

1　Select the Share workspace by clicking the Share tab in the Tasks panel.

2　Save your current project. It's always a good idea to save your Adobe Premiere Elements project file before burning a disc.

3　Click the Disc button (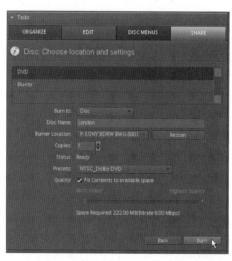) in the Start a new share: box to open the Disc: Choose location and settings view. Choose DVD from the list at the top of the view. To burn a Blu-ray Disc, select Blu-ray from that list.

4　Make sure Disc is selected in the "Burn to" menu. Select the option to burn to a folder on your hard drive if you prefer to use an alternative program to burn your discs.

5　In the Disc Name field, type *London*. Software playing DVDs or Blu-ray Discs on a personal computer may display this disc name.

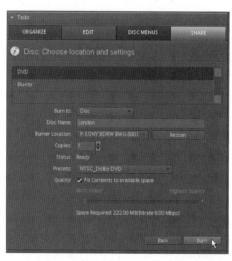

6　Select the desired DVD or Blu-ray Disc burner from the Burner Location menu. If you don't have a compatible disc burner connected to your computer, the Burner Location menu is disabled and the Status line reads "No burner detected."

7　If you want to create a DVD or Blu-ray Disc, ensure that you've inserted a compatible blank disc in the disc burner. If you insert a disc after you start this process, click Rescan to have Adobe Premiere Elements recheck all connected burners for valid media.

8　Next to Copies, select the number of discs you want to burn during this session. For this exercise, choose 1. When you select multiple copies, Adobe Premiere Elements asks you to insert another disc after the writing of each disc is completed, until all the discs you specified have been burned.

● **Note:** This exercise ends with the burning of a DVD. If you don't want to create a DVD, follow the steps of the exercise only up to the point of writing the disc. If you will be creating a DVD, I suggest using a DVD-RW (Rewritable) disc, if you have one available, so that you can reuse the disc later.

● **Note:** Adobe Premiere Elements detects only burners that are connected and turned on at the time you started Adobe Premiere Elements. If you connected and turned on any burners after that point, Adobe Premiere Elements will not recognize them until you restart the application.

9 Select the "Fit Contents to available space" check box to ensure that Adobe Premiere Elements maximizes the quality of your video based on disc capacity.

10 From the Presets menu, select the NTSC_Widescreen_Dolby DVD option. Adobe Premiere Elements is also capable of burning a project to the PAL standard (used in Europe, parts of Africa, South America, the Middle East, Australia, New Zealand, some Pacific Islands, and certain Asian countries) in both normal or widescreen format.

11 If you want to burn a disc at this point, click the Burn button. If you don't want to burn a disc, click the Back button.

Congratulations! You've successfully completed this lesson. You learned how to manually and automatically add scene markers to your movie, create an auto-play disc, and—by applying a menu template—a disc with menus. You added a submenu for a bonus clip and learned about stop and main menu makers. You customized the disc menus by changing text attributes, background images, button labels, and image thumbnails. You added sound and video clips to the menu background, and activated motion menu buttons. Finally, you learned how to burn your movie onto a DVD or Blu-ray Disc.

Choosing Blu-ray Disc Quality Options

When burning to Blu-ray Disc, you have multiple compression and resolution options. In general, recording to MPEG-2 is much faster than H.264 and quality is very similar at high to moderate data rates. Unless you're recording two or more hours to a Blu-ray Disc, MPEG-2 should deliver equal quality in much less time.

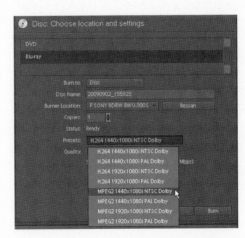

When choosing a target resolution, use the native resolution of your source footage. For example, HDV has a native resolution of 1440x1080, so if you recorded in HDV, you should produce your disc at that resolution. If you have a recent AVCHD camcorder, you may be recording in native 1920x1080, so use that resolution for your Blu-ray Disc. If you're not sure what resolution you're recording in, check the documentation that came with your camcorder.

Review Questions

1 What is an auto-play disc? What are the advantage and disadvantage of creating one?

2 How do you identify separate scenes for use in your disc menu?

3 What is a submenu, and how would you add one to your disc menu?

4 Which menu button text properties can you change, and how are these properties modified?

5 Which type of menu template should you choose if you want to insert a still image or video file as a full-screen background for your disc menus?

Review Answers

1 An auto-play disc allows you to create a DVD or Blu-ray Disc quickly from the main movie of your project. The advantage of an auto-play disc is that it can be quickly and easily created, whereas the disadvantage is that it doesn't have a menu for navigation during playback.

2 Separate scenes can be defined by placing a scene marker on a specific frame in the Timeline. Scene markers are set in the Timeline using the Add Menu Marker button.

3 A submenu is a button on your main disc menu that points to a specific section of your project, such as a credit sequence or a bonus clip. Submenus are created by adding a main menu marker to your Timeline.

4 You can change the font, size, color, and style of your text buttons. Changing the properties of your text is done inside Properties view for objects selected in the Disc Layout panel.

5 You should choose a template that does not include a drop zone. If you insert a still image or video into a menu template with a drop zone, Adobe Premiere Elements will display that content within the drop zone.

12 SHARING MOVIES

This lesson is based on a project that you finished in a previous chapter, which you'll now share using multiple techniques. In this lesson, you'll learn how to send your completed video project to the digital media or device of choice, for example, a DV camera. You will also learn the different ways you can export movies to view online or on a personal computer. Specifically, you'll learn how to do the following:

- Upload a video file to YouTube and Photoshop.com
- Export a video file for subsequent viewing from a hard drive
- Export a video file for viewing on an iPod or other mobile device
- Record your video file back to DV/HDV tape
- Export a single frame as a still image
- Use the Quick Share feature to save and reuse your favorite sharing methods

 This lesson will take approximately 1.5 hours.

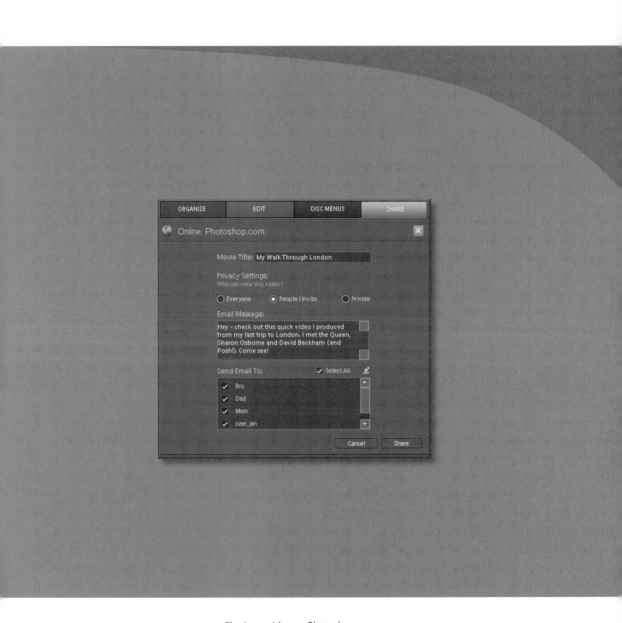

Sharing a video on Photoshop.com.

Sharing and Exporting Video

Apart from creating DVDs or Blu-ray Discs, you can export and share movies, still images, and audio in a variety of file types for the web, computer playback, mobile devices, and even videotape. The Share workspace in the Tasks panel is your starting point for exporting your finished project. Here you choose your target and configuration options.

Selecting any of the options listed under Start a new share: opens a view in the Tasks panel that provides output-specific options and settings. Share view simplifies sharing and exporting by providing presets of the most commonly used formats and settings. If you want to specify unique settings for any format, you can click Advanced options and make changes.

When exporting using the Share workspace, you can create a Quick Share preset to save and reuse your favorite sharing method for future projects, along with all the settings. Whenever you want to share a project using those settings, just select that preset and click the Share button.

The first step for all sharing is choosing your desired target. The exercises in this chapter walk you through examples of the available targets in the Share workspace.

Getting Started

To begin, you'll launch Adobe Premiere Elements and open the project used for this lesson. Then you'll review a final version of the project you'll be creating.

1   Before you begin, make sure that you have correctly copied the Lesson12 folder from the DVD in the back of this book onto your computer's hard drive. See "Copying the Classroom in a Book files" in the Getting Started section of this book.

2   Start Adobe Premiere Elements, click the Open Project button in the Welcome screen, and then click Open. If Adobe Premiere Elements is already open, choose File > Open Project.

3   Navigate to the Lesson12 folder and select the project file Lesson12_Start.prel. Click the Open button to open your project. The Adobe Premiere Elements work area appears with the Edit workspace selected in the Tasks panel.

4   The project file opens with the Media, Monitor, and My Project panels visible. Choose Window > Restore Workspace to ensure that you start the lesson with the default panel layout.

Viewing the Completed Movie for the First Exercise

To see what you'll be exporting in this lesson, play the completed movie.

1   In the Organize tab of the Tasks panel, click Project ( ). In Project view, locate the file Lesson12_Movie.wmv, and then double-click it to open the video into the Preview window.

2   In the Preview window, click the Play button ( ) to watch the video about a walk through London, which you will render in this lesson.

3   When done, close the Preview window by clicking the Close button ( ) in the upper-right corner of the window.

If the movie looks familiar, that's because it's the project you finished back in Lesson 9 after adding a soundtrack and narration. Now it's time to share the fruits of your hard work with the world!

Rather than duplicating the project file and content from Lesson 9 to Lesson 12, I inserted the rendered file that you just played onto the Timeline in Lesson12_Start. prel, since it simulates the Lesson 9 project completely and saved a few hundred megabytes on the DVD that accompanies this book. The experience will be *exactly* the same as if you were working with the original content and project file.

Still, if you'd like to work with the original assets, you can load the Lesson09_End. prel file that you created in Lesson 9, or load Lesson09_Work.prel (if you didn't make it to the end), and follow the instructions in this chapter to render those contents. Obviously, those projects would be in the Lesson09 folder, not the Lesson12 folder. In your shoes, I would simply use the Lesson12_Start.prel project you currently have loaded, but feel free to work with the original content if that's your preference.

Uploading to YouTube

Adobe Premiere Elements provides presets for four online destinations—YouTube, Photoshop.com, and PodBean, as well as configurable FTP settings for your own website. The workflow is very similar for all with a simple wizard guiding your efforts. Here I'll work through the first two, starting with YouTube. It's faster if you already have an account with YouTube, but if not, you can sign up as part of the process. Follow these steps to upload your project to YouTube.

1   Click Share in the Tasks panel, and then click Online ( ).

2   Choose YouTube from the list at the top. Adobe Premiere Elements uses the Flash preset for YouTube for all files produced to upload to YouTube.

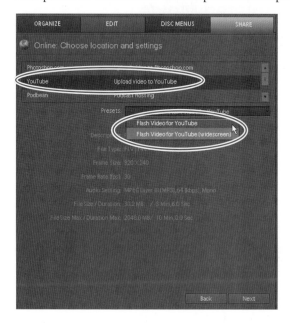

3   Choose a preset. Use Flash Video for YouTube for 4:3 projects like this one and Flash Video for YouTube (widescreen) for 16:9 projects.

4   If desired, click the Share WorkArea Bar Only to upload only the work area bar. It's not shown in the immediately preceding figure because it's hidden behind the Preset drop-down list box, but you'll see it after selecting your preset.

5   Click Next.

6 Log in to YouTube. If this is your first time uploading to YouTube, click Sign Up Now and register. Then log in.

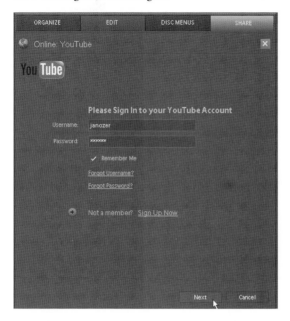

7 Click Next.

8 Enter the required information about your project: Title, Description, Tags, and Category, and then click Next.

9 Choose whether you want to allow the public to view your project or to keep it private, and then click Share. Adobe Premiere Elements renders the project and starts uploading to YouTube.

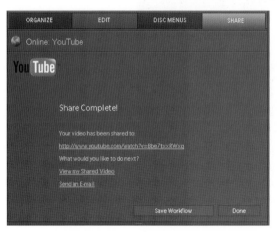

10 When the share is complete, the URL appears in the Share workspace. You can choose View My Shared Video to open YouTube and watch your video, or choose Send an E-mail to alert friends to your new posting.

Note: We're pretty sure that there will be (at least) dozens if not hundreds of copies of this video on YouTube by sometime in late 2009. It might be a better idea if you follow these latter steps to upload your own video to YouTube, or if you do upload this sample movie, that you later delete it.

11 Do *one of the following:*

- To save your workflow as a Quick Share preset, click Save Workflow, and follow the instructions in the Adding a Quick Share Preset below. Note, however, that if you create a YouTube Quick Share Preset, the preset will use the title, description, and tags entered for the video uploaded when you created the preset; there is no opportunity to edit these. For this reason, I don't recommend creating a Quick Share preset for any online destination.

- To return to the main Share workspace without saving a Quick Share preset, click Finish.

Uploading to Photoshop.com

YouTube is a great location to upload your video to for it to be seen by the multitudes, but video quality ranges from fair to poor, and some of the comments can be, well, rude. If you'd like to upload a video primarily for friends and family, at very good quality, your Photoshop.com account is ideal, and the workflow is exceptionally simple. Here's how.

1 Click Share in the Tasks panel, and then click Online (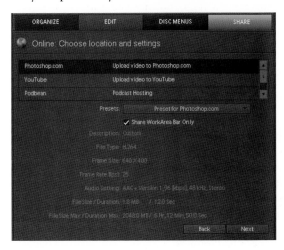).

2 Choose Photoshop.com. There's currently only a single preset for Photoshop.com, so there are no options available. If desired, click the Share WorkArea Bar Only to upload only the work area bar.

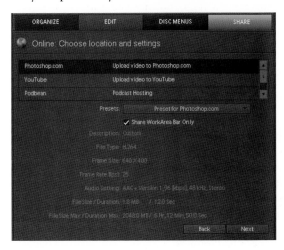

3 Click Next.

4 If you're not already logged into Photoshop.com, you'll see the login screen. Log in to Photoshop.com. If you don't have a Photoshop.com account, click Create New Adobe ID and sign up. Then enter your account name and password, and click Sign In. Click OK to close the Success dialog.

5 Enter the required information about your project: Movie Title, Privacy Settings, Email Message, and Send Email To addresses, and then click Share.

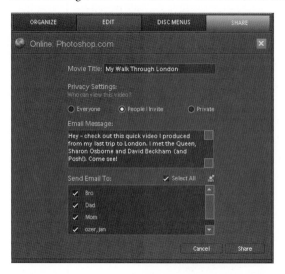

Note: We're pretty sure that there will be (at least) dozens if not hundreds of copies of this video on YouTube by sometime in late 2009. It might be a better idea if you follow these latter steps to upload your own video to YouTube, or if you do upload this sample movie, that you later delete it.

6 When the share is complete, Adobe Premiere Elements will display a hyperlink that you can click to view your online video.

7 Do *one of the following:*

- To save your workflow as a Quick Share preset, click Save Workflow, and follow the instructions in the Adding a Quick Share Preset below. Note, however, that if you create a Photoshop.com Quick Share Preset, the preset will use the metadata entered for the video uploaded when you created the preset; there is no opportunity to edit these. For this reason, creating a Quick Share preset for any online destination is not advised.

- To return to the main Share workspace without saving a Quick Share preset, click Finish.

Sharing on Your Personal Computer

In the previous exercise, you exported an Adobe Premiere Elements project to YouTube. In this exercise, you'll export your project as a stand-alone video file to play on your own system, upload to a website, email to friends or family, or archive on DVD or external hard drive.

As you'll see in a moment, Adobe Premiere Elements lets you output in multiple formats for all these activities. Each file format comes with its own set of presets available from the Presets menu. You can also customize a preset and save it for later reuse, which you'll do in this lesson.

See the sidebar "Choosing Output Formats" for more information on which preset to choose. In this exercise, you'll output a file using the Windows Media format.

1   In Share view, click the Personal Computer button (■).

2   In the list at the top of Share view, choose Windows Media.

3   In the Presets list box, choose Local Area Network (LAN).

4   Enter *Lesson12_SharePC* in the File Name field, and then click Browse to select the Lesson12 folder as the Save in folder.

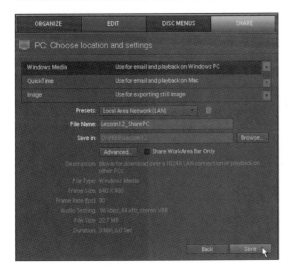

5   If desired, select the Share WorkArea Bar Only check box.

Formats

- **Adobe Flash Video:** Adobe Flash Video is a very high-quality format that's used by the majority of sites on the Internet for playback via the ubiquitous Adobe Flash Player. Use this format if you're producing files to be distributed from a website. However, the FLV files produced by this format require a stand-alone player to play back from a hard drive outside of the browser environment, which many viewers don't have. Accordingly, the format is not appropriate for creating files to view on other computers outside the browser environment, whether by email, file transfer protocol (FTP), or via a Universal Serial Bus (USB) drive.

- **MPEG:** MPEG is a very widely supported playback format, though it is used almost exclusively for desktop or disc-based playback rather than for streaming. Use MPEG to create files for inserting into Blu-ray or DVD projects produced in other programs. For most casual hard drive-based playback, however, either QuickTime or Windows Media offer better quality at lower data rates, making them better options for files shared via email or FTP.

- **DV AVI:** This is the format used by DV camcorders. DV AVI is an excellent archival format for standard-definition (SD) productions and is a good choice for producing files to be further edited in other programs. However, DV AVI files are too large for casually distributing via email or FTP.

- **Windows Media:** Windows Media files—whether distributed via a website, email, or FTP—can be played by virtually all Windows computers via the Windows Media Player. Quality is good at low bitrates, making Windows Media a good choice for producing files to be distributed via email to other Windows users. However, Macintosh compatibility may be a problem because Microsoft hasn't released a Windows Media Player for OS X, forcing users to download a third-party solution from Flip4Mac. When producing files for viewing on Macintosh computers, use the QuickTime format.

- **QuickTime:** QuickTime is the best choice for files intended for viewing on both Macintosh and Windows computers, whether distributed via the web, email, or other technique. All presets use the H.264 codec, which offers very good quality but can take a long time to render.

When producing a file for uploading to a website like Yahoo Video, Facebook, or Blip.tv, check the required file specifications published by each site before producing your file.

6 To start exporting your movie, click Save.

Adobe Premiere Elements begins rendering the video and displays a progress bar in Share view and an estimated time to complete each phase of the rendering process. Click Cancel at any time to stop the exporting process. Otherwise, you'll see a Save Complete! message in Share view when the rendering is complete.

7 Don't click either Click Save As Quick Share or Done, because you'll be saving this Windows Media output to a Quick Share preset in the next exercise.

⬤ **Note:** Most Adobe Premiere Elements standard definition (SD) presets are for 4:3 projects. When producing a 16:9 project, you'll have to change the preset to a 16:9 output resolution. Do this by clicking the Advanced button shown in the preceding screen to open the Export Settings dialog. Click the Video tab to reveal those settings, and then adjust the Frame Width [pixels] and Frame Height [pixels] text boxes to a 16:9 output resolution. For your reference, the most common 16:9 SD output resolutions are 640x360, 480x270, and 320x180. Click OK to close the Export Settings dialog. You'll be prompted to save the preset, and then you'll return to the Share screen.

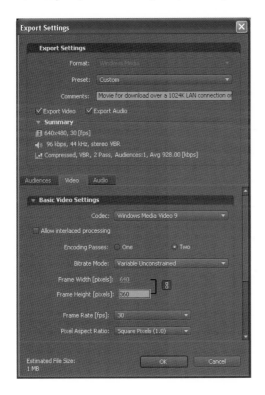

Adding a Quick Share Preset

Quick Share presets are located in an easily accessible box in the Share interface. If you'll be using a preset frequently, you should save that preset as a Quick Share preset. Here's the procedure.

1   After sharing your project using the preset that you want to convert to a Quick Share preset, click Save As Quick Share.

Adobe Premiere Elements opens the Save As Quick Share dialog.

2   Type a name and description, and click Save.

3   Adobe Premiere Elements saves the output preset in the Quick Share dialog. To share using this preset in the future, click the Share tab in the Tasks panel, then the desired Quick Share preset, and then the Share button. Adobe Premiere Elements will share the project using the selected Quick Share option.

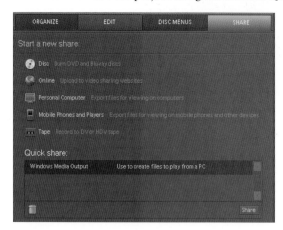

Exporting to Mobile Phones and Players

Adobe Premiere Elements also includes an option for producing files for mobile phones and players such as the Apple iPod or iPhone, the Creative Zen, and the Microsoft Zune. Note that most of these devices have very specific and inflexible file and format requirements, so you shouldn't change any parameters in the Export Settings window, since you may produce a file that's unplayable on the target device.

In this lesson, you'll learn how to create a file for the iPod; if producing for a different device, just choose that device and preset in the appropriate steps.

1   In Share view, click the Mobile Phones and Players button (▣).

2   In the list at the top of Share view choose Apple iPod and iPhone.

3   In the Presets list box, choose iPod and iPhone – High Quality to produce a high-quality file compatible with iPods, iPhones, the iPod touch, and similar, newer portable media players, keeping in mind that this file won't play on some older portable players. Choose iPod and iPhone – Medium Quality for a lower-quality file that should be playable on all iPods and iPhones, past and present, as well as many other portable media players. For the purposes of this exercise, choose iPod and iPhone – High Quality.

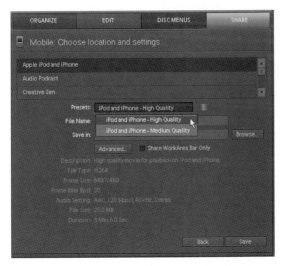

4   Next to File Name, enter *Lesson12_iPod*, and then click Browse to select your Lesson12 folder as the Save in folder.

5   If desired, select the Share WorkArea Bar Only check box.

6 To start exporting your movie, click Save.

Adobe Premiere Elements starts rendering the video and displays a progress bar in Share view and an estimated time to complete each phase of the rendering process. Click Cancel at any time to stop the exporting process. Otherwise, you will see a Save Complete! message in Share view when the rendering is complete.

7 Click Save As Quick Share to save the preset, or click Done to return to the Share workspace.

After producing the file, transfer it to your device in the appropriate manner. For example, use iTunes to upload the file to your iPod or iPhone.

Preparing to Export to Tape

The final Share option is Tape. If you have access to a DV camera, you may want to use it for this exercise. We'll proceed as if a DV camera is connected to your system, but if not, follow along with the exercise anyway.

To begin, connect your DV camera to your personal computer, turn it on, and then open Adobe Premiere Elements. In most cases, if Adobe Premiere Elements is already open, it will recognize a DV camera when it is attached and turned on; however, we've found this happens more reliably if the DV camera is connected first and turned on prior to launching Adobe Premiere Elements.

When writing videos to tape, it's good practice to add some excess video to the start of the project to prevent your recording device from accidentally cutting off the first few seconds of your project. In this regard, Adobe Premiere Elements lets you create either a 5-second black video file or a universal counting leader, which looks like the countdown video that preceded older movies you may have viewed in the theater. In this exercise, you'll add a universal counting leader to your project before writing it to tape.

1 Connect your DV camera to your computer. For help, refer to your owner's manual or the diagram located in the section "Connecting Your Device" in Lesson 3.

2 Turn on your DV device and switch it to the VTR (or VCR) mode. If a Digital Video Device dialog appears, click the Cancel button to close it.

3 Start Adobe Premiere Elements and open the project file Lesson12_Start.prel in the Lesson12 folder. If a dialog appears asking for the location of rendered files, click the Skip Previews button.

4 In the Timeline of the My Project panel, press Home to move the current-time indicator to the start of the project.

5 In the upper-right corner of Project view, click the New Item button ( ), and then choose Universal Counting Leader from the menu that appears.

6 Adobe Premiere Elements opens the Universal Counting Leader Setup dialog. Leave all items at their default settings, and click OK to close the dialog.

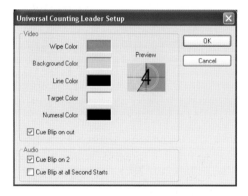

A new item called Universal Counting Leader appears in your Media panel, and Adobe Premiere Elements adds it to your Timeline after the first scene.

7 In the Timeline, drag the newly added Universal Counting Leader to the beginning of the movie, waiting for about two seconds for the Lesson12_Movie. wmv clip to shift to the right before releasing the pointer. Adobe Premiere Elements moves the Universal Counting Leader to the beginning of the movie and shifts the Lesson12_Movie file to the right.

(See illustration on next page.)

8 Choose File > Save As. Rename this file *Lesson12_DV.prel*.

Exporting to Tape

Let's write the project to DV tape. If you connected an analog device such as a VCR to your DV camcorder, you can follow these steps as well to dub the video through your DV camcorder to the VCR.

1 Make sure your DV camcorder is turned on and in VTR (or VCR or Play) mode, and that you have enough blank tape to record your project.

When writing video to tape, Adobe Premiere Elements records only the video within the work area, not the entire project. So before starting, make sure that the work area includes the entire project.

2 In the Timeline of the My Project panel, press the Backslash key (\) on your keyboard to display the entire project.

3 Double-click the work area bar beneath the time ruler to make sure it extends to the end of the project.

Work area bar   Work area end

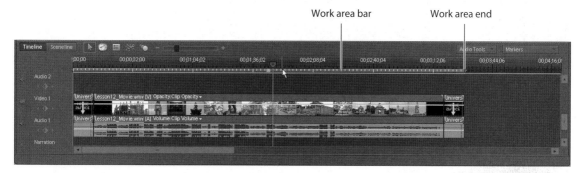

4 Select the Share tab in the Tasks panel, and then click the Tape button () at the bottom of Share view.

If your recording device is properly connected to your computer, the Export to Tape dialog opens.

5 If you're recording to a DV device, make sure the Activate Recording Device check box under Device Control is selected. This ensures that Adobe Premiere Elements can communicate with the device.

6 If you are using a DV device, click the Record button. After rendering project components as necessary, your DV device will begin to record as Adobe Premiere Elements begins to play the Timeline from the beginning. If you are recording with an analog device, you must manually press the Record button on your device when Adobe Premiere Elements starts playing the Timeline.

● **Note:** If you're recording to a DV device and Device Control is unavailable, click Cancel, choose Edit > Preferences > Device Control, make sure that your device is set up properly in the Device Control options, and then try recording to tape again.

7   When the end of the project has been reached, the recording will stop automatically if you are using a DV device. If you're recording to an analog device, you must manually press its Stop button to stop recording.

8   Click the Cancel button to close the Export to Tape dialog.

Export to Tape Options

- **Activate Recording Device:** This option lets Adobe Premiere Elements control your DV device.

- **Assemble at timecode:** This option indicates the place on your DV tape that you want the recording to begin, if you have a tape that already has timecode recorded, or striped, on it. You stripe a tape by first recording only black video before you record your footage. You usually record black video by recording with the lens cap on. If your tape is not striped, leave this option deselected to have recording begin at the location where you have cued the tape.

- **Delay movie start by *n* frames:** Here you specify the number of frames that you want to delay the start of the movie so that you can synchronize it with the DV device recording start time. Some devices need a delay between the time they receive the Record command and the time the movie starts playing from the computer. Experiment with this setting if you are experiencing delays between the time you enable record and the time your DV device begins recording.

- **Preroll by *n* frames:** The number you enter here specifies the number of frames that you want Adobe Premiere Elements to back up on the recording deck before the specified timecode. Specify enough frames for the deck to reach a constant tape speed. For many decks, 5 seconds or 150 frames is sufficient.

- **Abort after *n* dropped frames:** Here you type the maximum number of dropped frames you want to allow before Adobe Premiere Elements aborts the recording. If you choose this option, you generally want to type a very low number because dropped frames will cause jerky playback, and are indicative of a hard disk or transfer problem.

- **Report dropped frames:** This specifies that Adobe Premiere Elements displays the number of dropped frames.

—From Adobe Premiere Elements Help

Exporting a Frame of Video as a Still Image

Occasionally, you may want to grab frames from your video footage to email to friends and family, include in a slide show, or use for other purposes. In this exercise, you'll learn to export and save a frame from the project. To perform this exercise, reload Lesson12_Start.prel as detailed in the Getting Started section near the start of this chapter.

1 In the Timeline, drag the current-time indicator to timecode 00;00;0;32, or click the current timecode box on the lower left of the Monitor panel, type in *3200*, and press Enter.

2 Click the Freeze Frame button () in the lower-right corner of the Monitor panel. You might have to enlarge the Monitor panel to see the Freeze Frame button. Adobe Premiere Elements opens the Freeze Frame dialog.

3 In the Freeze Frame dialog, click Export to create a separate still image, or Insert in Movie to insert the frame into the movie. You can also click the checkbox to Edit the captured frame in Adobe Photoshop Elements if you choose the Import in Movie option.

4 In the Export Frame dialog, locate the Lesson12 folder and name your file *Big Ben*. Click Save to save the still image onto your hard drive. Then click Cancel to close the Freeze Frame dialog.

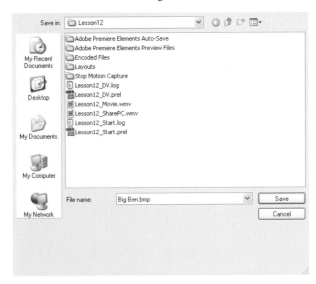

▶ **Tip:** The snapshot export function is very quick and easy but outputs only BMP files at the resolution of your current project (720x480 in this case). For more control over export size and formats, click Share, then Personal Computer, and choose Image, which exposes multiple presets that you can customize by clicking the Advanced button.

▶ **Tip:** You can also export Audio only from the Personal Computer output group.

Review Questions

1 What's the best format to use for creating files to view on Windows computers or to share with other viewers with Windows computers?

2 Why shouldn't you change any encoding parameters for files produced for iPods or other devices?

3 Why should you add a universal counting leader to the beginning of a file before writing it to DV or analog tape?

4 What's the easiest way to write a project to an analog tape format such as VHS?

5 What's the easiest way to upload your movie to a website such as YouTube or Photoshop.com?

Review Answers

1 Windows Media is the best format for Windows because it combines small file size with high quality. Though virtually all computers can play MPEG-1 or MPEG-2 files, the files are usually too large for easy transport. QuickTime files may pose a problem because not all Windows computers support QuickTime, and Adobe Flash Video files with an FLV extension require a stand-alone player, which not all computers have installed.

2 Devices have very specific playback requirements, and if you change a file parameter and deviate from these requirements, the file may not load or play on the target device.

3 You should add a Universal Counting Leader or simply a black video file to the start of a project before writing it to tape to prevent the recording device from cutting off the initial frames of the video file.

4 Connect a VHS recorder to your DV camcorder via composite or S-Video connectors plus audio while writing your project to DV tape. Most DV camcorders will display the recorded signal out the analog ports while recording, which you can record on the VHS deck by clicking the Record button on the deck.

5 Switch to Share view, and then click the Online button. Choose YouTube or My Website, and then follow the instructions in Share view to render and upload your movie.

13 WORKING WITH ADOBE PHOTOSHOP ELEMENTS

Adobe Photoshop Elements and Adobe Premiere Elements are designed to work together and let you seamlessly combine digital photography and video editing. You can spice up your video projects with title images or customized menu templates created in Adobe Photoshop Elements, or build slide show presentations in Adobe Photoshop Elements, and then use parts of them in Adobe Premiere Elements for further editing.

To work on the following exercises, you must have Photoshop Elements installed on your system. In this lesson, you will learn several techniques for using Photoshop Elements together with Adobe Premiere Elements. Specifically, you will learn how to do the following:

- Use the Send To command in Adobe Photoshop Elements to create a slide show in Adobe Premiere Elements

- Access Albums created in Adobe Photoshop Elements in Adobe Premiere Elements

- Paste images into Adobe Premiere Elements

- Create a Photoshop file optimized for video

- Edit a Photoshop image from within Adobe Premiere Elements

 This lesson will take approximately 1.5 hours.

A cool text title created in Adobe Photoshop Elements
for use in Adobe Premiere Elements.

Viewing the Completed Movie Before You Start

To see what you'll be creating, let's take a look at the completed movie.

1   Before you begin, make sure that you have correctly copied the Lesson13 folder from the DVD in the back of this book onto your computer's hard drive. See "Copying the Classroom in a Book files" in the Getting Started section of this book.

2   Navigate to the Lesson13 folder, and double-click Lesson13_Movie.wmv to play the movie in your default application for watching Windows Media Video files.

Getting Started

You'll now open Adobe Photoshop Elements 8 and import the files needed for the Lesson13 project.

1   Launch Photoshop Elements.

2   In the Welcome screen, click the Organize button to open the Photoshop Elements Organizer.

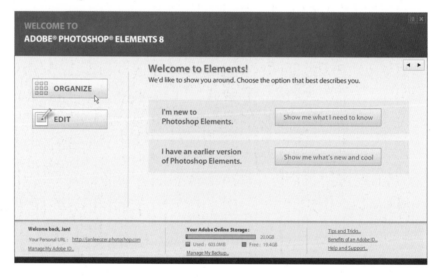

3   If you've previously used Photoshop Elements, your Organizer may be
    displaying the photos in your current catalog. If this is the first time you've
    launched Photoshop Elements, you may receive a message asking if you would
    like to designate a location to look for your image files. Click No to work with
    an empty Organizer panel.

4   Choose File > Get Photos and Videos > From Files and Folders. Navigate to your
    Lesson13 folder and select—but do not open—the images subfolder. Then click
    Get Media. Photoshop Elements will import the photos.

5   If a message appears telling you that only the newly imported files will appear,
    click OK. In the Organizer, you should see nine thumbnail images from the walk
    through London. Thumbnail images are small versions of the full-size photos.
    You will be working with the full-size photos later in this lesson.

6   Under Albums in the Tagging window, click the Create new album or album
    group button (![+]), and choose New Album. Adobe Premiere Elements opens
    the Album Details dialog.

7 In the Photoshop Elements menu, choose Edit > Select All to select the nine new images. Then click on any one image, drag all the images into the Items window on the right, and release the pointer.

8 In the Album Name field in the Album Details dialog, type *London Pix*.

9 On the lower left of the Album Details dialog, click Done to save the Album.

As you may recall from Lesson 4, Adobe Premiere Elements and Adobe Photoshop Elements use the same Organizer, which Adobe Premiere Elements can access from the Media view in the Edit workspace. You'll review how to access the newly created London Pix album from Adobe Premiere Elements in a later exercise.

Using the Send To Command in Adobe Photoshop Elements

You learned back in Lesson 1 that you can create a project in Adobe Premiere Elements after selecting video files in the Organizer. Similarly, you can create an Adobe Premiere Elements project from images using the same technique. Let's review that quickly in this exercise.

Briefly, if you have a project open in Adobe Premiere Elements when you use this technique, the Organizer will add the selected files to the current project at the end of the current Sceneline or Timeline. If no project is open, the Organizer will create a new project, which is the workflow you will follow in this exercise. Accordingly, if you have a project open in Adobe Premiere Elements, please close it (after saving if necessary) before starting this exercise.

To sort images in the Organizer, Photoshop Elements uses the date and time information embedded in the image file by the digital camera. In the Organizer menu, choosing to show the oldest files first by selecting Date (Oldest First) enables you to create a slide show in chronological order when transferring the photos to Adobe Premiere Elements.

1 Right-click the first image (Victoria Memorial.jpg) and choose Show Properties. Properties view opens to Properties-General view, which displays the name of the image and also details the file size, the date the photo was taken, and its location on your hard drive. The date the picture was taken is also displayed below the image thumbnail in the Photo Browser if you select the Details check box on the upper right of the Photo Browser. To show filenames in the Photo Browser, choose View > Show File Names.

2 Press and hold the Ctrl key on your keyboard, and then in the Photo Browser click five images—Palace Guard.jpg, Treelined lane.jpg, Wellington Arch.jpg, Albert Memorial.jpg, and Albert Hall.jpg—to select them. A blue outline appears around the thumbnail to indicate a selected image. In the next step, Photoshop Elements will process only the selected images.

● **Note:** Before performing the next step, make sure you do not have a project open in Adobe Premiere Elements. Otherwise, the images will be placed in the open file.

3 In the Fix Panel, click the downward triangle on the top right of the Fix tab, and choose Edit Videos. A dialog may appear informing you that the files will be inserted at the end of your Timeline and that the Adobe Premiere Elements defaults will be used. Click OK. If Adobe Premiere Elements is not already open, it will launch automatically.

4 In the Adobe Premiere Elements New Project dialog, type *Lesson13_Start* in the name field. Click the Browse button. In the Browse For Folder dialog, navigate to the Lesson13 folder located on your hard drive and select it. Click OK to close the Browse For Folder dialog.

5 If necessary, click the Change Settings dialog and change the preset to NTSC-DV-Standard 48kHz. Click OK to close the Setup dialog, and then click OK to close the New Project dialog.

An Adobe Premiere Elements project is created, and the images you selected in Photoshop Elements are now visible in the Organize view of the Tasks panel. They have also been added to Project view and placed in the Sceneline (or Timeline) of the My Project panel. The first image is displayed in the Monitor panel. In the Sceneline of the My Project panel you'll see all images as individual scenes.

6   With all scenes selected in the Sceneline, choose Clip > Group to place the entire group onto one target that can be moved as a single clip. Then choose Clip > Ungroup to treat each still image as its own scene in the Sceneline.

7   Press the spacebar to play your project. Adobe Premiere Elements uses the default duration of five seconds for each still image and applies a cross-dissolve as the default transition between each clip.

● **Note:** Although you might assume that the total length of the slide show is equal to the number of images multiplied by the default duration for still images, it's actually less than that. This is because Adobe Premiere Elements inserts the transition effect between the images by overlapping the clips by the default length of the transition effect. Note that you can change the default still image duration and transition duration in the Adobe Premiere Elements Preferences panel. See the section in Lesson 2 titled "Working with Project Preferences," for more details.

8   Return to the Organizer by clicking the Elements Organizer button at the bottom of your screen in the Windows taskbar (if it's visible) or by holding down the Alt key and pressing Tab until you see the icon for the Elements Organizer. Release the Alt key and the Elements Organizer opens.

Note: Because you're sending only a single image from Photoshop Elements to Adobe Premiere Elements, no transition has been placed on the image. In this case, if you wanted to add a transition, you would have to do so manually, but do not add one at this time. See Lesson 7 for more information about adding transitions.

9 Click to select only one image, the one named Victoria Memorial.jpg, and then choose Edit > Edit with Premiere Elements. Click OK to close the Edit with Premiere Elements dialog if it appears. Your open application should switch to Adobe Premiere Elements, and the image will be placed at the end of your Sceneline or Timeline.

10 Choose File > Save As and save this project file into your Lesson13 folder as *Lesson13_Work*.

Moving Images Manually into Adobe Premiere Elements

Using the Send To Premiere Elements command in Photoshop Elements will not only add the images to Project view, but also place them in the Sceneline. At times you may prefer to add only the images to Project view so that you can manually place them in the My Project panel. To do this, you can copy images from the Organizer in Photoshop Elements and paste them into Adobe Premiere Elements, or open an Album created in Photoshop Elements in Adobe Premiere Elements. In this lesson, you will learn both these methods to transfer images from Photoshop Elements to Adobe Premiere Elements.

Using Copy and Paste to Add Images

The fastest way to move one or two images from the Organizer to Adobe Premiere Elements is to use the Copy and Paste commands. Remember that you can press the Shift key to select sequential images to copy or press the Ctrl key to select random images.

1 Make sure the Organizer is your active application.

2 Press the Ctrl key, and then click to select Palace longshot.jpg and Wellington Arch - traffic.jpg. Then choose Edit > Copy. Alternatively, you could use the keyboard shortcut Ctrl+C or right-click the image thumbnail and choose Edit > Copy.

3 Switch to Adobe Premiere Elements by clicking the Adobe Premiere Elements button at the bottom of your screen in the Windows taskbar or by holding down the Alt key and pressing Tab until you see the icon for Adobe Premiere Elements. Release the Alt key and Adobe Premiere Elements opens.

4 Select Project in the Organize tab of the Tasks panel to open Project view.

5 Choose Edit > Paste to add the images to Project view. You can also use the keyboard shortcut Ctrl+V or right-click inside Project view and select Paste. The files appear at the bottom of Project view.

After you've pasted the images into Project view, you can use them just like any image that you imported into Adobe Premiere Elements.

Loading an Album from Adobe Photoshop Elements

Copying and pasting images works well for small numbers of images, but sometimes you'll want to access the entire album. No problem, since as mentioned, Adobe Premiere Elements can open albums created in Photoshop Elements. Once open, you access the images just like content that you imported directly into Adobe Premiere Elements. You learned how to create and open albums back in Lesson 4; here's a brief refresher course.

1 In Adobe Premiere Elements, click the Organize tab to open the Organizer workspace in the Media view.

2 In the Filter by: list box, scroll down and select the desired album—in this case, the London Pix album that you created earlier in the chapter.

Adobe Premiere Elements displays the Album's contents in Organizer view.

From the Organizer you can drop assets directly onto the Sceneline or the Monitor panel to add them to your project. Assets added from the Organizer will also be automatically added to Project view and tagged with a project-specific keyword tag. For more information on catalogs, keyword tags, and the Organizer view, see "Tagging in the Organizer" section in Lesson 4, "Organizing Your Content."

Creating a New Adobe Photoshop File Optimized for Video

The first part of this lesson focused on importing image files from Adobe Photoshop Elements into Adobe Premiere Elements. In this exercise, you'll create a new still image in Adobe Premiere Elements, modify it in Photoshop Elements, and then use it in your Adobe Premiere Elements project.

One of the more common workflows between the two programs is to create a project title in Adobe Premiere Elements, edit it in Adobe Photoshop Elements, and then deploy the title in Adobe Premiere Elements. That's what you'll do in this and the following exercise.

1 Make sure you're in Adobe Premiere Elements. Choose File > New > Photoshop File. In the Save Photoshop File As dialog, navigate to your Lesson13 folder and name the file *Title.psd*. Select the Add to Project (Merged Layers) check box, and then click Save. This will create a new Photoshop file in your Lesson13 folder and add a blank placeholder image in Project view.

● **Note:** If the file opens in an application other than Photoshop Elements, see the sidebar "Microsoft Windows File Associations" at the end of this chapter. You might have to open the file manually from within Photoshop Elements.

2 Your application will automatically switch to Photoshop Elements. Click No if you see a dialog notifying you that the file you are about to see was meant to be viewed on a TV screen, and then click OK if you see another dialog about viewing the new image on a video monitor. The file Title.psd opens in the Photoshop Elements Editor.

Photoshop Elements has multiple components. The Organizer, which you used in the beginning of this lesson, enables you to sort and categorize your digital media files. The Editor, which you'll use now, enables you to enhance and modify your digital images using a series of image-editing tools.

3 In the Editor, make sure EDIT Full mode is selected on the extreme upper-right side of the interface. If necessary, click the EDIT button and choose EDIT Full.

The Title image was automatically formatted for your digital video project using the dimensions 720 pixels wide by 480 pixels high. The checkerboard that you see indicates that the image is on a transparent background.

Now you'll add the Big Ben image that you captured in the last chapter as a background for this title, and then customize the image and add some text.

4 In Adobe Photoshop Elements, choose File > Open. The Open dialog opens. Navigate to the Chapter13 folder on your hard drive, choose Big Ben.bmp, and click Open to load the image into Adobe Photoshop Elements.

5 In the Adobe Photoshop Elements menu, choose Select > All to select the image, and then choose Edit > Copy to copy the image to the clipboard.

6 Click Title.psd to make it active and choose Edit > Paste to paste the copied Big Ben image into Title.psd. If you see an error message about the background of the image being locked, click OK to enable the paste.

7 You need to expand the size of the image Title.psd within the Adobe Photoshop Elements interface. To do this, drag the bottom right edge of the Title.psd image to expand the image palette so you can see the bounding box of the pasted image, which is a dotted line with boxes at each edge and in the middle of each side.

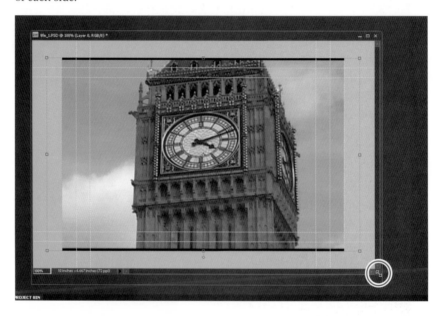

8 You'll need to adjust the size of the pasted image to fit Title.psd, which you accomplish by clicking and dragging any of the eight small squares on the edges and sides of the bounding box. Drag the top and bottom lines of the bounding box *outward* from the center to eliminate the black lines on the top and bottom of the image, and drag the right and left lines *inward* as far as possible without revealing the black bars on the sides. Then click the Free Transform check mark on the lower right to set the adjustment.

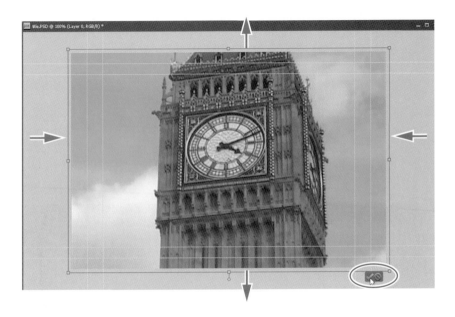

9   On the upper-right side of the Adobe Photoshop Elements interface, in the
    EFFECTS tab, click the second icon from the right (), click the drop-down
    list, and then choose the Vintage Photo effect.

10 Drag the Vintage Photo effect onto Title.psd and release. Adobe Photoshop
    Elements applies the effect to the image.

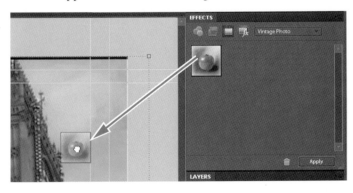

11 Drag the edges of the bounding box in the Title.psd image outward to exclude the blue edges from each side. Then click the Free Transform check mark on the lower right to set the adjustment.

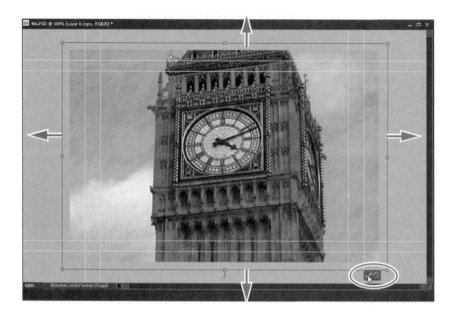

12 Let's add a text title to Title.psd. Click the Horizontal Type Text (T) tool in the Toolbox.

13 In the Text tool options bar, choose the Calligraph421 BT font, Roman style at 55 pts, center text alignment, and set the font color to black.

A. Font **B.** Style **C.** Font Size **D.** Alignment **E.** Color **F.** Create Warped Text.

14 Click Big Ben near the "VI" on the clock face and type *My Walk* (carriage return) *Through London.*

15 Click the Move tool ( ) in the Toolbox to return to the selection arrow. Now you need to make the text more legible. To do this, right-click the text box and choose Edit Layer Style.

16 Let's make several adjustments in the Style Settings dialog:

- Add inner and outer glows by clicking the Glow check box, then clicking the Inner and Outer check boxes, and then conforming their settings to the figure.

- Add a Stroke by clicking the Stroke check box and otherwise make sure that your settings match those in the figure.

- Click OK to close the dialog.

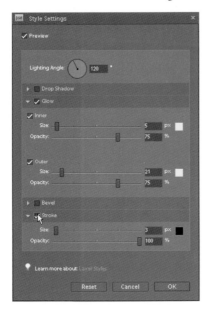

17 Much better. Now let's warp the text around Big Ben. Double-click the text box to select all text, and then click the Create Warped Text icon on the text tools option bar.

18 In the Warp Text dialog, click the Style drop-down list and choose Arc.

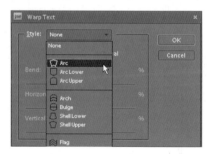

19 In the Warp Text dialog, click the Bend text box and type -50. Then click OK to close the dialog.

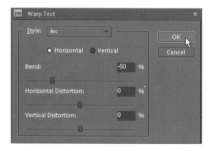

20 Choose File > Save. The Save As dialog should show the Lesson13 folder. If not, navigate there now. Make sure that the check box Save in Version Set with Original is deselected. The filename should default to Title.psd. Click Save.

21 When the Alert dialog appears notifying you that the file already exists, click OK. If an Adobe Photoshop Elements Format Options dialog appears, click OK to close it using the default settings. Then choose File > Close.

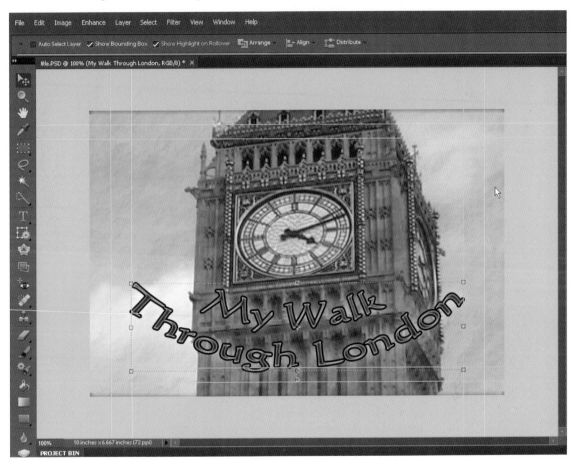

22 Switch to Adobe Premiere Elements by clicking the Adobe Premiere Elements button at the bottom of your screen in the Windows taskbar or by holding down the Alt key and pressing Tab until you see the icon for Adobe Premiere Elements. Release the Alt key and Adobe Premiere Elements opens. The Title. psd file has automatically been updated in Project view.

23 In the Timeline, drag Title.psd to the beginning of the movie, waiting for about two seconds for the other images to shift to the right. Then release the pointer. If Adobe Premiere Elements opens the SmartFix dialog, click No. Adobe Premiere Elements will insert Title.psd at the start of the movie and shift all other content to the right.

24 Save your work. Your title should look like the one shown in the Monitor panel in the next figure.

Editing an Adobe Photoshop Image in Adobe Premiere Elements

You can edit an Adobe Photoshop Elements image (or any image for that matter) while you're working in Adobe Premiere Elements, using the Edit in Photoshop Elements command. Changes you make to the image will be updated automatically, even if the clip is already placed in your Sceneline or Timeline. Let's add a bit of color to the currently drab title.

► **Tip:** When in the Timeline, pressing the equals sign (=) on your keyboard is a quick way to zoom in to better view the clips.

1 Right-click the Title.psd clip in the Timeline and choose Edit in Adobe Photoshop Elements. The Title.psd file opens in Adobe Photoshop Elements.

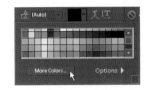

2 Double-click the My Walk Through London text box to make it active.

● **Note:** If Photoshop Elements is closed, it will automatically launch and open the file.

3 In the tool options bar, click the color swatch to open the Select Color dialog.

4 In the Select Color dialog, enter the values R: *209*, G: *39*, and B: *38* to set the color, and then click OK.

5 Click the Move tool (![move tool]) in the Toolbox to return to the selection arrow. Then right-click the text box and choose Edit Layer Style.

6   In the Style Settings dialog, click the Inner Glow check box to deselect that style setting. Click OK to close the dialog.

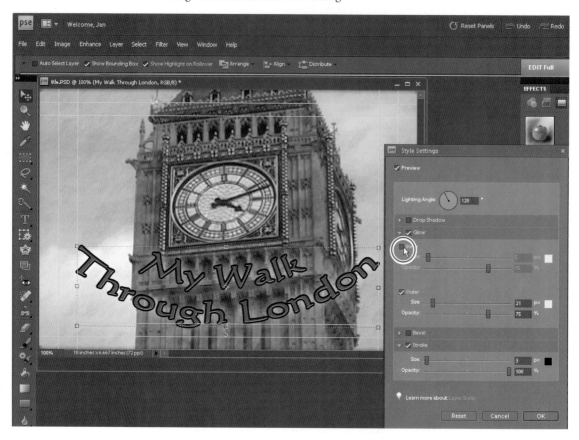

7   Choose File > Save, overwriting the Title.psd file in the Lesson13 folder. Close the file, and then switch to Adobe Premiere Elements.

The changes made to the Title.psd file in Adobe Photoshop Elements have automatically been updated in the Adobe Premiere Elements project. This is very useful because it eliminates the need to reimport an image file every time a change is made.

Microsoft Windows
File Associations

The Edit Original command can be very useful when there are changes to be made to an image. However, you need to be aware of a few possible pitfalls. When you use the Edit Original command on an image, Windows XP opens the file in the application that is associated with the filename extension. For example, using the Edit Original command on the .jpg files used in this lesson may very well open them on your machine in another program such as a web browser. You can force Windows XP to use Adobe Photoshop Elements as the associated application for your image files using the following steps. Be aware that you will need to perform these steps each time for different file types, .jpg, .gif, .tiff, etc. Additionally, if you happen to have both Adobe Photoshop and Adobe Photoshop Elements on the same machine, you will need to choose one to be the default application for opening image files.

To change file associations in Windows XP, do the following:

1   Choose Start > My Computer.

2   Double-click a drive or folder.

3   Right-click the selected image file and choose Open With > Choose Program.

4   In the Open With dialog, select Adobe Photoshop Elements (Editor) if it's in the list of Recommended Programs. If it's not in the list, click Browse and locate the application on your hard drive.

5   In the Open With dialog, make sure the check box Always Use the Selected Program to Open this Kind of File is selected.

The procedure is the same in Microsoft Windows Vista with two exceptions: In step 1, choose Start > Computer; in step 4, in the Open With dialog, if Adobe Premiere Elements does not appear in the list of Recommended Programs, select Choose Default Program at the bottom of the dialog and browse for the application on your hard drive.

For more information, see the Help documentation that came with your copy of Microsoft Windows.

8 Click the top of the Timeline to select it, and then press the Home key to place the current-time indicator at the beginning of the Timeline. Press the spacebar to play your project. When you're finished reviewing, save your work.

Congratulations! You've finished the lesson on working with Adobe Photoshop Elements. You've discovered how to get photos from the Organizer and how to enhance them using the Editor. You've also learned how to create a title in Adobe Photoshop Elements for use in Adobe Premiere Elements.

This is the last lesson in this book. We hope that you have gained confidence in using Adobe Premiere Elements 8, developed some new skills, and increased your knowledge of the product and the many creative things you can accomplish with it.

But this book is just the beginning. You can learn more by studying the Adobe Premiere Elements 8 Help system that is built into the application. Simply choose Help > Adobe Premiere Elements Help and browse or use the search functionality to find what you need. Also, don't forget to look for tutorials, tips, and expert advice on the Adobe Systems website at www.adobe.com.

Review Questions

1   Where can you find the command to place images from Adobe Photoshop Elements into Adobe Premiere Elements? Where are the images placed after they are sent to Adobe Premiere Elements?

2   What are additional ways to transfer images from Adobe Photoshop Elements to Adobe Premiere Elements?

3   How do you create an Adobe Photoshop file in Adobe Premiere Elements? What are the advantages of doing so?

Review Answers

1   In the Adobe Photoshop Elements Organizer, choose File > Send to Premiere Elements. All files selected in the Photo Browser will be sent to Adobe Premiere Elements and added at the end of your Timeline. You can select individual images in the Adobe Photoshop Elements Photo Browser by Ctrl-clicking them.

2   You can transfer images from Photoshop Elements to Adobe Premiere Elements by selecting them in Photoshop Elements, choosing Edit > Copy, switching to Adobe Premiere Elements, and then choosing Edit > Paste. From the Organizer view in Adobe Premiere Elements, you can open a Photoshop Elements album without having to open Adobe Photoshop Elements.

3   The command File > New > Photoshop File will create a blank Adobe Photoshop file that matches the dimensions and aspect ratio of the current project. This will enable you to use the various image-editing tools in Photoshop Elements to modify or create images for use in your video project

INDEX

effects. *See also specific effects*
  adjusting speed of clip, 130–131
  animating with keyframes,
    137–140
  applying to multiple clips, 129
  audio, 213
  choosing and applying, 126–127
  compositing clips with
    Videomerge, 143–144
  copying to other clips, 140–141
  deleting, 127
  effect masking, 147–148
  exploring, 148
  fade-out using keyframes,
    134–136
  fixed, 119, 122–125
  image pan, 132–134
  Motion Track, 145–147
  Picture-in-Picture overlay,
    141–143
  reframing clip with Motion
    controls, 123–125
  rendering in background, 90–91,
    125–126
  replaced when theme applied,
    219
  Reverse Speed, 131
  Shadow/Highlight filter, 127–129
  sharpening, 126–127
  Stabilize filter, 129–130
  Time Stretch, 130–131, 144–145
  toggling on/off, 121
  types of, 117–119
  using for titles, 182–184
error during capture, 50
Export to Tape dialog, 277, 278
exporting movies. *See also* uploading
    movies
  to mobile phones and players,
    273–274, 281
  single frames, 93
  to tape, 276–278, 281
  uploading to websites, 269, 271,
    281
eye icon, 121

F

fade-in/-out
  titles using, 182–184
  transitions creating, 163–164
  using keyframes, 134–136
  volume, 207–209
files
  Blu-ray compression and
    resolution options, 257

changing associations in
    Windows, 303
  compatible movie formats, 270,
    281
  finding, 61–63
  opening, 64–66
  optimizing for video, 293–300
  Project view of, 79–80
  sending from Photoshop
    Elements to Premiere
    Elements, 305
  synchronizing video on
    Photoshop.com, 78
  uploading to Photoshop.com.,
    75–78
Fix panel, 11–13
fixed effects
  applying and resetting, 122–123
  reframing clip with Motion
    controls, 123–125
  working with, 119, 123
Flash Memory camcorders presets,
    29
Flash preset, 264
FLV (Adobe Flash Video) format, 270
font size of text, 177–178
frames. *See also* keyframes
  exporting single, 93
  moving to specific, 92
  scene markers on, 258
  sharing single movie, 279–280
  timecode and, 92
  trimming, 105–106
Freeze Frame dialog, 279–280

G

gain controls to adjust audio, 203–
    205, 206, 207
GPU (Graphics Processing Unit)
    transition effects, 164

H

hard disk
  importing video content from, 54
  space required for DV editing, 41
hard disk camcorder presets, 29
HDV presets, 29
History panel, 20
Horizontal Type tool, 174

I

IEEE 1394 connector, 40, 42
IEEE 1394 port, 41
Image Control effects, 119, 122–123
image pan, 132–134

images
  adding to menu, 246–249
  adding to titles, 181–182
  changing menu thumbnail,
    238–241
  combining with video, 111–112
  editing Photoshop image in
    Premiere Elements, 301–
    302, 304
  file associations for, 303
  sending from Photoshop
    Elements to Premiere
    Elements, 287–290, 305
importing
  audio and video clips, 60–61
  content from hard disk, 54
  images with Photoshop's Send
    To Premiere Elements
    command, 287–290, 305
  Photoshop Elements file into
    Premiere Elements, 299–300
  Photoshop images by copying/
    pasting, 290–291
  video with Media Downloader,
    39–40, 51–54
In/Out points, 98, 104–105
Info panel, 19
InstantMovie
  about, 218
  breaking apart to edit, 75, 223
  creating, 72–75, 223
  Movie themes vs., 219, 223
Interest Level threshold (Smart
    Trim), 110, 111
iPod and iPhone movies, 273–274,
    281

J

J-cuts, 211

K

kerning text, 178–179
keyframes
  about, 131–132
  animating effects with, 137–140
  audio adjustments using, 207–
    209, 214
  fade-out using, 134–136
  image pan using, 132–134
  working with, 136–137
keyword tags
  about, 64, 70
  adding, 67–69

properties
    menu button text, 250–251, 258
    preset audio effect, 214
    viewing transition, 156–158
Properties view
    about, 19
    adjusting fixed effects in, 119, 123
    current-time indicator in, 134
    customizing menus in, 245–246
Push transition, 156–158

Q

Quality Level threshold (Smart
    Trim), 109, 110–111
Quick Share preset
    creating, 262, 272
    saving workflow as, 266, 268
QuickTime, 270

R

recording narration, 201
reframing clip with Motion controls,
    123–125
replacing transitions, 160–162
repositioning
    scene markers, 234
    text, 175
restoring workspace defaults, 33
reversing clip playback, 131
ripple deletion, 97
rolling credits, 189–191
rough cuts, 82–84

S

saving
    captured files, 53
    projects automatically, 30, 31
Scene Detect, 43–44
scene markers
    about, 258
    adding, 229–230
    automatically generating,
        232–234
    changing button labels and image
        thumbnails, 238–241
Sceneline view
    adding clips, 94–96
    current-time indicator on, 89
    defined, 14
    deleting in, 97
    dragging clips to, 84
    moving clips, 96–97
    Split Clip tool in, 99–100
    trimming clips in, 98–99
scenes, 43–44

Scratch Disk preferences, 31
scrubbing, 90
searching for files, 61–63
Send To Premiere Elements
    command (Photoshop
    Elements), 287–290, 305
Shadow/Highlight filter, 127–129
Share workspace, 18, 262
sharing movies, 260–281
    about, 262
    adding Quick Share preset, 262,
        272
    creating Universal Counting
        Leader, 274–276, 281
    exporting movies to mobile
        phones and players, 273–
        274, 281
    exporting to tape, 276–278, 281
    options for Export to Tape dialog,
        277, 278
    sending from your computer,
        269, 271
    sharing single frame from movie,
        279–280
    uploading movies to Photoshop.
        com, 266–268
    uploading movies to YouTube,
        264–268
Sharpen filter, 130
sharpening clips, 126–127
simulated DVD remote control, 241
single-sided transitions, 153,
    163–164
slide show
    creating, 111–112
    using Photoshop Elements image
        for, 287–290
Smart Albums, 78
Smart Tags
    about, 64
    Instant Movie and, 223
    running Auto Analyzer, 69–71
    working with clips after, 71
Smart Trim
    about, 108–110
    Manual and Automatic mode for,
        110–111
SmartFix, 119–121
SmartMix
    about, 214
    Audio Mixer vs., 209
    volume adjustments with, 200,
        202–203
SmartSound Quicktracks, 197–199
smoothing transitions, 162
sound. See audio

source footage. See also clips
    challenges of indoor and outdoor,
        122
    choosing for Media Downloader,
        53
    selecting presets for, 26
    types of, 38
spacing between lines, 179
speed
    changing rolling title, 190–191
    effects controlling, 118
    stretching clip, 130–131, 144–145
    using Reverse Speed effects, 131
split editing, 211
splitting clips
    in Sceneline, 99–100
    in Timeline, 106–108
Stabilize filter, 129–130
stacking order, 188
star ratings
    about, 64, 70
    adding, 66–67
stop markers, 242, 244, 245
stop-motion video, 49
storyboard-style editing. See
    Sceneline view
submenus
    about, 258
    creating bonus video clips on,
        241–245
synchronizing video on Photoshop.
    com, 78

T

tagging
    adding star ratings, 66–67
    clips in Organizer, 64–66
    creating InstantMovie after,
        72–75, 223
    making Smart Albums using, 78
tape-based devices
    capturing stop-motion from, 49
    exporting movies for, 276–278,
        281
    options for Export to Tape dialog,
        277, 278
Tasks panel
    effects on, 117
    illustrated, 13
    Transitions view of, 153–155
    unable to close or dock, 33
    workspaces of, 15–18
television. See TV
templates. See also disc menu
    templates
    drop zones in, 246–247, 248, 258
    title, 172, 191–192